Discover the White Mountains

Second Edition

AMC's Guide to the Best Hiking, Biking, and Paddling

JERRY AND MARCY MONKMAN

Appalachian Mountain Club Books
Boston, Massachusetts

The AMC is a nonprofit organization and sales of AMC books fund our mission of protecting the Northeast outdoors. If you appreciate our efforts and would like to make a donation to the AMC, contact us at Appalachian Mountain Club, 5 Joy Street, Boston, MA 02108.

http://www.outdoors.org/publications/books/

Cartography by Ken Dumas
Book Design by Eric Edstam
All cover and interior images by Jerry Monkman unless otherwise noted

Library of Congress Cataloging-in-Publication Data
Monkman, Jerry.
  Discover the White Mountains: AMC's guide to the best hiking, biking, and paddling / by Jerry and Marcy Monkman.
    p. cm.
  Includes index.
  ISBN 978-1-934028-22-3 (alk. paper)
    1. Hiking—White Mountains (N.H. and Me.)—Guidebooks. 2. Cycling—White Mountains (N.H. and Me.)—Guidebooks. 3. Canoes and canoeing—White Mountains (N.H. and Me.)—Guidebooks. 4. White Mountains (N.H. and Me.)—Guidebooks. I. Monkman, Marcy. II. Title.

  GV199.42.W47M66 2009
  917.42'204—dc22

                                                                    2008050466

The paper used in this publication meets the minimum requirements of the American National Standard for Information Sciences-Permanence of Paper for Printed Library Materials, ANSI Z39.48-1984. ∞

Outdoor recreation activities by their very nature are potentially hazardous. This book is not a substitute for good personal judgment and training in outdoor skills. Due to changes in conditions, use of the information in this book is at the sole risk of the user. The author and the Appalachian Mountain Club assume no liability for accidents happening to, or injuries sustained by, readers who engage in the activities described in this book.

Printed in the United States of America.
Printed on paper that contains 30 percent post-consumer recycled fiber, using soy-based inks.

10 9 8 7 6 5 4 3 2 1   09 10 11 12 13 14 15 16

Locator Map

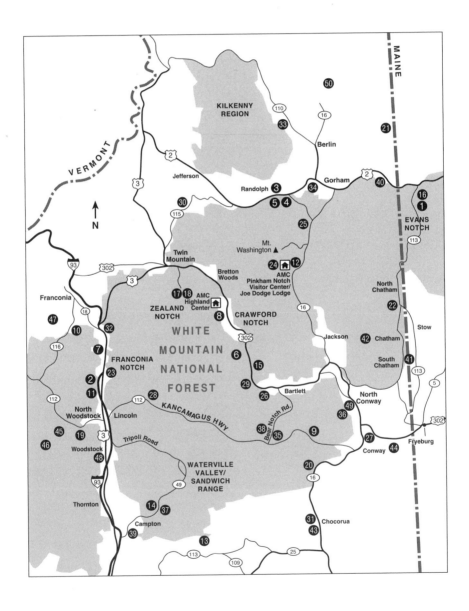

Contents

Nature and History Essays

At-a-Glance Trip Planner

	Trip	Page	Location	Distance and elevation gain	Difficulty
HIKES					
1	The Roost	5	Evans Notch	1.8 mi, 550 ft	Easy
2	Cascade Brook and the Basin	8	Franconia Notch	2.0 mi, 500 ft	Easy
3	Lookout Ledge	13	Northern Presidentials	2.6 mi, 1,000 ft	Moderate
4	Stairs, Coosauk, and Hitchcock Falls	16	Northern Presidentials	2.0 mi, 650 ft	Easy
5	Northern Presidentials Waterfalls	20	Northern Presidentials	2.5 mi, 600 ft	Easy
6	Arethusa Falls with Frankenstein Cliff	26	Crawford Notch	3.0 mi, 900 ft to the falls; 6.2 mi, 1,300 ft to the cliffs	Moderate
7	Lonesome Lake	30	Franconia	3.2 mi, 950 ft	Easy
8	Mount Willard	33	Crawford Notch	3.2 mi, 900 ft	Easy
9	Kancamagus Boulder Loop	36	Kancamagus Highway	3.1 mi, 950 ft	Moderate
10	Bridal Veil Falls	39	Franconia Notch	5.0 mi, 1,100 ft	Moderate
11	Mount Pemigewasset	44	Franconia Notch	3.6 mi, 1,150 ft	Easy

Estimated time	Fee[1]	Good for kids[2]	Dogs allowed[3]	X-C skiing	Snow-shoeing[4]	Trip highlights
1.25 hrs	$	kids	dog		snowshoe	Excellent views of the Evans Notch area
1.5 hrs		kids	dog		snowshoe	Waterfalls and countless cascades
2 hrs		kids	dog		snowshoe	Panoramic views of the Presidential Range
2 hrs		kids	dog		snowshoe	Wildflowers and waterfalls
1–2 hrs	$	kids	dog		snowshoe	Woodland walk to four waterfalls
1.5–3 hrs		kids	dog		snowshoe	Tallest waterfall in New Hampshire
2 hrs		kids	dog		snowshoe	High mountain lake with views of Franconia Ridge
2 hrs		kids	dog		snowshoe	Spectacular view of Crawford Notch
2 hrs	$	kids	dog		snowshoe	Great views of the Kancamagus Region
2–3 hrs		kids	dog		snowshoe	Woods walk to a beautiful waterfall
2.75 hrs		kids	dog		snowshoe	Views of Mount Moosilauke, Mount Osceola

Estimated time	Fee[1]	Good for kids[2]	Dogs allowed[3]	X-C skiing	Snow-shoeing[4]	Trip highlights
2.75 hrs		🚶	🐕		❄️	Views of Mount Adams, Mount Madison, and Wildcat Mountain
3 hrs		🚶	🐕		❄️	Excellent views of the Sandwich Range and the Lakes Region
3 hrs	$	🚶	🐕		❄️	Big views from small peaks
4 hrs	$		🐕		❄️	Unique views of the Presidential Range-Dry River Wilderness Area
4.5 hrs		🚶	🐕		❄️	Great views of the Caribou-Speckled Mountain Wilderness Area
5 hrs	$		🐕		❄️	Mountain views and Thoreau Falls
5.5 hrs	$		🐕		❄️	Excellent views of the Pemigewasset Wilderness Area
6 hrs			🐕			N.H.'s westernmost alpine peak
6 hrs	$		🐕			One of the most photographed mountains in New England
6 hrs			🐕			Spectacular views in the Mahoosuc Range
7 hrs	$		🐕			More than 3 miles of hiking above treeline
8 hrs			🐕			Longest above-treeline hike in the WM outside of the Presidential Range
8 hrs			🐕			New England's tallest peak
3–4 days						Three days of spectacular views

	Trip	Page	Location	Distance and elevation gain	Difficulty
BIKE TRIPS					
26	Bartlett Experimental Forest	124	Crawford Notch	4.8 mi, 400 ft	Easy to Moderate
27	Conway Recreation Trail	127	Conway	6.0 mi, 200 ft	Easy
28	Lincoln Woods	130	Kancamagus Highway	6.4 mi, 300 ft	Easy except for crossing the Pemi
29	Sawyer River Road	137	Crawford Notch	8.0 mi, 750 ft	Easy to Moderate
30	Pondicherry Rail Trail	140	Northern Presidentials	7.2 mi, minimal	Easy
31	Chocorua-Tamworth Loop	145	Conway	11.4 mi, 600 ft	Easy to Moderate
32	Franconia Notch Bike Path	148	Franconia	18.4 mi, 600 ft	Easy to Moderate
33	Kilkenny Road Trip	154	North Country	17.5 mi, 1,150 ft	Easy to Moderate
34	Presidential Rail Trail	157	Northern Presidentials	13.75 mi, 500 ft	Moderate
35	Lower Nanamocomuck Ski Trail	163	Kancamagus Highway	8.4 mi, 800 ft	Moderate
36	Mineral Site and Moat Mountain	166	Conway	8.6 mi, 1,000 ft	Easy to Difficult
37	Sandwich Notch Road	170	Waterville Valley	8.0 mi, 1,270 ft	Moderate to Strenuous
38	Rob Brook Road	173	Kancamagus Highway	12.5–15.8 mi, 200–500 ft	Moderate
39	Beebe River Road	177	Waterville Valley	17.2 mi, 1,100 ft	Easy to Moderate
40	Shelburne to Evans Notch	183	Northern Presidentials	37.2 mi, 2,200 ft	Easy to Strenuous

Estimated time	Fee[1]	Good for kids[2]	Dogs allowed[3]	X-C skiing	Snow-shoeing[4]	Trip highlights
1 hr			🐕			Smooth ride through beautiful forest; bumpy stretch of single-track
1.5 hrs		🚶	🐕	🎿	⛄	Ride through tall pines
1.5 hrs	$	🚶	🐕	🎿	⛄	An easy ride along the rushing waters of the Pemigewasset River
1–2 hrs	$		🐕	🎿	⛄	Beautiful forests and the rushing Sawyer River
1.5 hrs		🚶	🐕	🎿	⛄	Abundant wildlife and spectacular views
1.5 hrs			🐕			Ride through tranquil forests of Tamworth
2.5 hrs				🎿	⛄	One of the most scenic places in the WM
2–3 hrs			🐕			Beautiful, undeveloped forests in the North Country
2–3 hrs			🐕			Occasional views of the Presidential Mountains
2.5 hrs			🐕	🎿	⛄	One of the more scenic backcountry rides in the White Mountains
2–3 hrs			🐕			Fast downhill run over rocky single-track; miles of quiet forest roads
2–3 hrs			🐕			Big elevation gain and a great downhill thrill
3–4 hrs			🐕	🎿	⛄	Easy woods riding on a gravel road; adventurous single-track
5.5 hrs			🐕			Many opportunities for riverside photos and snack stops
3–4 hrs			🐕			Long ride on back roads and along the Wild River

	Trip	Page	Location	Distance and elevation gain	Difficulty
	PADDLING TRIPS				
41	Upper Kimball Pond	190	Conway	3.4 mi	Quietwater
42	Mountain Pond	192	Conway	1.7 mi with 0.3 mi portage	Quietwater
43	Chocorua Lake	195	Conway	3.3 mi	Quietwater
44	Conway Lake	201	Conway	7.5 mi	Quietwater
45	Long Pond	204	Western Whites	2.5 mi	Quietwater
46	Lake Tarleton	210	Western Whites	3.5 mi	Quietwater
47	Pearl Lake	213	Western Whites	1.5 mi	Quietwater
48	Pemigewasset River—Woodstock to Thornton	216	Franconia Notch	12.3 mi	Flatwater, Quickwater, Class I
49	Saco River—North Conway to Conway	219	Conway	8.5 mi	Flatwater, Quickwater, Class I
50	Northern Forest Odyssey—Androscoggin River and Umbagog Lake	224	North Country	9.0 mi	Quietwater

NOTES

1. The White Mountain National Forest Parking Pass is required at most national forest trailheads. Passes can be purchased at WMNF ranger stations, AMC visitor centers, and other retail outlets. For a complete list, visit www.fs.fed.us/r9/forests/white_mountain/passes/. Federal Interagency, Golden Eagle, Golden Age, or Golden Access holders are not required to purchase a pass.
2. All families hike at different levels. We have marked trips as kid-friendly assuming the kids are between the ages of 8 and 13 and are comfortable in the outdoors.

Estimated time	Fee[1]	Good for kids[2]	Dogs allowed[3]	X-C skiing	Snow-shoeing[4]	Trip highlights
2 hrs		✓	✓			An easy paddle with views and excellent bird-watching opportunities
1 hr	$	✓	✓			Excellent views of the surrounding mountains
2 hrs		✓	✓			Loons, pines, and spectacular views of Mount Chocorua
4 hrs		✓	✓			Mountain views and miles of varied wildlife-filled shoreline
1.5 hrs	$	✓	✓			One of New Hampshire's most scenic ponds
2 hrs		✓	✓			Views of Mount Moosilauke
1 hr		✓	✓			A quietwater paddle in the rural western foothills of the Whites
5 hrs			✓			A long, enjoyable paddle through the countryside
4 hrs			✓			An easy paddle close to town with great scenery
5 hrs			✓			A true wilderness paddle in New Hampshire's wild Northern Forest

3. While dogs are allowed on all national forest lands, they must be under verbal or physical control at all times. While we've listed dogs as allowed for most of the bike trips, use common sense when riding with your dog, and leave him or her at home on the road bike trips.

4. We have listed trips as showshoeing-friendly if they are primarily below treeline, thus avoiding the need for crampons, ice axes, and mountaineering experience. However, winter trail conditions can vary widely from year to year and month to month, so be prepared to turn back during any winter hike if trail or weather conditions become unsafe.

Preface

NEW HAMPSHIRE'S WHITE MOUNTAINS ARE A SPECIAL PLACE FOR US. It is where we first learned to hike after moving to New England from the very flat land around Chicago. A visit to Zealand Falls was soon followed by our first foray above treeline on Mount Jefferson. We were in awe that a place so beautiful was so close to our new home. The vastness of the Pemigewasset Wilderness Area and the drama of the glacial cirques of the Northern Presidentials got us hooked on exploring the White Mountains as often as possible, and now these places feel like familiar stomping grounds, though no less awesome than during those first visits. Now we have two young children and we are reveling at seeing these mountains through their young eyes and hearts.

"The Whites" are well known for their spectacular scenery and rugged topography. More than 7 million people a year visit the region—that's more people than those who visit such well-known national parks as Yosemite and Grand Canyon. The most popular activities include ascending Mount Washington by foot, car, or cog railway, paddling the gentle waters of the Saco River, fishing for trout below the cliffs of Cannon Mountain, and, yes, shopping the outlet malls of North Conway. However, this book celebrates the fact that the White Mountains have a lot more to offer than the usual tourist destinations. Since we wrote the first edition of this book eight years ago we have continued to explore the region, so we have added a dozen new trips that we feel fit well in a book about the best the White Mountains have to offer. Exploring a place in different ways lets you see things from different perspectives, which is why we encourage you to discover the region on a bike, in a boat, and on your own two feet. Along the way, you might find tiny plants that live nowhere else in the world, giant moose that make your heart race, and waterfalls that soothe your soul.

Acknowledgments

REVISING THIS BOOK HAS BEEN A TRUE JOY because we have been lucky enough to spend a dedicated amount of time in the White Mountains on behalf of the AMC, but also because of the input of new voices to what we hope will become a trusted resource to those who enjoy the White Mountains. Dan Eisner, Heather Stephenson, and Kevin Breunig at AMC Books were instrumental in helping to shape and focus this new version of *Discover the White Mountains*, with its fresh mix of trips that we hope will appeal to newcomers and experienced outdoors enthusiasts alike. Doug Mayer, Matt Bowman, and Jenna Bowman, who over the years have worn various hats at the AMC and now generously display our artwork at their White Mountain Café in Gorham, N.H., provided some great suggestions for additional biking and hiking trips for us to explore. Wesley Tucker, the Excursions Committee Chair for the AMC's New Hampshire Chapter provided valuable input, as did David Ross, also of the New Hampshire Chapter. Jana Johnson and Mary Anne Lieberman of the U.S. Forest Service were very helpful in providing updated information on bike routes in the national forest. We also want to thank our families—Jeff and Pat Monkman, the entire Wolin clan, and Clare and Dick Lesser—for their unwavering support and belief in our career as "ecophotographers." Lastly, we would like to dedicate this book to our two children, Acadia and Quinn, who never fail to inspire us in life and in our belief in conserving our natural world.

Stewardship and Conservation

Protect the Resource!

With so many people enjoying the White Mountains' limited resources, it is imperative that everyone learn and adhere to Leave No Trace principles. These principles were developed and are updated regularly by the Leave No Trace Center for Outdoor Ethics in order to promote and inspire responsible outdoor recreation. How we use the forest now determines what the forest will be like in the future. Whether you are hiking, biking, or paddling, follow these principles:

Plan Ahead and Prepare

When going into the backcountry, plan a trip that you know everyone in your group can finish. Be prepared for unexpected events by having extra food, water, and clothing. A well-planned day will prevent the need for an unnecessary night out in the woods, where you may be forced to build fires and trample delicate vegetation. Keep your group size to ten or less, splitting into smaller groups if necessary (this is required in designated wilderness areas). Try to avoid travel in wet and muddy conditions, and use extra care when in the delicate alpine zone. Planning ahead also means confirming that you are traveling and/or camping in an area where it is legal to do so.

Camp and Travel on Durable Surfaces

When hiking, try to stay on trails and rocks. Stay in the center of the trail, even when it is wet and muddy. Use your boots! Trails are hardened sites where use should be concentrated. Avoid contributing to the widening of trails and their erosion. Hiking off-trail into pristine areas is allowed, but requires greater understanding and effort and is especially discouraged above treeline. First, consider if hiking off-trail is necessary. If you decide to hike off-trail use durable surfaces such as rock, gravel, or grasses. Spread your group out, take different routes, and avoid places where unofficial "social" trails are just beginning to show. While mountain biking, always stay on the trail. Camping in the backcountry should be at designated sites, sites that have already been affected, or 200 feet from trails and water sources. Avoid moderately affected sites where your visit could create more damage.

Dispose of Waste Properly

Pack out *all* that you bring in. This includes any and all food you may drop while eating. Urinate at least 200 yards from any water source and pack out your used toilet paper. To dispose of solid human waste in the backcountry, dig an individual "cathole" at least 200 yards from a trail or water source. Organic topsoil is preferable to sandy mineral soil. Dig a hole 4 to 8 inches deep and about 6 inches in diameter. After use, mix some soil into the cathole with a stick and cover with the remainder of the soil. Disguise the hole by covering it with leaves or other brush. Pack out your toilet paper in a Ziploc bag. It is especially important not to pollute near any watercourse, as it probably leads to a campground or town water source.

Leave What You Find

Leave all natural and historical items as you find them. There is much human history in and around the White Mountains that should be left for future visitors to enjoy. Eating a few blueberries on a hike or adding an edible mushroom to a camp dinner is OK, but it is illegal to harvest any forest product for commercial purposes without a permit from the Forest Service. Before picking any wild edibles, consider the number of other people who might be using the area and decide if you will be negatively affecting an important food source for wildlife.

Minimize Campfire Impacts

Use a lightweight backpacking stove when in the backcountry. Try to build campfires only in designated fire pits in campgrounds and picnic areas.

Respect Wildlife

Remain reasonably quiet while in the backcountry, and give animals enough space so that they feel secure. While watching wildlife, if you notice them changing their behavior, it is most likely because you are too close. In that case, back off and give the animals space. Avoid nesting or calving sites and *never* attempt to feed any wildlife, even those cute little red squirrels. For low-impact wildlife-watching tips, visit Watchable Wildlife's website, www.watchablewildlife.org.

Be Considerate of Other Visitors

Refrain from using cell phones and radios. When hiking, take rests on the side of the trail so that other hikers do not have to walk around you. When on the water, remember that sound carries a long, long way. Dogs are allowed on all trails in the national forest, but they must be under control, either verbally or on a leash. Leashes are required in campgrounds.

You can learn more about the Leave No Trace program by visiting the website www.lnt.org, or by writing to Leave No Trace, P.O. Box 997, Boulder, CO 80306. Information on Leave No Trace Master Educator training by the AMC can be found at www.outdoors.org/education. A good book for learning more about ethics in the backcountry is *Backwoods Ethics: Environmental Issues for Hikers and Campers* by Laura and Guy Waterman, published by Countryman Press.

Introduction to the White Mountains

THE WHITE MOUNTAINS HAVE BEEN DRAWING TOURISTS to their lofty heights since the mid-1800s, when most visitors made the trip from cities to the south by train or horse-drawn carriage to spend a month or more taking in the fresh air and sublime views. Today's visitors might spend only the weekend or a couple of weeks, but they are still enticed by the incredible scenery provided by the highest peaks in the Northeast, which culminate in the summit of Mount Washington at 6,288 feet. Hiking is the traditional and most popular outdoor sport in the area, and, with more than 1,200 miles of trail to choose from, hikers can visit the mountains again and again without hiking the same stretch of trail twice. Of course, the beauty of places like the above-treeline world of Franconia Ridge or the Presidential Range ensures that most hikers will visit those places over and over again. While there are few water-based miles of recreation in the Whites, it is still a great place to enjoy a quiet paddle in a mountain setting or the adrenaline rush of whitewater. And exploring the back roads and rail trails of the region on two wheels is an exhilarating way to enjoy both the frontcountry and portions of the backcountry in the White Mountains.

Sections 1 through 3 give detailed descriptions of hiking, biking, and paddling trips, from one-hour excursions to all-day adventures. The rest of this introductory chapter provides some basic information you can use to get started on your visit to the White Mountains.

Climate

The White Mountains are notorious for their bouts of bad weather anytime of the year, with storms that seem to come out of nowhere. Despite this reputation, the weather in the area is generally similar to what you'll find throughout northern New England. The winters are long and cold, with daytime highs in the 20s and 30s and lows in the 10s and below. The average winter snowfall is around 100 inches. Springs are usually wet and muddy, with daytime highs in the 40s and 50s and lows in the 20s and 30s. Summers are warm with afternoon thunderstorms fairly common, particularly at higher elevations. Average highs are in the 70s and 80s with lows in the 50s and 60s. Fall is cool with occasional heavy rains. Highs are in the 50s and 60s and lows are in the 30s and 40s. These averages, however, are only for the valleys. As you gain elevation in the mountains, the temperature can drop dramatically (often by 30 degrees), the winds can get very strong, and rain, sleet, or snow can fall even on a day when it is sunny in the valleys. Current weather forecasts can be obtained by calling the AMC weather line at 603-466-2721 (option 4) or the National Weather Service at 603-225-5191 or online at www.nws.noaa.gov/. Winter backcountry conditions can be found on AMC's website at www.outdoors.org/tripplanner/go.

Getting There

The White Mountains are readily accessible by car, with the major access routes being I-93, NH 16, US 2, and US 302. Several airlines service the airports in Manchester, N.H., and Portland, Maine, both of which are approximately a 90-minute drive from the mountains. Bus service to several locations in the White Mountains is provided by Concord Trailways. For a schedule, call 800-639-3317 or visit the website www.concordtrailways.com.

Once in the Whites, you can take advantage of the AMC Hiker Shuttle, which provides transportation between various AMC facilities and trailheads for a flat fee. The shuttle runs only in the summer, but it is a great way to plan one-way trips without the need to spot a car. For a current schedule or to make reservations, contact the AMC at 603-466-2727 or visit the AMC website, www.outdoors.org.

Lodging

Literally hundreds of choices for lodging exist in and around the White Mountains. They range from basic campgrounds to very expensive, luxurious hotels and inns.

U.S. Forest Service Information

To request information about the White Mountains before your trip, you can contact the U.S. Forest Service at White Mountain National Forest, P.O. Box 638, Laconia, NH 03247; 603-528-8721; TTY 603-528-8722; www.fs.fed. us/r9/white/. Once in the Whites, you can visit one of five regional ranger stations:

- Ammonoosuc Ranger Station, located 1.0 mile from the intersection of US 3 and US 302 on Trudeau Road in Bethlehem, N.H.
- Androscoggin Ranger Station, located 0.5 mile south of US 2 on NH 16 in Gorham, N.H.
- Evans Notch Ranger Station, located on US 2 and Bridge Street in Bethel, Maine
- Pemigewasset Ranger Station, located on NH 175 in Plymouth, N.H. Take Exit 25 on I-93
- Saco Ranger Station, located on NH 112 (Kancamagus Highway), just west of NH 16, in Conway, N.H.

A U.S. Forest Service information center is also located in Lincoln, N.H., on NH 112, just off of Exit 32 on I-93. In addition to these Forest Service offices, the AMC Pinkham Notch Visitor Center is an excellent source of visitor information. It is located on NH 16 about 20 miles north of Conway and 11 miles south of Gorham. You can also find recent trip reports, trail conditions, and safety warnings on White Mountain Guide Online (www. outdoors.org/wmgonline).

Fees

Recently, the Forest Service has instituted a parking pass program, which requires cars parked at trailheads and along most roads in the national forest to display a White Mountain National Forest parking pass. As of 2008, annual passes for $20 ($25 for two vehicles in one household) and one-week passes for $5 were available at Forest Service offices, Pinkham Notch Visitor Center, and selected outfitters. Self-serve pay stations are located at many parking areas, where you can pay a one-day, $3 fee to park. Ninety-five percent of parking fees go back to the White Mountain National Forest for recreation services and facilities repairs. National forest campground fees range from $14 to $20 per site per night depending on the facilities. Some backcountry sites also have fees, which are usually under $10. State campground fees usually range from $21 to $35 per night.

Universal Access

The Forest Service and state of New Hampshire offer campgrounds with universally accessible facilities. The Forest Service is constantly adding accessible facilities, and they can mail you a list of these facilities as well as a list of suggested wheelchair-friendly hikes. Just call the Forest Service headquarters at 603-528-8721, TTY 603-528-8722. One great option for visitors with disabilities is the Franconia Notch Bicycle Path, a paved path that is accessible from most of the parking areas along the Franconia Notch Parkway—see trip 32.

Emergencies

In an emergency situation, you should call 911, as New Hampshire has recently implemented a statewide 911 system. Backcountry accidents and search-and-rescue situations can also be reported to the New Hampshire State Police at 800-852-3411, the U.S. Forest Service at 603-528-8721, or the AMC at Pinkham Notch at 603-466-2727.

Choosing Your Trip

The 50 hiking, biking, and paddling trips in this book provide a variety of outdoor experiences. Before heading out on the trail or on the water, you should decide what the focus of your trip is (paddling, mountain views, wildlife watching, etc.). You should also decide how strenuous a trip you and your group are willing to take and able to complete. The trip highlights chart following this introduction has an easy-to-follow listing of all the trips, including their difficulty, length, and trip highlights. Once you have narrowed down your choices, read the detailed trip descriptions in the individual hiking, biking, and paddling chapters to get a better idea of what the trip entails and what you might encounter.

Hunting Season

Hunting is allowed in the White Mountain National Forest. Hunting accidents are rare in New Hampshire, but everyone in your group, including dogs, should wear at least one piece of blaze-orange clothing during hunting season, particularly during November when deer hunters are allowed to hunt with rifles. Hunting seasons are set by the New Hampshire Fish and Game Department and are posted on its website, www.wildlife.state.nh.us. In general, the various hunting seasons are as follows:

- *Deer:* Archery—middle of September through middle of December; muzzle-loader—end of October through first week of November; regular firearms (shotguns and rifles)—early November through early December
- *Black bear:* Early September through early December
- *Moose*: Nine days, starting on the third Saturday in October
- *Turkey:* Archery—middle of September through middle of December; archery and shotgun—May
- *Birds and small mammals:* Usually early October through December

Logging

The White Mountain National Forest is managed for multiple uses, including timber harvesting. While you will most likely never encounter a logging operation while hiking or paddling, some of the bike trips in this book use active logging roads. While traveling these roads, be prepared to move aside for logging vehicles. Although logging has been done for more than 150 years in the White Mountains, the White Mountain National Forest sees a relatively low amount of harvesting compared to other national forests.

Don't Drink the Water

While the water in many White Mountain streams is most likely safe to drink, there is no way to tell a safe water source from a contaminated one. Even water bubbling up from a spring can contain bacteria, viruses, or protozoa that can cause illness. If you are just out for the day, the easiest thing to do is bring enough water with you. If you are camping or prefer to fill up on an "as needed" basis, use one of the following procedures for purifying your water:

- *Boiling:* Boiling water for one to three minutes is a surefire way of killing any diseases that may be in the water. The down side is having to set up a stove and then wait for the water to boil and cool down before drinking.
- *Filtering:* Using a portable water filter is a convenient way to get potable water. There are several different types of filters—some use glass, carbon, or ceramic elements to strain the nasty elements from water. These filters do not rid the water of viruses, which are rare in the American backcountry, but do eliminate bacteria and protozoa and are adequate in the White Mountains—just make sure the filter element has a pore size of 0.2 microns or smaller. If you want extra protection, buy a filter that also passes the water through a layer of iodine, which will kill viruses.

- *Chemical treatments:* Dropping a few tablets of a chemical purifier, such as Potable Aqua or Polar Pure, into your water is a simple, lightweight water purification solution. The side effect is that your water will have an unpleasant iodine taste. To a certain extent, this can be masked with powdered drinks like Gatorade or Tang. Be sure to add your powdered drink *after* the chemical purifier has had sufficient time to work—usually 30 minutes to two hours. Also, chemical treatments cannot kill crypto-sporidium, a protozoan that can cause flulike symptoms, including diarrhea and severe bloating. We carry Potable Aqua in our first-aid kit for emergency purposes on day hikes when we don't want to carry the extra weight of a filter.

Backcountry Camping

The trips in this book are all day trips, but several trips pass by backcountry campsites or shelters that are good places to spend a night in the woods, away from the crowds. Camping is allowed anywhere in the forest, with the following exceptions:

- No camping or wood or charcoal fires are allowed within 0.25 mile of any hut, shelter, cabin, picnic area, campground, or trailhead. This rule is also in effect near most roads in the national forest, as well as near popular waterfalls and ponds.
- The 0.25-mile restriction is reduced to 200 feet in designated wilderness areas and in posted Forest Protection Areas along popular trails, as well as a few other locations. Before a backcountry trip, you should confirm the location of Forest Protection Areas with a ranger station or by visiting the Forest Service website at www.fs.fed.us/r9/forests/white_mountain/recreation/camping/.
- Camping and hiking group size is limited to ten people in designated wilderness areas.
- No camping or wood or charcoal fires are allowed within the Bartlett Experimental Forest, Mount Chocorua Scenic Area, Greeley Ponds Scenic Area, or the islands in Long Pond.
- No wood or charcoal fires are allowed in the Great Gulf Wilderness Area, and no camping is allowed between the intersection of the Great Gulf and Sphinx Trails and Spaulding Lake.
- No camping in Tuckerman or Huntington Ravines (above or below treeline) except at the Harvard Mountain Club Cabin (December 1–March 31

only) and Hermit Lake Shelters (no dogs allowed overnight). No wood or charcoal fires are allowed at any location in either ravine.

- Camping is allowed in the alpine zone (where trees are less than 8 feet tall) *only* on 2 or more feet of snow and not on frozen bodies of water. No wood or charcoal fires are allowed above treeline.

Available Maps

Many mapping resources are available to help you find your way as you take the trips suggested in this book. The Appalachian Mountain Club produces the detailed, waterproof White Mountain National Forest Trail Map Set that covers the entire White Mountain region. Hikers interested in a single map of the entire WMNF may be interested in the *White Mountain National Forest Map and Guide* published by the AMC. It is available at Pinkham Notch Visitor Center and Highland Center and from the AMC's online store at www.outdoors.org/amcstore. The United States Geographical Survey (USGS) also produces maps that are available for purchase at store.usgs.gov. The summary box at the beginning of each trip includes information about which maps to use. The White Mountain Guide Online is another helpful resource that offers trail descriptions and an interactive map of the entire White Mountain region. Visit www.outdoors.org/wmgonline to sign up.

hikeSafe Hiker Responsibility Code

The White Mountain National Forest and New Hampshire Fish and Game Department joined forces to create the hike-Safe Hiker Responsibility Code to educate hikers on the inherent risks of hiking and how they can become better prepared before beginning any hike. The Hiker Responsibility Code was created to help hikers become more self-aware about their responsibility for their safety. It also acknowledges the inherent danger of hiking in the backcountry and encourages hikers to be better prepared every time they are on the trail.

You are responsible for yourself, so be prepared:

1. *With knowledge and gear.* Become self-reliant by learning about the terrain, conditions, local weather, and your equipment before you start.
2. *To leave your plans.* Tell someone where you are going, the trails you are hiking, when you will return, and your emergency plans.

3. *To stay together.* When you start as a group, hike as a group, end as a group. Pace your hike to the slowest person.

4. *To turn back.* Weather changes quickly in the mountains. Fatigue and unexpected conditions can also affect your hike. Know your limitations and when to postpone your hike. The mountains will be there another day.

5. *For emergencies.* Even if you are headed out for just an hour, an injury, severe weather, or a wrong turn could become life-threatening. Don't assume you will be rescued; know how to rescue yourself.

6. *To share the hiker code with others.*

hikeSafe: It's Your Responsibility

The Hiker Responsibility Code was developed and is endorsed by the White Mountain National Forest and New Hampshire Fish and Game.

1

Hiking in the White Mountains

HIKING IN NEW HAMPSHIRE'S WHITE MOUNTAINS is one of the oldest outdoor sports activities in America. By the 1850s, tourists were flocking to the White Mountains to hike Mount Washington and other peaks. Those early visitors enjoyed the same rewards that today's hikers find: incredible views from the tallest mountains in the Northeast and lush forested valleys filled with wildlife, serene mountain ponds, and thunderous waterfalls. While hiking in the White Mountains, you can study alpine flora that remains from the last ice age, watch an otter at play in a backcountry pond, and traverse a knife-edge ridge with 2,000 vertical feet between you and the valley floor. Hundreds of miles of hiking trails in the White Mountains allow for just about any kind of hiking experience, from a one- or two-hour hike to a waterfall or a several-day exploration of the high ridges. We have suggested 25 hikes in this section that will take you to some of the most scenic spots in the White Mountains. If you have an insatiable appetite for White Mountain hiking, you should also pick up a copy of the AMC *White Mountain Guide*, which describes in detail more than 500 trails in the White Mountains.

Hiking Times

Our hiking times are based on estimates in the *White Mountain Guide*, and our own experiences as average 30-something hikers carrying 15 to 30 pounds of gear. As a general guideline, the *White Mountain Guide* estimates 30 minutes for each 0.5 mile traveled and 30 minutes for every 1,000 feet of elevation gain traveled. Obviously, these times can vary based on the weather, physical fitness, and the amount of gear in your pack. While we think these times are useful for planning a trip, your hiking times will undoubtedly vary from ours, and you should always be prepared to spend a longer time outdoors than planned due to factors such as weather and fatigue.

Trip Ratings

Trip ratings vary in difficulty based on mileage, elevation gain, and trail conditions. *Easy* trips are suitable for families with kids; however, even hikes listed as easy may have short sections of significant climbing or rough footing—the White Mountains are a rugged place and easy is a relative term. *Moderate* hikes entail more mileage than easy hikes, usually between 5 and 10 miles, and can require as much as 2,500 feet of elevation gain. The hikes in this chapter listed as moderate will challenge most hikers at some point along the way, but they can still be fun for older children who have experience hiking steep and rocky trails and are willing to hike for more than a few hours. *Strenuous* trips usually take an entire day to complete due to the significant mileage and elevation gain involved, as well as the possibility for one or more scrambles over steep rock faces. Only hikers in good physical condition with some hiking experience should consider undertaking a strenuous trip.

Safety and Etiquette

With proper planning, each of the hikes offered in this section will provide an enjoyable and safe experience. Be especially careful when you see an exclamation point (⚠) in the margin of the text. This symbol indicates that you should be aware of a potential danger. Before heading out for your hike, please consider the following tips:

- Select a trip that is appropriate for everyone in the group. Match the hike to the abilities of the least capable person in the group.
- Plan to be back at the trailhead before dark. Determine a turnaround time and stick to it—even if you have not reached your goal for the day.
- Check the weather. Weather in the White Mountains is notoriously changeable and potentially dangerous. It is not uncommon to be hiking above treeline and suddenly experience conditions with visibility of only a few yards. Combine this with high winds and wet weather and you are suddenly in a life-threatening situation. Lightning is also a serious threat above treeline—take shelter if you hear thunder or see thunderstorms

approaching. Rain and fog can make steep trails over rock ledges dangerous. We have needed our fleece, Gore-Tex, wool hats, and mittens during every month of the year in the White Mountains, so do not assume that a hike to the summit in July is going to be shorts and T-shirt weather. Know the weather forecast before you begin your hike, monitor the sky for changing weather, and be prepared to alter your route or end your hike early. For daily weather updates, you can call the AMC weather and trail information line at 603-466-2721 (option 4).

- Bring a pack with the following items:
  - ✓ Water: Two quarts per person is adequate depending on the weather and length of the trip (be sure to bring water purification items for long trips)
  - ✓ Food: Even for a short one-hour hike, it is a good idea to bring some high-energy snacks like nuts, dried fruit, or snack bars. Bring a lunch for longer trips.
  - ✓ Map and compass: Be sure you know how to use them!
  - ✓ Headlamp or flashlight, with spare batteries and lightbulb
  - ✓ Extra clothing: Rain gear, wool sweater or fleece, hat and mittens
  - ✓ Sunscreen
  - ✓ First-aid kit: Adhesive bandages, gauze, nonprescription painkiller
  - ✓ Pocketknife
  - ✓ Waterproof matches and a lighter
  - ✓ A trash bag
  - ✓ Toilet paper
  - ✓ Binoculars for wildlife viewing (optional)
- Wear appropriate footwear and clothing. Wear wool or synthetic hiking socks and comfortable, waterproof hiking boots that give you good traction and ankle support. Even if the weather is sunny and pleasant, bring rain gear because unexpected rain, fog, and wind is possible at any time in the White Mountains. Avoid wearing cotton clothing, which absorbs sweat and rain, making for cold, damp hiking. Polypropylene, fleece, silk, and wool all do a good job of keeping moisture away from your body and keeping you warm in wet or cold conditions.

In addition to practicing the Leave No Trace techniques described in the Stewardship and Conservation section, it is wise to keep the following things in mind while hiking:

- Try not to disturb other hikers. While you may often feel alone in the wilderness, wild yelling or cell phone usage will undoubtedly interfere with another person's quiet backcountry experience.
- When you are in front of the rest of your hiking group, wait at all trail junctions. This avoids confusion and keeps people in your group from getting lost or separated.
- If you see downed wood that appears to be purposely covering a trail, it probably means the trail is closed due to overuse or hazardous conditions.
- If a trail is muddy, walk through the mud or on rocks, never on tree roots or plants. Having waterproof boots will keep your feet comfortable, and by staying in the center of the trail you will keep the trail from eroding into a wide "hiking highway."
- If you decide to take an impromptu swim in a trailside stream or pond, be sure to wear sturdy sandals or old tennis shoes to protect your feet and give you traction on slippery surfaces. Also, wipe off sunscreen and bug spray to avoid polluting water on which animals, plants, and other hikers rely.

By taking the above precautions, you can spend your trip focusing on the pleasures of exploring the wilderness that exists in the White Mountains. Most of the hikes in this book will take you through multiple natural habitats, giving you the opportunity to see a variety of flora and fauna. You probably won't see something as exciting as a moose on every trip, but you will always be surrounded by the wonders of nature, whether it is the fresh tracks of an otter in the mud next to a stream, the jungle-like sounds of the northern hardwood forest in the spring, or the delicate details of alpine azalea growing on the slopes of Mount Washington.

TRIP 1
THE ROOST

Rating: Easy
Distance: 1.8 miles round-trip
Elevation Gain: 550 feet
Estimated Time: 1 hour, 15 minutes
Maps: AMC White Mountain Trail Map #5: E13, USGS Speckled
Mountain (Maine) Quadrangle

This steep but short climb will take you to excellent views of the Evans Notch area.

Directions
From the intersection of US 2 and ME 113 in Gilead, Maine, head south on ME 113. In 3.0 miles, park in the small parking area on the right just before Wild River Road.

Trip Description
Compared to the rest of the White Mountains, Evans Notch is remote, out-of-the-way, and one of the less-visited areas of the White Mountain National Forest. Straddling the Maine-New Hampshire border, Evans Notch provides access to excellent hiking, biking, and camping opportunities. This trip makes a short but steep climb to the Roost, a small peak at the northern end of the notch with great views to the south and west. The Roost sits high above the Wild River, a beautiful mountain stream that was once a major route for loggers 100 years ago. Today the forest along the Wild River and throughout Evans Notch has recovered from that logging and seems particularly wild.

From the small parking area on the west side of ME 113 just north of Wild River Road, walk north on 113 over the bridge that crosses Evans Brook. The trailhead for the Roost Trail is across the street just after the bridge. Although the trail immediately climbs very steeply, the footing is good and the climbing is not technically difficult. The ascent soon moderates as you climb gradually through a beautiful northern hardwood forest that includes northern red oaks and a few very large white pines. At 0.3 mile you cross a small brook and climb more steeply for the remaining 0.2 mile to the summit of the Roost, which is covered in a forest of mixed conifers.

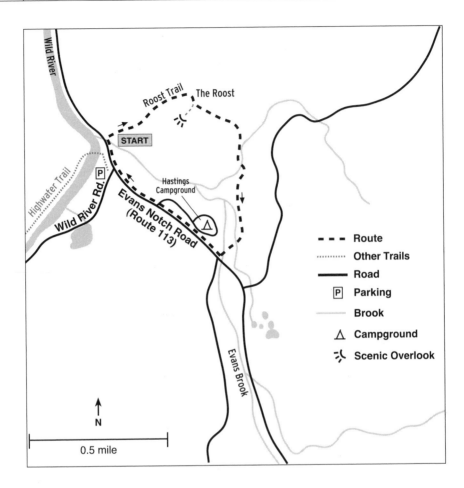

Although the summit doesn't offer any views, a side trail leads down and to the right about 150 yards to open ledges. From these ledges you will get excellent views of Mount Moriah, North and South Baldface (see trip 22), Royce Mountain, and the Wild River. Blueberries, checkerberries, and fragrant white pines have found enough soil to grow in isolated pockets. The ledges are composed of metamorphic schist, and you can see where the rock was bent and folded by forces that came from deep within the earth's crust. Shiny mica and quartz crystals sparkle in the sun when not covered by gray, green, or black lichens. To continue this trip, return to the summit of the Roost.

From the summit, follow the Roost Trail southeast (on your right as you face the trail sign). The trail descends this side of the Roost much more mod-

Northern hardwood forests such as this one are prominent throughout the White Mountains.

erately than its climb to the summit. The trail becomes level as you reach Evans Brook, which is lined by dark green hemlock. Cross the brook and then turn right as the trail follows an old woods road. As the trail crosses another brook, look for an old cellar hole on the left. This area was once the town of Hastings, Maine, during the logging boom on the Wild River in the late 1800s. The town and the logging trains are long gone, with beaver now doing the construction. The trail can be very wet at times due to that beaver activity, and you should be able to see trees that have been cut recently or gnawed on by these large rodents.

The Roost Trail ends on ME 113, which was built by the Civilian Conservation Corps in 1936. Turn right on ME 113 to complete your loop. The parking area is 0.6 mile ahead on the left.

TRIP 2
CASCADE BROOK AND THE BASIN

Rating: Easy
Distance: 2.0 miles up and back
Elevation Gain: 500 feet
Estimated Time: 1 hour, 30 minutes
Maps: AMC White Mountain Trail Map #2: H4, USGS Franconia and
     Lincoln Quadrangles

**This easy family hike begins in Franconia Notch and will take
you to waterfalls and countless cascades.**

Directions

This hike begins from the exit marked The Basin on the Franconia Notch
Parkway, just north of the Flume Gorge Visitor Center and about 6.0 miles
north of NH 112 in Lincoln. Separate parking areas are on the northbound
and southbound sides of the highway. Either parking area is fine.

Trip Description

This hike in Franconia Notch is great for families, as it follows Cascade Brook
for nearly 1.0 mile, visiting two waterfalls and numerous cascades along the
way. Excellent views can also be seen from spots where the brook cuts a wide
swath through the forest. The elevation gain is easy to tackle for enthusi-
astic children who love exploring the mountains, although the footing can
be rough at times due to exposed tree roots. The falls are most spectacular
in the spring, but in very high water the crossing of the brook at Kinsman
Falls can be too much for smaller children. Since both Lonesome Lake and
Kinsman Pond feed Cascade Brook, it has plenty of water throughout most
of the year. For a longer day hike, this trip can be combined with trip 7, the
Lonesome Lake hike (see alternate description at the end of this trip).

From either the northbound or southbound parking area on the Franconia Notch Parkway, follow signs to the Basin, an impressive circular pool
of water in the Pemigewasset River that was carved into the rock by thousands of years of rushing water. For this hike take the Basin-Cascade Trail,
which starts at an intersection of trails just to the west of the Basin. At the
trail junction follow the Basin-Cascade Trail toward Lonesome Lake. Stay on

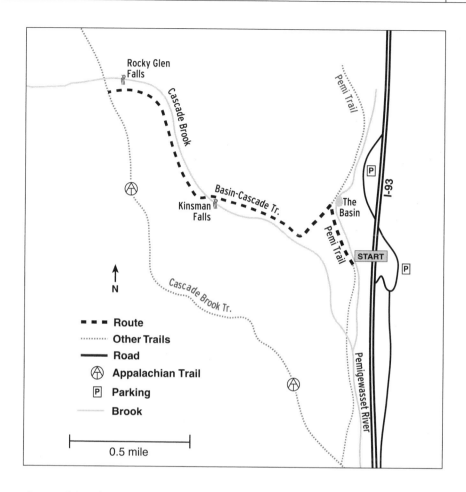

Rocky Glen Falls

Cascade Brook

Pemi Trail

P

I-93

Basin-Cascade Tr.

Kinsman Falls

The Basin

Pemi Trail

START

P

N

Cascade Brook Tr.

Pemigewasset River

- - - **Route**

.... **Other Trails**

—— **Road**

Ⓐ **Appalachian Trail**

P **Parking**

—— **Brook**

0.5 mile

this trail for the entire hike. Almost immediately the trail begins to parallel Cascade Brook, which will be on your left. Water cascades over smooth rock, and the ledges next to the water provide nice views to the east. On a sunny day, you may find that you have no need to explore farther than the first 0.25 mile, but if you do, you will find ever more dramatic cascades, and ever fewer people.

A side trail soon leads left to the base of a wide, unnamed waterfall that is worth a look. The trail climbs moderately to the top of these falls, where there are more good views. The forest next to the brook varies; you will see hardwoods and conifers, as well as flowery shrubs like hobblebush and shadbush. The trail continues to climb moderately over a rough trail that can be slippery in wet weather due to exposed tree roots. You will pass a seemingly endless series of cascades, small waterfalls, calm pools, and even a

While hiking along the Basin-Cascade Trail, you may want to stop for a moment to enjoy Kinsman Falls.

small gorge on your way to the base of Kinsman Falls, where the trail crosses Cascade Brook about 0.5 mile from the Basin. This crossing can be difficult in high water. Try the crossing yourself before letting small children forge ahead. Kinsman Falls is a series of 10-foot cascades where the water plunges from pool to pool before being forced through a small gorge for the final drop.

Continue hiking on the Basin-Cascade Trail for a moderate climb to Rocky Glen Falls at 0.9 mile. This is our favorite waterfall of the trip. At Rocky Glen Falls water tumbles over a series of falls through a narrow gorge of gray rock, which is topped by the cool green of balsam fir and red spruce. Viewing the falls from the bottom of the gorge is a refreshing experience, as the cold mountain water chilling the air can make the temperature much cooler than it is in the surrounding forest. Continuing up the trail will provide different views of the falls. This trip ends at the junction with Cascade Brook Trail. For one final look at the falls, follow the bank of the brook south from this trail junction for about 60 yards to the top of the falls. Be careful: it is a long, rocky ride down if you slip and fall. To return to the parking area, retrace your steps down the Basin-Cascade Trail.

Alternate trip: To combine this trip with the Lonesome Lake trip, turn right onto the Cascade Brook Trail when you reach the end of the Basin-Cascade Trail. From this point it is 1.3 miles and 650 feet of elevation gain to Lonesome Lake and the Fishin' Jimmy Trail. At the junction with the Fishin' Jimmy Trail, turn left to head to Lonesome Lake Hut or turn right to follow the shore of the lake to the Lonesome Lake Trail, which will take you down to Lafayette Campground. From the campground, you can take either the Pemi Trail or the Franconia Notch Bicycle Path 1.9 miles back to the Basin parking area.

Fall Foliage: Why Leaves Change

Autumn is one of the busiest seasons in the White Mountains as millions of "leaf peepers" crowd the area's highways hoping to witness the peak of one of nature's most beautiful displays of color. In the White Mountains, peak fall colors usually occur some time between the last week of September and Columbus Day weekend. River valleys and mountain slopes below 3,000 feet are covered in northern hardwood forests, where beech, maple, birch, and other hardwoods provide dramatic colors—yellow, orange, gold, red, and purple. New England's climate tends to create conditions for what many people consider the best foliage displays in the world. Generous summer rainfall followed by a September of cool nights and sunny days is generally thought to provide the most brilliant colors. The state of New Hampshire provides foliage forecasts on its website at foliage.visitnh.gov.

During the summer months, tree leaves produce food for the tree in the form of chlorophyll, which is green. As summer nears an end, cold weather causes the tree to stop producing chlorophyll as it prepares to go dormant for the winter. As this chlorophyll breaks down, the colors of other chemicals in the leaves begin to show through. The decomposition of chlorophyll is hastened

Fallen red maple leaves dot the ground throughout the Whites in autumn.

by cool weather and sunshine. Pigments such as carotene and xanthophyll are present in the leaves year-round, but their orange and yellow colors do not become visible until chlorophyll production stops. Dry weather can increase the concentration of sugars in leaves, leading to the production of anthocyanin, which is responsible for the brilliant reds and purples found in red maple, sumac, red oak, and other trees. As winter nears, leaves that manage to stay on the trees eventually turn brown, a result of a waste product known as tannin.

Popular foliage driving tours include NH 112 (Kancamagus Highway), US 302 through Crawford Notch, and US 2 north of the Presidential Range. During peak foliage weekends, traffic on these routes can be very heavy, so it is probably best to leave your car and venture out onto the trails. Any bike ride in this book will give you a good look at the foliage from within the forest, and getting above the trees can give you a good overall look. Easier fall foliage hikes include the Roost in Evans Notch (trip 1), Lookout Ledge (trip 3) in Randolph, Mount Willard in Crawford Notch (trip 8), the Boulder Loop Trail (trip 9) on the Kancamagus Highway, and Mount Pemigewasset in Franconia Notch (trip 11).

TRIP 3
LOOKOUT LEDGE

Rating: Moderate

Distance: 2.6 miles up and back

Elevation Gain: 1,000 feet

Estimated Time: 2 hours

Maps: AMC White Mountain Trail Map #6: E9, USGS Mount
Crescent and Mount Washington Quadrangles

This short hike will provide panoramic views of the Presidential Range.

Directions

From the northern intersection of US 2 and NH 16, drive west on US 2 for 4.6 miles and turn right onto Durand Road, then left at the T intersection in 0.1 mile. The parking area is on the right in another 1.0 mile, next to the Ravine House Site.

Trip Description

This hike is short, though steep at times, but rewards hikers with panoramic views of the northern Presidential Range from a small ledge in Randolph. The hike follows the Ledge Trail, which is just one of numerous trails in the Northern Presidentials and Kilkenny Range that are maintained by the Randolph Mountain Club. The town of Randolph is a small, tightly knit community that has been home to many dedicated hikers for more than a century, and many homes are connected to each other and the surrounding mountain trails by casual footpaths that wind throughout the community. Lookout Ledge is accessible from many points within Randolph, but the Ledge Trail is the most direct route.

From the parking area, walk up the paved driveway for about 30 yards and then turn right onto the trail. The hike begins climbing at a moderate pace almost immediately as it works its way up through a northern hardwood forest that still shows signs of damage from a major ice storm that hit the area in 1998. Despite the damage, numerous woodland wildflowers like

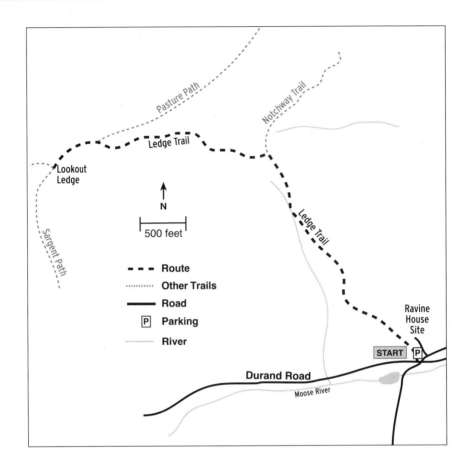

trilliums, clintonia, and trout lily can be found blooming here in mid-May among the modest-sized sugar maples and yellow birch in the forest. At 0.6 mile, the Notchway Trail comes in from the right. Turn left to stay on the Ledge Trail. The grade gets steeper, though still not too taxing by White Mountain standards.

At 1.2 miles, continue on the Ledge Trail at its intersection with the Pasture Path. The last 0.1 mile of the hike is completely different than the previous section, as the hardwoods give way to a dark, fragrant grove of spruce trees. The trail gets rockier and you start to see glimpses of the view through the trees on your left. At 1.3 miles from the parking area, you reach an intersection with the Crescent Ridge Trail with Lookout Ledge just below. Considering the low amount of effort needed, the view is one of the best in

Trout lillies grow best in deciduous shade.

the Whites, with Mounts Madison, Adams, and Jefferson looming above the valley, seemingly almost close enough to touch. The view into the glacial cirque known as King Ravine below Mount Adams is spectacular, and with binoculars you can see hikers climbing the headwall or walking the ridges above.

As you hike back to the car, you should thank the foresight of the people of Randolph and surrounding communities who spent much of the first half of this decade negotiating purchase rights and raising money to create the 10,000-acre Randolph Community Forest, which includes much of the land on this hike. The creation of the town forest (at the cost of $4 million) provides an important ecological link between the Presidential Range to the south and the Kilkenny Range and beyond to the north. Formerly owned by timber management companies, this community forest should continue to be sustainably harvested and allow for traditional recreation uses like hiking and hunting, while preventing development of the land. The Randolph Community Forest has since been used as a model for creating other community forests in the region such as the Errol Town Forest in Errol, N.H., and the Brushwood Community Forest in West Fairlee, VT.

TRIP 4
STAIRS, COOSAUK, AND HITCHCOCK FALLS

Rating: Easy
Distance: 2.0 miles up and back
Elevation Gain: 650 feet
Estimated Time: 2 hours
Maps: AMC White Mountain Trail Map #1: E9, USGS Mount
Washington Quadrangle

**In the spring, this great family hike will give you views of
wildflowers and waterfalls.**

Directions
From the western intersection of NH 16 and US 2, head west on US 2 for 4.5
miles and turn left onto Pinkham B Road (also called Dolly Copp Road). The
parking area for the Howker Ridge Trail is on the right in another 0.2 mile.

Trip Description
This hike on the lower end of the Howker Ridge Trail visits three waterfalls
along a mile of Bumpus Brook, a stream that begins on the upper slopes of
Mount Madison. This is a great hike for families, particularly in May when
the brook is running high and the wildflowers are in full bloom. Later in the
summer the falls tend to be less impressive, particularly Stairs Falls, which
practically disappears, so wait for a heavy rainfall if you plan to do this hike
long after the snow has melted. Although the hike is rated easy, the elevation
gain is 650 feet, so you may breathe heavily once in a while. However, the
trail surface is in good shape with good footing and the grades are moderate. Because this hike offers much to explore, you will be able to easily turn
around if the kids get tired without feeling that you have missed much.

Leaving the south side of Pinkham B Road, the Howker Ridge Trail coincides with the Randolph Path for about 30 yards. Soon after crossing an
abandoned railroad bed, turn left where the two trails diverge, continuing
on the Howker Ridge Trail. The trail climbs gradually through a forest recovering from several years of logging and soon crosses an old logging road.

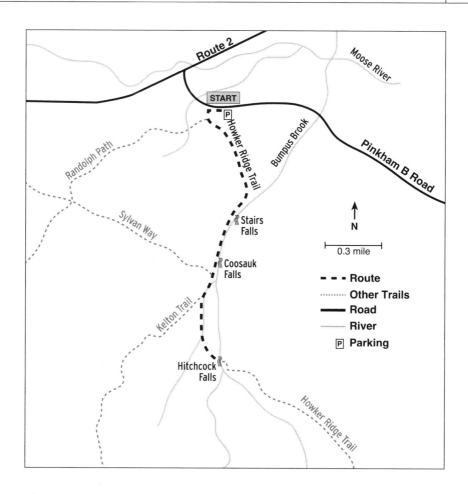

The Howker Ridge Trail continues straight across the road and comes to the banks of Bumpus Brook, about 0.4 mile from the parking area. Bumpus Brook is named after the Bumpus family, some of the earliest settlers of this area. With the brook on the left, the trail begins to climb moderately. In high water, the cascades along this lower section of the brook are worth visiting, even if you do not plan to continue to the falls higher up.

In spring, you will be surrounded by many of the wildflowers that are common in the lower forests of the White Mountains, finding yourself in a forest of green accented by red, white, yellow, and pink. These flowers include red and painted trilliums, wild lily of the valley, trout lilies, clintonia, bellwort, wild oats, rose twisted stalk, and Indian cucumber. Keep your eyes

Coosauk Falls, in the background, drops 40 feet into Bumpus Brook and may be the most picturesque of the three waterfalls you will find on this trip.

and ears open for songbirds such as American redstart, Canada warblers, black-throated blue warblers, and hermit thrushes, which forage among the understory of striped maple and hobblebush. On a lucky day you might even spot a snowshoe hare or a moose.

You will soon reach an outlook to Stairs Falls, which tumbles 15 feet over a natural rock staircase from a tributary on the opposite side of Bumpus Brook. In high water, the waterfall is about 10 feet wide and water splashes in all directions, but when the mountains dry out, it is a disappointing trickle. Just beyond Stairs Falls is the Devil's Kitchen, a beautiful, richly shaded gorge with 40-foot-high rock walls. Bumpus Brook runs through the center of the gorge, while hemlock trees lean over the gorge from the banks above. Keep an eye on small children while viewing the Devil's Kitchen from above, as the drop-off is sudden.

Next is an outlook to Coosauk Falls, which drops into Bumpus Brook from a tributary on the opposite bank. Coosauk Falls may be the most picturesque of the three waterfalls on this trip. It falls about 40 feet in a delicate, thin stream, framed by hemlock and birch trees and surrounded by lush ferns. According to *The White Mountains: Names, Places, and Legends* by John T. B. Mudge, Coosauk Falls was named by William Peek, a summer resident of Randolph, N.H., who mistakenly thought the Abenaki Indian word "coos" meant "rough." Coos is generally thought to mean "place of pines."

Continuing on toward Hitchcock Falls, the Howker Ridge Trail passes both the Sylvan Way and Kelton Trail. Continue straight at both intersections and climb moderately away from Bumpus Brook and through more wildflower habitat. The trail crosses a few small streams before returning to Bumpus Brook at the foot of Hitchcock Falls 1.0 mile from the parking area. Hitchcock Falls is a tall waterfall that plunges about 60 feet over large boulders. Tall cliffs protect the banks on both sides of the stream, making it somewhat difficult to explore the upper reaches of the falls; however, resting on the rocks at the base of the falls is a great way to spend a lunch break. The Howker Ridge Trail crosses the brook at this point on its way to the summit of Mount Madison (a very strenuous 4-hour hike from here). This trip, however, ends at Hitchcock Falls.

TRIP 5
NORTHERN PRESIDENTIALS WATERFALLS

Rating: Easy
Distance: 2.5 miles round-trip
Elevation Gain: 600 feet
Estimated Time: 1 to 2 hours
Maps: AMC White Mountain Trail Map #1: E9, USGS Mount
   Washington Quadrangle

This easy woodland walk leads to four waterfalls.

Directions
From the northern intersection of US 2 and NH 16, drive west on US 2 for 5.5 miles to the Appalachia parking area on the left.

Trip Description
If you are in the mood for a walk through beautiful forests to tumbling White Mountain waterfalls, this is the trip to take. The hike won't overwhelm you with dramatic mountain views, but it also won't overwhelm you with strenuous uphill hiking. It starts with an easy climb along Snyder Brook, quickly passing three waterfalls before heading back down and to the west for a visit to the biggest falls of the trip, Cold Brook Falls. The hike presents the creativity of the early twentieth century Randolph path builders who recognized that the mountains offered beauty beyond the alpine world of the high peaks.

The hike starts on the Fallsway Trail at the eastern end of the Appalachia parking area on US 2. Follow the trail for a few yards to the Presidential Rail Trail, and follow the rail trail to the left for 100 yards or so to the Brookbank Trail, which is on the right just beyond an old railroad bridge. The Brookbank Trail climbs moderately, parallel to Snyder Brook, and soon reaches Gordon Falls in a beautiful grove of old hemlocks. Gordon Falls is a modest 15-foot-high cascade with numerous smaller cascades and pools below the main falls. Above the fall, the trail passes Sylvan Way and continues to climb at a moderate pace through the hemlock forest to Lower and Upper Salroc Falls.

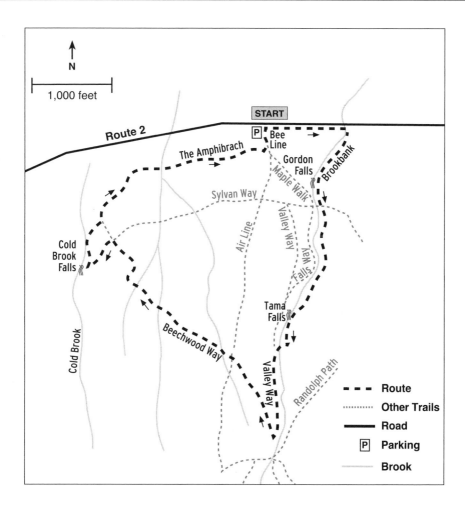

About 0.7 mile from Appalachia, the Brookbank Trail reaches the base of Tama Falls, which tumbles in two big drops, making it the most dramatic of the three Snyder Brook falls. On a hot summer day, there are several places to wade into the stream and cool off or you can explore the shady hemlock grove, which boasts some very large trees. The trail climbs to the top of the falls, where it crosses the stream and ends at the Fallsway Trail. Turn left and follow the Fallsway Trail for about 100 yards to the Valley Way, where you should continue hiking uphill.

In another 0.1 mile, turn right on the Beechwood Way Trail, which gradually descends through a classic northern hardwood forest that is especially

Cold Brook Falls tumbles 30 feet into a deep pool.

beautiful in spring with its thick understory of blooming hobblebush and woodland flowers like trilliums and trout lilies. Turn left onto Sylvan Way 0.7 miles from the Valley Way for a short walk to Cold Brook Falls. Here, Cold Brook tumbles about 30 feet through a gorge-like cleft in the bedrock to a deep pool at its base. It makes a good place to spend some time having a picnic lunch or taking a dip in the pool, while listening to the soothing sounds of the rushing water.

From the falls, continue downhill on the trail next to the stream for about 100 yards to the Link and Memorial Bridge. The bridge is unusual for White Mountain trail bridges, with its wooden railings and deck resting on a beautiful fieldstone foundation. Next to the bridge is a granite stone inscribed with a memorial to several of the early trail builders in this area, including J.R. Edmunds, E.B. Cook, and Gordon Lowe. To return to the Appalachia parking area, head east on the Link (right as you are facing downstream) and walk the almost flat 0.7 miles back to your car.

The Geology of the White Mountains

Five-hundred million years ago, the land that is now New Hampshire lay under a vast ancient ocean known as the proto-Atlantic. The North American continent ended around the present-day eastern border of Vermont. Over millions of years, sedimentary rock formed at the bottom of this ancient ocean. Between 500 million and 300 million years ago, multiple mountain-building events took place as the European and African continents merged with the North American continental plate. First, the Taconian event created an ancient mountain range. As ancient Europe moved across the Atlantic, it pushed a volcanic chain of islands, much like Japan and the Philippines, into the North American continent. The pressures of this collision transformed sedimentary rocks like sandstone, shale, and limestone into much harder metamorphic rocks like quartzite, schist, gneiss, and marble. By the end of this collision, around 435 million years ago, new mountains stood in Vermont and far western New Hampshire; however, the rest of what would become the White Mountains still lay at the bottom of the ocean.

Much of the mountains built during the Taconian event eroded away into the proto-Atlantic, creating new layers of sedimentary rock over what would become the rest of New Hampshire. Between 335 and 375 million years ago, the European and African plates eventually collided with North America in what is known as the Acadian mountain-building cycle or Acadian Orogeny. This event created a mountain range where the White Mountains now stand. Again, sedimentary rocks were metamorphosed into much harder rocks, the most resistant of which is still visible today and is known as Littleton schist. The Presidential Range consists of Littleton schist, which was much more resistant to erosion than other rocks. According to this picture of history, New Hampshire and the White Mountains were once part of Africa or Europe.

The mountain building did not end with the Acadian Orogeny, however. As the continents once again separated to re-form the Atlantic Ocean about 200 million years ago, the earth's crust was stretched and fractured, allowing magma to bubble up from deep within the earth. This is when most of New Hampshire's granite was formed in underground magma plutons and above ground in volcanic lava flows. The most common rocks from this era include Moat volcanics (still seen on Moat Mountain), Conway granite, Mount Osceola granite (seen on most of Mount Chocorua), and Winnepesaukee granite. The Moat volcanics once covered most of the White Mountains in more than 9,000 feet of rock, but it has mostly eroded away. Conway granite is now the most common granite in the area. It formed underground in a huge sea of lava, which as it hardened became what is now known as the White Mountain batholith. The granite of this batholith now forms the base of the White Mountains.

Millions of years of erosion have taken place since these mountain-building events, leaving behind a mountain range with a complex composition. Sedimentary rocks have completely disappeared from the New Hampshire land-

Moving glaciers formed Tuckerman Ravine.

scape, leaving a mixture of igneous rocks, like granite and basalt, and metamor-phic schists and gneisses. Since schists are the most durable of these rocks, they make up the tallest peaks, while granite is more common on lower peaks. Over the last 2 or 3 million years, much of the erosion in New England has occurred during periods of heavy glaciation. During this time frame, there have been sev-eral periods of glaciation, known as ice ages, where all of New Hampshire was covered in a layer of ice, sometimes more than a mile thick.

The last ice age, known as the Wisconsin glaciation, peaked around 18,000 years ago when a continental ice sheet reached as far south as Long Island. All of the White Mountains were completely covered with ice, and their smooth, rounded summits are a result of glacial scouring. Tongues of ice carved through weaker rocks to form the U-shaped valleys of Franconia Notch, Zealand Notch, and Crawford Notch. As the ice retreated, small remnant glaciers remained on the colder north and east facing slopes. These alpine glaciers eventually carved out several glacial cirques, including Tuckerman Ravine and Madison Gulf. The ice sheet also left behind huge boulders that it carried for miles. One of these "glacial erratics" is Glen Boulder, which can be seen from NH 16 as you approach Pinkham Notch from the south.

The ice completely retreated from the White Mountains at some point be-tween 12,000 and 14,000 years ago. For a while, the area resembled the high arctic, where only lichens and small tundra plants could survive. Remnants of this tundra community still exist in the White Mountains above treeline. As the climate slowly warmed, the composition of plant species began to change. Co-nifers like spruce and fir first grew in the recently thawed soil. Over time, hard-woods moved in: first birch and aspen, then beech, maple, and oak. About 3,000 years ago, the current makeup of the forests was reached, with northern hard-wood forests common at lower elevations and boreal forests dominant above 3,000 feet.

TRIP 6
ARETHUSA FALLS WITH
FRANKENSTEIN CLIFF

Rating: Moderate

Distance: 3.0 miles out and back for the falls, 6.2-mile loop to falls
and cliff

Elevation Gain: 900 feet to falls only, 1,300 feet to falls and cliff

Estimated Time: 1 hour, 30 minutes; 3 hours for entire loop

Maps: AMC White Mountain Trail Map #3: H8, USGS Crawford
Notch Quadrangle

**This short hike goes to the tallest waterfall in New Hamp-
shire, with an option to hike to Frankenstein Cliff.**

Directions

The Arethusa Falls Trailhead is located on a spur road on the west side of US
302, 8.5 miles north of Bear Notch Road in Bartlett, and 6 miles south of the
AMC Highland Center at Crawford Depot. The trail begins at the upper parking area, but if that lot is full, there is usually plenty of parking at the lower
parking area just off of US 302.

Trip Description

At 200 feet high, Arethusa Falls is the tallest waterfall in New Hampshire,
and in spring there is an impressive wall of water making the plunge down a
wall of reddish-brown rock on Bemis Brook. The hike to the falls is relatively
easy and suitable for most kids with some hiking experience who can go uphill at a moderate pace for more than a mile. If you feel like doubling your effort, you can make this a loop hike by adding Frankenstein Cliff to your itin-
erary. The views from the cliff are excellent, but it is a down-sloping ledge
with a very steep drop-off, so it is not appropriate for smaller children.

The Arethusa Falls Trail begins in the southwest corner of the parking
lot, across the railroad tracks, which are still used by the Conway Scenic Railway. It climbs at a moderate pace and soon intersects with the Bemis Brook
Trail, which parallels the Arethusa Falls Trail, offering a rougher but more

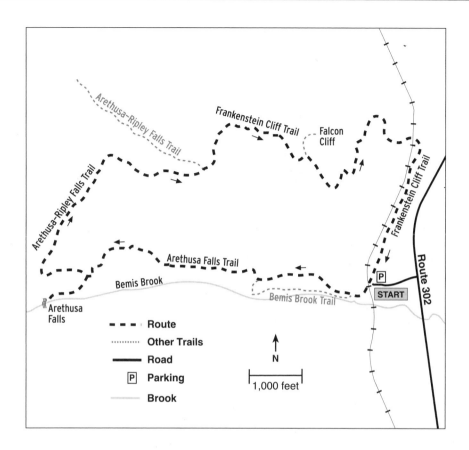

scenic hike next to the brook. If you decide to hike the Bemis Brook Trail, it reconnects with the Arethusa Falls Trail in about 0.5 mile. Shortly after the upper junction with the Bemis Brook Trail, the trail turns to the right and ascends at a gentler grade, soon entering a beautiful spruce forest with the sounds of Bemis Brook off to the left.

At 1.0 mile, the trail makes the first of two stream crossings over wooden bridges, and then makes a short, steep climb up to the Arethusa-Ripley Falls Trail at 1.3 miles. From here it is a steep 0.2 mile descent to Bemis Brook and a view of the falls. In high water, it is difficult to go much farther, but in lower water it is possible to carefully navigate to the base of the falls. Either way, you will be treated to the roaring sounds of the waterfall, cool temperatures as the air flows over the cold mountain stream, and the occasional dousing of mist from the tumbling water.

Hiking past Arethusa Falls, the tallest waterfall in the White Mountains. It was named after the Greek nymph of the same name who was turned into a fountain.

Once you have enjoyed the falls, head back up the trail to its intersection with the Arethusa-Ripley Trail. Continue straight on the Arethusa Falls Trail to head back to the parking area, or turn left on the Arethusa-Ripley Trail if you decide to make the journey to Frankenstein Cliff.

The Arethusa-Ripley Trail starts by making a short descent to a brook it parallels and then crosses at 0.1 mile from the Arethusa Falls Trail. The trail is much narrower and rougher than the Arethusa Falls Trail and it makes a 0.5 mile traverse of a side slope, crossing two more brooks in the process, the first of which has an interesting cascade that drops about 30 feet. After the second brook crossing, the trail climbs steeply for about 0.25 mile before leveling out and following the ridgeline to the Frankenstein Cliff Trail 1.1 miles from the Arethusa Falls Trail.

Turn right and follow the Frankenstein Cliff Trail, which continues on a relatively level grade through spruce and birch, reaching the height of land and an obstructed view of Mount Washington in 0.3 mile. From here, the hike begins a steep descent over rocky trail and through spruce woods to Frankenstein Cliff, which will be on the right, 0.8 mile from the Arethusa-

Ripley Trail. The drop-off at the edge of the cliff is significant, as the cliff top stands 800 feet about the valley floor, which is only 0.3 mile away as the crow flies. There are excellent unobstructed views of the nearby Saco River, Stairs Mountain, and Mount Crawford, as well as Mount Chocorua in the distance. In high water, you can even make out Arethusa Falls off to the right. On a day with little wind or road traffic, you can hear the rushing waters of the Saco River and the falls.

To complete the loop, continue the steep descent on the Frankenstein Cliff Trail. The trail eventually skirts the bottom of the cliffs where at times the trail can be challenging with loose rocks, especially in wet weather. This area is the staging area for ice climbers in the winter, as there are several popular ice-climbing routes on the cliffs. The trail crosses under a railroad trestle, then turns right and parallels the tracks back to the parking area, 1.3 miles below the top of the cliffs.

TRIP 7
LONESOME LAKE

Rating: Easy
Distance: 3.2 miles up and back
Elevation Gain: 950 feet
Estimated Time: 2 hours
Maps: AMC White Mountain Trail Map #2: H4, USGS Franconia
    Quadrangle

**This easy family hike in Franconia Notch will take you to a
high mountain lake with views of Franconia Ridge.**

Directions
From the Franconia Notch Parkway (I-93), follow signs to Lafayette Campground, 7.6 miles north of NH 112. Park in the hiker parking area at the Lafayette Campground in Franconia Notch State Park. The only exit for the campground is on the southbound side of the parkway, but hiker parking is available on the northbound side.

Trip Description
Lonesome Lake is one of those special places in the White Mountains, where families and friends build backcountry vacation memories that are never forgotten. Perhaps those memories are the result of the rustic comfort of Lonesome Lake Hut or the friendly conversations that begin there over a cup of hot chocolate. Most likely, they come from the incredible setting: the beautiful blue waters of the lake are surrounded by a rich green spruce-fir forest, and in the distance rising above the trees is the rugged, sharp-edged outline of Franconia Ridge, looking more like the Rockies than the mountains of New England. It is also relatively easy to get to Lonesome Lake. The well-graded path of Lonesome Lake Trail enables you to climb the 950 feet to the hut in a little more than an hour. This is a good hike for families, and Lonesome Lake Hut is the AMC "family hut," so it makes a great place to take children for their first overnight experience in the backcountry. It is a popular place in summer; if you plan on spending the night, you will need to make reservations well in advance.

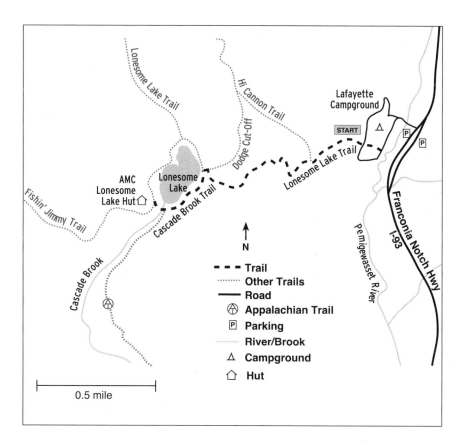

Trail legend:
- - - Trail
.... Other Trails
——— Road
Ⓐ Appalachian Trail
Ⓟ Parking
——— River/Brook
△ Campground
⌂ Hut

0.5 mile

The hike to Lonesome Lake begins from Lafayette Campground in Franconia Notch State Park. The Lonesome Lake Trail is about 50 yards south of the shower building on the back road of the campground. The trail begins in a mature northern hardwood forest typical of the lower slopes in Franconia Notch. Birch, beech, and maple are the dominant trees, and if you look carefully at the smooth bark of the beech trees, you might find the claw marks of black bears, which depend on beechnuts for a large part of their diets. Though you are unlikely to see one on your hike, bears are common in this area and can sometimes be seen on the ski slopes of Cannon Mountain foraging for raspberries.

The trail climbs moderately for the most part, though you will encounter a few steep sections, especially after the trail makes a sharp right. After this right the forest slowly transitions from northern hardwoods to a forest of fir and paper birch. When you reach the height of land, you have entered

Hikers relax at Lonesome Lake, enjoying the view of Franconia Ridge in the distance.

the boreal zone where the air is filled with the sweet smell of red spruce and balsam fir. At this point the trail levels out and you soon reach a trail junction near the eastern shore of Lonesome Lake. Turn left and follow the Cascade Brook Trail, which follows the eastern shore of the lake and has good views of the Kinsmans. At the next trail junction continue straight on what is now the Fishin' Jimmy Trail. You will soon reach Lonesome Lake Hut. Below the hut is a small dock where you can sit and absorb the views of Franconia Ridge or take a plunge into the lake, which averages 3 to 6 feet in depth and is 12 feet at its deepest.

While in the hut, pick up information for a self-guided nature tour of the area. In addition to the boreal forest, an extensive boggy area near the hut provides a good place for bird-watching or plant study. Plants such as leatherleaf, Labrador tea, and sheep laurel are common here, and you can also find the insectivorous, sticky-leaved sundew in nutrient-poor soils around the bog. To complete the hike, follow the Around-Lonesome-Lake Trail from the hut. This trail takes you along the western shore of the lake, over bog bridges with views of the Cannon Balls, and back to the Lonesome Lake Trail. Turn right on the Lonesome Lake Trail and follow it back down to Lafayette Campground. For a longer day hike, you can combine this trip with a hike along Cascade Brook (see trip 2).

TRIP 8
MOUNT WILLARD

Rating: Easy
Distance: 3.2 miles up and back
Elevation Gain: 900 feet
Estimated Time: 2 hours
Maps: AMC White Mountain Trail Map #3: G8, USGS Crawford
   Notch Quadrangle

This popular hike will give you a spectacular view of Crawford Notch.

Directions
Parking for the Mount Willard Trail is at the Crawford Depot next to the AMC's Highland Center in Crawford Notch, which is on US 302, 8.5 miles south of US 3 in Twin Mountain and 21.0 miles north of NH 16 in Glen.

Trip Description
This hike may offer the best effort-to-view ratio in the White Mountains, as its relatively easy climb takes you to wonderfully scenic views of Crawford Notch. While this hike is rated easy, 900 feet of elevation gain will seem difficult if you are unaccustomed to regular physical activity. However, if you are used to hiking and looking for an easy day, or if you want to bring along kids eager to climb their first mountain, this is a great choice. Of course, the relative ease of this hike does draw the crowds, so to ensure a more peaceful experience, hike Mount Willard at times other than summer and fall weekends. Getting an early start helps. Sitting alone in the sun on the ledges of Mount Willard early on a summer morning is one of the more relaxing experiences in the White Mountains.

The Mount Willard Trail begins across the railroad tracks from the Crawford Depot, which houses the Macomber Family Information Center. It coincides with the Avalon Trail for about 100 yards (you can follow the Avalon Trail to Mount Avalon if you are up for a longer, more strenuous hike to less crowded views of Crawford Notch). At its junction with the Avalon Trail, the Mount Willard Trail turns left and winds its way through a mixed forest as it parallels a brook and climbs moderately.

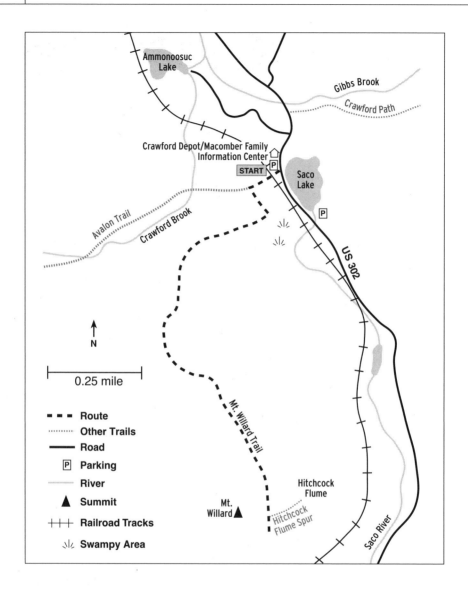

In spring and summer you might find warblers foraging for insects among the hobblebush, trilliums, and trout lilies. On your right at 0.5 mile you will find Centennial Pool, a basin of cool water sitting at the base of a small waterfall that tumbles 10 feet over square, fractured rocks.

After the trail reaches Centennial Pool, it leaves the brook and continues on a moderate grade over a pathway eroded from years of use as a carriage road and hiking trail. At times the footing is a bit rough due to exposed rocks,

These freshly created snowshoe tracks pass in front of Mount Webster.

but the hiking is relatively easy for the most part. As you climb higher, the forest becomes dominated by paper birch with an understory of balsam fir. Many of the birch trees are severely bent over as a result of a 1998 ice storm. The trail makes a long, moderate ascent of the western side of the mountain before turning sharply left, then right on its way to the summit, with the last 400 yards being an easy, mostly flat walk. As you reach the summit, you will emerge from the forest onto several acres of wide-open ledges with spectacular views to the south of Crawford Notch.

Crawford Notch is a classic U-shaped valley, carved by a glacier during the last ice age 15,000 to 18,000 years ago. On the eastern side of the notch, the Webster Cliffs rise dramatically from the floor of the notch and mark the southern extent of the ridge that forms the Southern Presidentials. On the western side of the notch is the Willey Range, with Mount Willey and Mount Field rising almost 3,000 feet from the Saco River, visible at the bottom of the notch. From this perspective it is easy to picture a river of ice flowing between the peaks. In addition to the great views, you are likely to see white-throated sparrows, slate-colored juncos, ravens, and possibly a soaring hawk while you are soaking in the sun on the granite ledges. To complete your hike, just retrace your steps back down the Mount Willard Trail.

TRIP 9
KANCAMAGUS BOULDER LOOP

Rating: Moderate
Distance: 3.1 miles round-trip
Elevation Gain: 950 feet
Estimated Time: 2 hours
Maps: AMC White Mountain Trail Map #3: I10, USGS Silver Lake
   and North Conway West Quadrangles

**This short hike leads to great views of the Kancamagus
Region.**

Directions
From NH 16 and NH 112 (Kancamagus Highway), drive west on NH 112 for
6.3 miles and then turn right on Dugway Road. Drive over the Albany Covered Bridge and turn right. Parking for the boulder loop trail is on the right
in another 0.1 mile.

Trip Description
The Boulder Loop Trail starts next to the Albany Covered Bridge and the
rushing waters of the Swift River. This starting location is itself a great place
to relax, have a picnic, and explore the banks of the river. The ledges at the
top of this hike offer the bird's-eye view of the area as they overlook the
river, the Kancamagus Highway, and the peaks of the Sandwich Range to
the south. Since the trail gains 1,000 feet in a little more than mile, you'll be
climbing at a steady pace for the first half of the trip, but the relatively short
distance ranks this hike on the easier end of the scale for White Mountain
hikes. If you have kids and want to impart some natural history lessons on
this hike, stop by the USFS ranger station near the intersection of NH 112
and NH 16, and pick up the interpretive leaflet that describes the flora and
geographical features along this trail.

The Boulder Loop Trail starts across the road from the parking area and
immediately starts climbing at a moderate pace, winding its way past white
pines and a jumble of large lichen-covered boulders that give the trail its
name. At 0.2 mile, you will reach the loop junction—turn left here. The trail

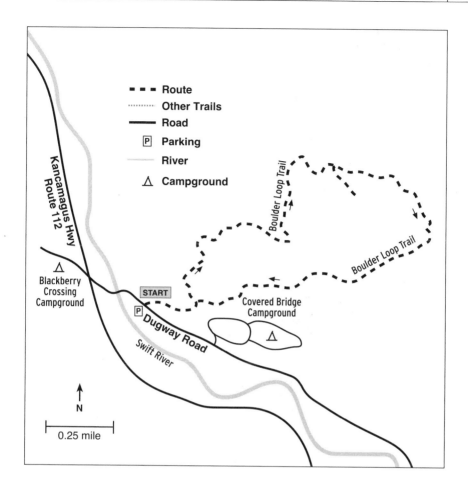

soon reaches the largest boulder on the hike, a house-sized behemoth that towers about 30 feet above the trail and is covered with leafy lichen known as rock tripe. Follow the trail to the right as it passes the boulder and continues its climb through a forest of northern hardwoods and the occasional spruce tree.

At 0.6 mile, you will pass a small outlook with views of the river and surrounding mountains, including the very tip of the summit cone on Mount Chocorua. You will notice that the forest has changed to spruce and fir, with pine and scrub oak hugging the ledges. After this viewpoint, the trail soon makes a short descent before beginning a moderate climb up to the main ledges. After a short, steep climb through a grove of hemlocks, the trail reaches a junction with the spur trail that leads to the ledges at 1.3 miles.

This hiker passes flowers (Bartram's shadbush) as he traverses the Kancamagus Boulder Loop Trail.

Follow the spur trail up to the right to reach the ledges after about two minutes of hiking. The ledges are spread out for several hundred yards and afford great views of the Swift River, nearby cliffs, Mount Chocorua, and other peaks in the Sandwich Range. Facing south, they get abundant sunshine so bring your sunscreen and stay awhile. There are also many wild blueberries growing here, so in midsummer, you can add some fresh fruit to your gorp, or trail mix.

To finish the loop, return to the trail junction and turn right. The trail soon begins a steep descent and winds its way below the ledges. As the grade eases, you will cross a stream at 2.3 miles, pass by some more large boulders and reach the end of the loop at 2.6 miles. From here, it is a 0.2 mile walk back to the parking area.

TRIP 10
BRIDAL VEIL FALLS

Rating: Moderate
Distance: 5 miles out and back
Elevation Gain: 1,100 feet
Estimated Time: 2 to 3 hours
Maps: AMC White Mountain Trail Map #2: G4, USGS Franconia
  Quadrangle

This nice woods walk will take you to a beautiful waterfall.

Directions
From Exit 38 on I-93 and the intersection of NH 18 and NH 116, head south
on NH 116. At 3.4 miles, turn left onto Coppermine Road, and park in the
parking area on the left. To reach the trailhead, you need to continue on foot
up Coppermine Road, staying to the right at a fork in the road and reaching
the Coppermine Trail on the left in about 0.25 mile. There is no parking at
the actual trailhead.

Trip Description
Bridal Veil Falls is a classic White Mountain waterfall, with a 30-foot tall wall
of water falling into a deep pool that empties over several smaller cascades
in Coppermine Brook. The hike, which starts near the farms of Franconia
to the west of the Cannon-Kinsman Range, is less traveled than the usual
White Mountain hot spots, but those who make the trek are rewarded with
quiet White Mountain forests and the cool waters of the falls. Overall, it is
a relatively easy hike with good footing on a trail that climbs a steady 1,100
feet over the 2.5 miles from the parking area to the base of the falls.

The Coppermine Trail begins as a wide former woods road in a stand of
big white pines, climbing at an easy pace. The forest during this part of the
hike shows signs of past harvesting, having grown back as a mosaic of both
hardwood and softwood species. After about half an hour of hiking through
these mixed woods, you will notice that the trees change to primarily hemlocks on your right as you come up to the rushing waters of Coppermine
Brook. You'll be tempted to take a break here and soak in the sounds of the

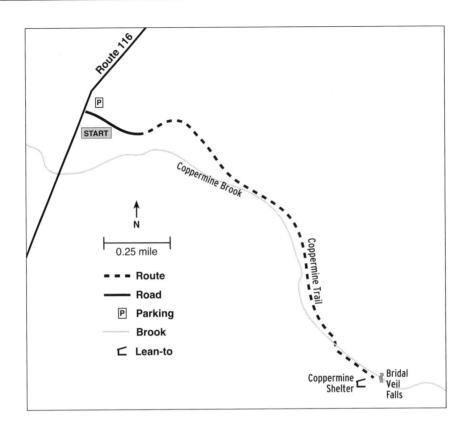

brook under the deep green canopy of the hemlocks—go ahead, you should have plenty of time. This is also a fine destination for a short walk with small children who will revel in playing among the big trees and throwing pebbles into the brook.

To continue to the falls, ignore the unmarked trail on the left and head straight up the Coppermine Trail, which becomes less woods road and more like a traditional narrow, rocky hiking trail. The grade gets a little steeper, but never too taxing, as it leaves the hemlock grove and enters a beautiful northern hardwood forest that is more typical for this elevation in the White Mountains. Spring is a great time for this hike. Not only are the falls more spectacular with spring snowmelt, but the wildflowers are abundant as the canopy created by the beeches, birches, and maples has yet to fully leaf out, flooding the forest floor with sunlight. If you can time your visit for mid-May, you will find large quantities of trout lilies, rose twisted stalk, red and painted trilliums, and spring beauties.

Bridal Veil Falls is considered by many to be one of the most attractive waterfalls in the White Mountains.

At the 2.3-mile point of the hike, the forest changes to spruce and paper birch just as you cross Coppermine Brook on a wooden bridge. The trail follows the brook, soon passes a lean-to, and then crosses the brook again (no bridge this time) before reaching the falls in a few hundred more yards. There are some good rocks for a lunch break at the bottom of the second cascade, from which you can see to the top of the main falls about 40 yards upstream. In high water, it can be difficult to reach the bottom of the main falls without getting seriously wet or trampling the streamside vegetation, so stay safe and use good Leave No Trace judgment before heading up to the falls. This is an out-and-back trip, so to return to your car, just turn around and head back on the Coppermine Trail.

Moose: An Animal Not Soon Forgotten

Moose are, by far, the largest animals you will encounter in the White Mountains. The average adult moose stands 6 feet tall at the shoulder and weighs in at 1,000 pounds—five times larger than the average black bear. A moose sighting is always memorable, and if you spend enough time in New Hampshire's backcountry, you are bound to have your own moose tales to tell. Moose are readily identified with the boreal forest, often called the "spruce-moose" forest, but you can find moose just about anywhere in New Hampshire since they feed on the twigs and bark of both hardwoods and softwoods (moose means "twig-eater" in Algonquin). They also enjoy eating aquatic plants such as water lilies. It may be hard to believe that a moose can grow so large eating twigs and lilies, but they are definitely strict vegetarians, eating 40 to 60 pounds of food a day.

Only adult male moose—known as bulls—grow antlers, which can weigh as much as 60 pounds. Every year bull moose grow new antlers, which fall off in December after the fall mating season known as the rut. A bull's antlers are covered with soft, blood-filled velvet during the spring and summer. About a month before the rut, the velvet dries up and falls off, leaving full-grown, hard-and-bony antlers used to attract mates and to spar with competing males. These sparring matches can be violent, but they rarely result in serious injury. During the rut, bull moose are quite cantankerous and care should be taken to stay out of their way.

Moose usually mate in late September. Calves are born about 240 days later in late May or early June. They stand 3 feet tall at birth and weigh around 25 pounds. Twins are common, occurring about 30 to 50 percent of the time. Moose calves stay with their mothers through their first winter, but they are usually chased off to fend for themselves by the next spring when their mother is preparing to give birth again. Mother moose can be even more dangerous than a rutting bull, and they will charge a person if they feel their calves are being threatened, so give moose cows and their calves a wide berth. A moose can seriously injure or kill a human. If a moose approaches you or if it shows irritation by folding its ears back, talk calmly to it (they have poor eyesight and might not realize you are a person) and slowly back away. If a moose charges you, run away. While you cannot outrun a moose, it should soon stop thinking of you as a threat and end its charge. Four subspecies of moose can be found across

An adult male moose relaxes near a pond.

northern North America, with Alaska and British Columbia having the largest populations.

In the lower 48 states, moose live from North Dakota east to Maine, as well as in the Northern Rockies south to Utah. In New Hampshire, moose were practically eliminated by hunting by the mid-1800s. Their population began to rebound in the 1970s and today about 9,600 moose live in the state. You are most likely to see moose in edge habitats, where forests abut beaver swamps, ponds, clearcuts, and roadsides. If you fail to find a moose while hiking, biking, or paddling, take a drive at dawn or dusk along the Kancamagus Highway, up NH 16 north of Milan, or on US 3 north of Lancaster—just drive slowly and keep your eyes peeled. Moose enthusiasts may also want to visit the annual North Country Moose Festival held in Colebrook and Pittsburg, N.H, and Canaan, Vt., during the last week of August. You can get more information about the festival by contacting the North Country Chamber of Commerce in Colebrook at P.O. Box 1, Colebrook, NH 03576; 603-237-8939; www.northcountrychamber.org.

TRIP 11
MOUNT PEMIGEWASSET

Rating: Easy
Distance: 3.6 miles up and back
Elevation Gain: 1,150 feet
Estimated Time: 2 hours, 45 minutes
Maps: AMC White Trail Mountain Map #2: H4, USGS Lincoln
   Quadrangle

This is a good first hike for families interested in exploring White Mountain peaks and will give great views with relatively little effort.

Directions
Parking for this trail is on US 3 at the Flume Gorge Visitor Center in Franconia Notch State Park. To get on US 3, you can take either Exit 33 on I-93 or Exit 1 on the Franconia Notch Parkway, which is 3.8 miles north of NH 112 in Lincoln.

Trip Description
Mount Pemigewasset, also known as Indian Head, is a small peak with a large treeless rock ledge that provides excellent views for a moderate effort. Pemigewasset is an Abenaki Indian word meaning "rapidly moving," which well describes the nearby Pemigewasset River. Pemigewasset was also a name given to a tribe of Native Americans who lived in the area during the seventeenth and eighteenth centuries. Two trails lead to the summit of Mount Pemigewasset: the Indian Head Trail and the Mount Pemigewasset Trail, both of which climb the peak from US 3 in Lincoln. This hike follows the Mount Pemigewasset Trail, which leaves from the Flume Gorge Visitor Center and entails 400 less feet of elevation gain than the alternate route.

From the north end of the Flume Gorge Visitor Center parking lot, follow the Franconia Notch Bicycle Path (see trip 32 for a description of this bike path) for about 150 yards to the Mount Pemigewasset Trail. Turn left onto the Mount Pemigewasset Trail. The trail crosses under US 3, passes a

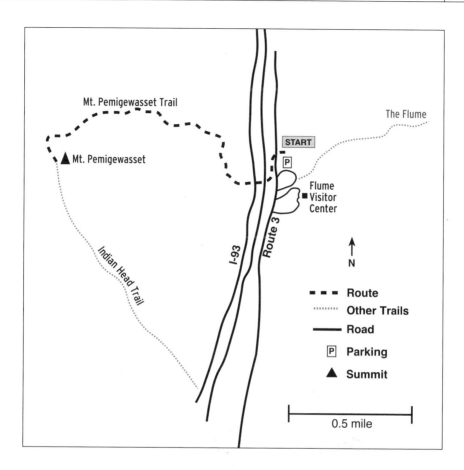

stream over a wooden bridge, and then tunnels under I-93. You soon leave civilization behind as you climb moderately through a northern hardwood forest filled with large yellow birch and American beech. The trail meanders over streams and past wildflowers, which depending on the season can include trout lilies, trilliums, star flowers, and rose twisted stalk. Shrubs include hobblebush, whose showy white flowers bloom in late May and early June. To keep the kids interested tell them which animals live in a northern hardwood forest: deer, bears, wild turkeys, ruffed grouse, and porcupines.

As you near the summit, the hardwoods are replaced by a spruce-fir forest, and at 1.7 miles the Indian Head Trail enters from the right. At 1.8 miles you suddenly emerge from the forest onto rock ledges (keep an eye on small children here) with excellent views to the south and west. After

Hikers can bring a dog on many of the trails in the White Mountains.

just an hour and a half of moderate hiking, you are looking out at Kinsman Ridge, Mount Moosilauke, Mount Osceola, and the peaks in the southern part of the Pemigewasset Wilderness Area. To get a view of Franconia Ridge to the northeast, continue past the first ledges to the true summit, which is on your left. On your way back down, be sure to stay to the right at the trail junction with the Indian Head Trail just below the ledges.

TRIP 12
LOW'S BALD SPOT

Rating: Moderate
Distance: 4.4 miles up and back
Elevation Gain: 900 feet
Estimated Time: 2 hours, 45 minutes
Maps: AMC White Mountain Trail Map #1: F9, USGS Mount
    Washington Quadrangle

This short, moderate hike from Pinkham Notch leads to good views of Mount Adams and Mount Madison. It's ideal for kids with some hiking experience.

Directions
This hike begins behind the trading post at the AMC Pinkham Notch Visitor Center. The visitor center is on NH 16, about 12.0 miles north of US 302 in Glen and 11.0 miles south of US 2 in Gorham.

Trip Description
Low's Bald Spot is an outcropping of rock that rises above the surrounding spruce to provide excellent views across the Great Gulf Wilderness. Its relatively low elevation and its proximity to the AMC Pinkham Notch Visitor Center make this a popular short hike. One scramble over steep rock near the top and the 900 feet of elevation gain results in some sections requiring substantial exertion; nonetheless, this is a good hike for families with hiking experience. This can be a fun hike for kids and adults as it crosses several small streams, passes through two forest types, and ends up with rewarding views from a prime wilderness lunch spot. Low's Bald Spot is most likely named after J. Herbert Low, who visited this spot in the early twentieth century.

The hike begins on the Old Jackson Road, a hiking trail that leaves from the Tuckerman Ravine Trail about 50 yards from its start at the AMC Pinkham Notch Visitor Center. The Old Jackson Road heads north, making a gentle ascent through a northern hardwood forest and crossing a small stream. The trail crosses several cross-country ski trails, and at 0.4 mile

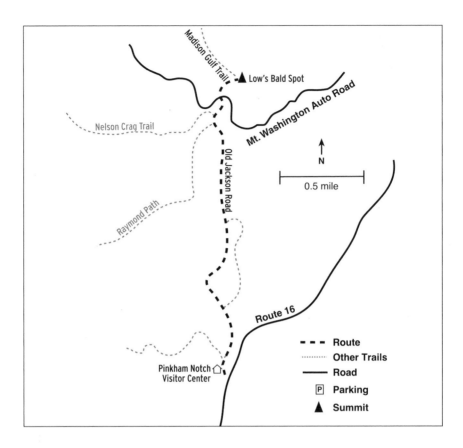

crosses a bridge and turns left (the Link is a ski trail that leads to the right at this point). After this left turn the trail begins a moderately steep climb, crosses another brook, and turns right for a long stretch of straight hiking that alternates between moderate climbs, descents, and flat sections.

In this section, the trail follows the contour line at the 2,600-foot level of Mount Washington, with the northern hardwood forest floor dropping quickly to the east. With the canopy of trees near eye-level to your right and the forest floor above you to the left, you can listen for a variety of woodland songbirds such as American redstart, white-throated sparrows, and hermit thrushes. After crossing several small brooks, the trail reaches a larger brook, makes a sharp left turn, and climbs steeply up a set of impressively placed rock stairs. At the top of these stairs, the trail turns right and continues at a relatively flat grade. The trail gets a little rockier as it passes the Raymond Path and the Nelson Crag Trail on its way to the Mount Washington Auto Road at 1.9 miles. This is the end of the Old Jackson Road.

A small spruce tree sits in the snow as Low's Bald Spot rises in the distance.

Cross the auto road and enter the Great Gulf Wilderness via the Madison Gulf Trail. Notice how the forest has changed to one filled with conifers: red spruce and balsam fir. You are now in the boreal forest, which is the dominant forest in Canada and along the United States-Canadian border. Turn right on the spur path 0.2 mile from the road, which leads to the summit of Low's Bald Spot. This 0.1-mile stretch of steep climbing to the open ledges above is the hardest part of the hike, with a scramble over a rock wall. Once at the top, you are rewarded with outstanding views across the Great Gulf Wilderness Area to Mount Adams and Mount Madison. The steep and impressive headwall of Madison Gulf can be seen between the two peaks. Madison Gulf is a glacial cirque formed by a glacier that flowed into the Great Gulf. Views to the north and east are also good from the summit's ledges, which are populated by scrubby spruce, blueberries, and sheep laurel. This is an out-and-back hike, so to complete your trip just retrace your steps back down the Madison Gulf Trail and Old Jackson Road.

TRIP 13
MOUNT ISRAEL

Rating: Moderate
Distance: 4.2 miles up and back
Elevation Gain: 1,700 feet
Estimated Time: 3 hours
Maps: AMC White Mountain Trail Map #3: L7, K7, USGS Center
  Sandwich Quadrangle

**This moderate hike takes hikers to excellent views of the
Sandwich Range and the Lakes Region.**

Directions

From the intersection of NH 113 and NH 109 in Center Sandwich, head west
on NH 113 for a few hundred yards and turn right (north) onto Grove Street
toward Sandwich Notch Road, following a sign for Mead Base. In 0.5 mile
take the left fork (straight) onto Diamond Ledge Road. In 1.0 mile the road
turns to gravel. One mile after this point, take the right fork, staying on Diamond Ledge Road and continuing to follow signs for Mead Base. Mead Base
will be in another 0.4 mile at the end of the road. Park in the lot on the left.

Trip Description

Mount Israel stands at the southern edge of the national forest, rising above
the pastoral setting of rural New Hampshire towns that fill the gap between
the lakes and the mountains. Despite its relatively low summit, which stands
no higher than 2,630 feet, Mount Israel provides excellent views of the surrounding mountains as well as the Lakes Region to the south. The hike via the
Wentworth Trail is more ambitious than you would expect, climbing 1,700
feet through a variety of forest types, including one of the more beautiful
stands of northern red oak in northern New Hampshire. Mead Base, where
the trail begins, is an Explorer Scout Camp that is used as a base for a variety
of outdoor activities, including trail maintenance.

This hike follows the Wentworth Trail for its entire length. The trail begins behind and to the left of the main building at Mead Base, climbing moderately through a mixed forest that fills with the colors of wildflowers in

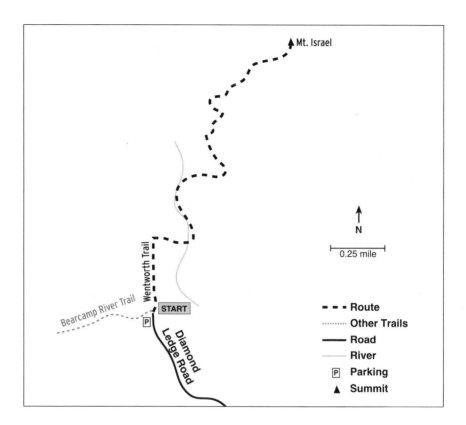

the spring. On your way up the mountain, you are likely to spot pink lady's slippers, star flowers, wild lily of the valley, wood sorrel, trilliums, violets, columbines, and other flowers growing beneath shrubs like hobblebush and striped maple. After a spring rain, you should also keep your eyes open for red efts, the land form of the aquatic red-spotted newt. Red efts are 1 1/2 to 3 3/8 inches long and their bright orange color stands out dramatically against the leaf litter on the forest floor. In the red-spotted newt's life cycle, efts are the stage between the larval stage and adulthood. Once red efts turn into newts, they can only breathe underwater through their gills.

The Wentworth Trail turns right at a stream crossing and angles up the south side of the mountain, paralleling a stone wall before turning left and following a brook while climbing moderately. The trail turns right again, leaving the brook at 0.8 mile, and winds its way up the mountain via switchbacks. Soon, northern red oaks are practically the only trees in the forest on the rocky southwest side of the mountain. The oaks create a high canopy

Northern red oaks grow from the north end of the Great Lakes, east to Nova Scotia, and south to Georgia.

that allows occasional glimpses to the southwest of Squam Lake. At 1.5 miles the trail passes under a rocky cliff on the right. A side trail on the left leads ten yards to nice views of the Lakes Region. The Wentworth Trail makes a right turn and climbs steeply to attain the ridgeline above the cliff. After this short, steep climb, you will find the hiking easier as you enter a spruce-fir forest and more level terrain.

The ridge walk through the dark green conifers is relatively flat and easy, until you make a short climb to a rocky knob that lies to the west of the true summit. From here, excellent views of the mountains are to the north. As you continue toward the summit, you reenter the forest, which occasionally thins out as you walk over gray rock ledges lined with veins of quartz and covered with reindeer lichen. Just below the summit, you will pass the Mead Trail on your left, which leads 1.7 miles to Sandwich Notch Road. A short climb brings you to the summit of Mount Israel, which has excellent 180-degree views to the north, particularly of the Sandwich Range. While on the summit, you are likely to see dark-eyed juncos, yellow-rumped warblers, and signs of coyote.

Suggested Snowshoe Hikes

Snowshoeing is a great way to experience the beauty of winter in the White Mountains. The trails are less crowded, the black flies and mosquitoes are nowhere to be found, and a quiet peace envelops the forests. Mountain streams are muffled under ice and powdery snow, animal tracks crisscross the landscape, and skies turn a deep blue with the sun hanging low in the sky. Experienced mountaineers will ascend to the high country using crampons and ice axes, but for the casual hiker there are many great hikes that can be accomplished with just a pair of snowshoes and basic winter hiking skills. To learn about keeping warm, dry, and safe in the winter, try a hike with an experienced winter hiker or take one of the many winter hiking courses offered by the AMC in the White Mountains or by local AMC chapters. *AMC Guide to Winter Hiking and Camping* by Yemaya Maurer and Lucas St. Clair is also a good resource.

The following trips in this book also make great snowshoeing excursions. Expect your hiking times to be longer in winter (as much as twice as long) due to deep snow.

- Lonesome Lake, trip 7. In winter, Lonesome Lake is a quiet windswept place, and the view to the snowcapped peaks of Mount Lafayette and Mount Lincoln is spectacular. Those seeking to spend an evening there can stay at Lonesome Lake Hut.
- Mount Willard, trip 8. Crawford Notch seems to get more snow than any other part of the mountains with the exception of the ravines in the Presidentials. The hike up Mount Willard is often filled with powdery bliss, and the view is the best for the effort.
- Mount Israel, trip 13. Tucked in between the Lakes Region and the Sandwich Range, Mount Israel is a wonderful winter climb past stone walls and through an interesting mix of forests. The savannah-like oak forest higher up on the mountain affords views in the winter that just don't exist in the summer. Up top, the views are even better.
- Boulder Loop Trail, trip 9. An easy hike in the summer, the Boulder Loop Trail makes for a great 3-hour adventure in winter, as you pass by giant snow-covered boulders and through quiet, mature forests. The view of the Swift River Valley and the Sandwich Range to the south is well worth the effort.

This snowshoer steps through freshly fallen snow on Mount Willard.

- Arethusa Falls, trip 6. The spruce forest near Arethusa Falls is a quiet, magical place in the winter, and you can usually walk right up to the base of the frozen falls, something that is often impossible to do in the warmer months. You might also get to watch ice climbers in action.
- Northern Presidentials Waterfalls, trip 5. More great forests, snowy trails, and winter solitude.
- Lookout Ledge, trip 3. Hiking Lookout Ledge in winter feels a little like cheating. You get great Northern Presidential views without the effort and risk of climbing the high peaks. This trip rivals Mount Willard for best views for the effort.

TRIP 14
WELCH AND DICKEY MOUNTAINS

Rating: Moderate
Distance: 4.4 miles round-trip
Elevation Gain: 1,800 feet
Estimated Time: 3 hours
Maps: AMC White Mountain Trail Map #3: J6, K6, USGS Waterville
Valley Quadrangle

This is a moderate hike to relatively small peaks with big views.

Directions

From I-93, take Exit 28 and head east toward Waterville Valley on NH 49. In
5.6 miles turn left onto Upper Mad River Road. In 0.6 mile turn right onto
Morris Road, following signs for the Welch-Dickey Loop Trail. In another 0.6
mile turn right onto a gravel road, which leads 50 yards to the parking area
for the Welch-Dickey Loop Trail.

Trip Description

Welch and Dickey Mountains were two of the mountains visited earliest by
regular summer tourists. In the 1850s, Nathaniel Greeley, who had pioneered
in Waterville Valley in the 1830s, created a system of trails in the area for
visitors to his inn. This was the first true system of trails in the White Mountains. Today the Welch-Dickey Loop Trail is a popular hike with families because it has good views for a relatively low amount of effort, as most of the
hike follows moderate grades. Welch and Dickey Mountains are well below
3,000 feet in elevation, but they both have several open rocky ledges. Natu-
ralists also will enjoy this hike because of its high diversity of trees, including
one of only four stands of jack pine in New Hampshire. The hike is close to
Waterville Valley and is one of the first White Mountain hikes reached from
Boston via I-93. This is a great hike to do in the off-season, when the crowds
are nonexistent and the weather on higher peaks may be uncertain.

The Welch-Dickey Loop Trail leaves the north end of the parking lot and
immediately offers you the choice of climbing Welch or Dickey Mountains;

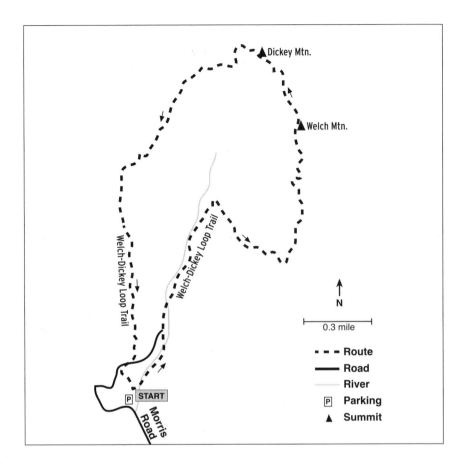

Dickey Mtn.

Welch Mtn.

Welch-Dickey Loop Trail

Welch-Dickey Loop Trail

N

0.3 mile

- - - Route

—— Road

—— River

P Parking

▲ Summit

P START

Morris Road

either direction loops over both peaks. This trip describes the route in a counterclockwise direction, climbing Welch Mountain first in order to hike up its steep south ridge, which is preferable to climbing down it. Following the right fork of the trail quickly brings you to a beautiful rushing stream surrounded by hemlock trees. The trail follows the brook for 0.5 mile before turning right and heading south and east toward the south ridge of the peak. At 1.3 miles you reach the first open ledges on the hike in an area filled with revegetation zones marked by stone circles. The maintainers of this trail are attempting to encourage the regrowth of the subalpine plants that usually grow here but die off when trampled by hikers. Please use care when hiking over these ledges.

From these first ledges, the trail climbs steeply over rock for 0.6 mile, passing in and out of the trees on its way to the summit of Welch Mountain.

The summit ledges provide excellent views in most directions, especially down into the Mad River valley. They also provide the opportunity to study the southernmost occurrence of jack pine in New Hampshire. Jack pine is a very common tree in the boreal forests of Canada, but it is relatively rare in New Hampshire. Its 1-inch-long needles grow in bundles of two, and are easily distinguished from the much longer needles of the more common red and white pines you will also find in this area. Jack pines are highly resistant to fire and they actually depend on fire to reproduce, as the extreme heat of a forest fire is needed to open up their cones and release their seeds.

From the summit of Welch Mountain, the Welch-Dickey Loop Trail continues north to Dickey Mountain. On the way, it first descends into an open area between the peaks populated by red spruce and shrubs that are typical in the ledgy areas of New England: sheep laurel, rhodora, blueberries, and pin cherry. Silvery mats of reindeer lichen are also common. At 2.4 miles after a short but steep climb, you reach the summit of Dickey Mountain, which has open ledges on all sides of its wooded summit. You have good views of the nearby Sandwich Range and Franconia Ridge, which are about 15.0 miles to the north. In fall, the summits of both mountains are good places to watch for migrating hawks, falcons, and monarch butterflies.

The trail continues by descending the rocky ledges of Dickey Mountain's west ridge. Views are abundant from these ledges as you hike in and out of the trees. If you look closely, you can see glacial striations in the ledges. These striations were created when boulders trapped under glacial ice carved lines in the rock as the ice moved over the mountain. These ledges are also home to a spruce forest that provides good habitat for spruce grouse, a rare cousin of the common ruffed grouse found at lower elevations. Just before entering the forest for good, you traverse a long ridge of bare rock perched over the northwest wall of the valley that sits between Welch and Dickey. Excellent views can be seen from here of Welch Mountain and the northern hardwood forest below.

Below this last ledge the trail makes a moderate descent to the trailhead for the final 1.2 miles. During this time the forest becomes a northern hardwood forest rich in northern red oaks, whose acorns provide an important food source for many animals, including white-tail deer, wild turkeys, and black bears. Other trees you can find here include sugar maple, American beech, yellow birch, mountain ash, large-tooth aspen, and Eastern hophornbeam.

TRIP 15
MOUNT CRAWFORD

Rating: Moderate
Distance: 5.0 miles up and back
Elevation Gain: 2,100 feet
Estimated Time: 4 hours
Maps: AMC White Mountain Trail Map #3: H8, USGS Stairs
Mountain and Bartlett Quadrangles

This moderate hike climbs to unique views of the Presidential Range and the Presidential Range-Dry River Wilderness Area.

Directions
From the intersection of US 302 and NH 16 in Glen, follow US 302 west for 12.1 miles. The parking area for the Davis Path will be on the right.

Trip Description
Mount Crawford is a relatively low peak just to the south of Crawford Notch. It is the first peak reached by hikers using the Davis Path, which makes a 15.0-mile ascent of Mount Washington through the Presidential Range-Dry River Wilderness Area. The peak is just one of several landmarks in the area named after the legendary Crawford family, who were the first settlers in Crawford Notch and provided mountain hospitality and guide services to travelers in the area for much of the nineteenth century. The hike up Mount Crawford begins on US 302, along the banks of the Saco River, and climbs steadily to the summit, which has excellent 360-degree views.

To start your hike, follow the gravel road at the north end of the parking lot for about 100 yards to a footbridge over the Saco River. This is the beginning of the Davis Path, which was built in 1845 by Nathaniel Davis, Ethan Crawford's son-in-law. The Davis Path is also the beginning link in the Cohos Trail, a new long-distance trail that starts in Crawford Notch and ends at the Quebec border. On the other side of the river, the trail crosses private property and passes many unmarked side trails and woods roads; keep an eye out for signs that help you stay on the right path, which follows telephone lines for a short distance before entering the White Mountain

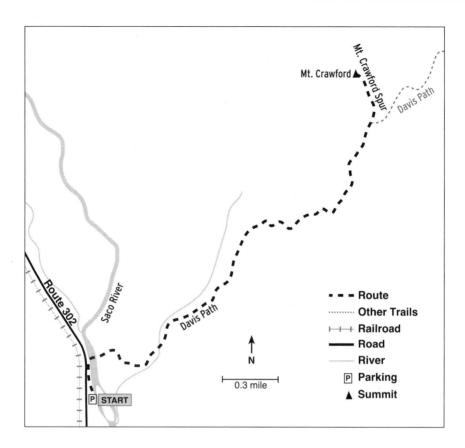

National Forest. At this point, you will notice you have entered a northern hardwood forest that includes many northern red oak. While it is most often associated with the oak-hickory forests to the south and west of the White Mountains in northern New England and Canada, northern red oak is often found in low-elevation northern hardwood forests. Like most oaks they can grow to be tall, stately trees, producing bumper crops of acorns every three or four years.

The trail crosses an often dry, rocky stream just before it enters the Presidential Range-Dry River Wilderness Area. This stream might look like the namesake of the wilderness area, but the Dry River actually lies to the north and west of Mount Crawford, where it drains the southern slopes of the Presidential Range. After crossing the stream, the Davis Path climbs moderately, increasing in steepness as you gain elevation. At 0.9 mile, the trail makes a sharp right-hand turn and follows a zigzag course on its way to the

A hiker takes a break while hiking Mount Crawford to enjoy views of the Presidential Range.

ridge between Mount Hope and Mount Crawford. Conifers become more common as you climb, and by the time you reach the ridgeline, you are in a pure boreal forest. The trail follows the ridge to the north, and at 1.9 miles you reach the first of several open ledges on your way to the summit. Views are particularly good to the south and west, with Mount Carrigain the dominant peak. At 2.2 miles turn left onto the Mount Crawford spur path. The spur path climbs steeply over bare rock ledges for most of its 0.3 mile to the summit. Small spruce trees, as well as sheep laurel, creeping snowberry, and alpine willows populate the summit area. Ledges on each side of the summit provide views in all directions. The views of Mount Washington and the Southern Presidentials are excellent, as the high alpine peaks rise above the vast forests of the Dry River valley and the long craggy ridge of the Dry River Range.

To complete your hike, follow the Mount Crawford spur path and Davis Path back to your car. If you feel like exploring the area a little further, you can continue north on the Davis Path from the Mount Crawford spur path for 0.7 mile. At this point you will reach a ledgy outlook on Crawford Dome, which provides good views of the steep, rocky east side of Mount Crawford.

TRIP 16
CARIBOU MOUNTAIN

Rating: Moderate

Distance: 7.0 miles round-trip

Elevation Gain: 1,900 feet

Estimated Time: 4 hours, 30 minutes

Maps: AMC White Mountain Trail Map #5, USGS Speckled
Mountain (Maine) Quadrangle

This hike through a mature northern hardwood forest leads to great views of the Caribou-Speckled Mountain Wilderness Area.

Directions

From the easternmost intersection of NH 16 and US 2 in Gorham, New Hampshire, drive east on US 2 for 11.1 miles and turn right on ME 113 in Gilead. The parking area will be 4.7 miles on the left.

Trip Description

This hike takes you through the 12,000-acre Caribou-Speckled Mountain Wilderness on the way to the summit of Caribou Mountain. While Caribou is a relatively low peak (2,800 feet), its summit is bare and provides views in all directions. Caribou is in the less visited Maine portion of the White Mountain National Forest. While you will see other hikers on a summer weekend, you are much more likely to encounter long moments of solitude than in the Presidentials or on Franconia Ridge. The unique perspective from the summit also makes this a nice change of pace from bagging all of those 4,000-footers to the west.

For this trip you will complete the loop made by the Caribou and Mud Brook Trails, both of which begin from the Caribou Mountain parking area on ME 113. Begin your hike on the Caribou Trail, which leaves from the northeast corner of the parking lot. You immediately enter a beautiful, mature northern hardwood forest that is rich with sugar maple and feathery-needled hemlock. Except for the area near the summit, you will be walking through various versions of this forest for the entire hike. The trail descends

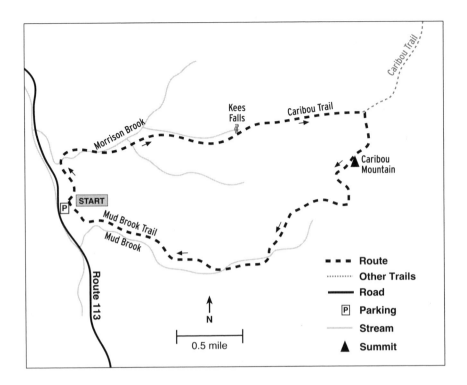

gradually to cross Morrison Brook over a wooden bridge. It then climbs gradually before crossing the brook and becoming steeper. Typical of a northern
hardwood forest in northern New England, the understory on this part of
the hike is populated by hobblebush, striped maple, and wildflowers such as
wood sorrel, bunchberries, and trilliums.

Two miles from the parking area, the trail crosses the brook at Kees Falls,
where the water drops 25 feet over a moss-covered rock wall into a deep,
circular pool. At this point you will begin to notice that the forest canopy
was heavily damaged by the 1998 ice storm. The storm injured or destroyed
scores of birch and beech trees, but the understory is taking advantage of
the extra sunlight reaching the forest floor, growing thick and bushy. After
Kees Falls the trail crosses the brook several times before climbing steeply to
its junction with the Mud Brook Trail in a col between Caribou and Gammon
Mountains (3.0 miles from the parking area). A boggy area to the left of the
trail junction is frequented by moose, as is much of the forest adjacent to the
Mud Brook Trail.

This hiker takes a break to enjoy sweeping views of the Caribou-Speckled Mountain Wilderness Area.

Turn right on the Mud Brook Trail for a steady 0.6-mile climb to the summit. Along the way, the hardwood forest gives way to a boreal forest of spruce and fir mixed with some paper birch and mountain ash. Caribou Mountain's summit is a large open area of granite ledges with scattered small spruce and fir, pin cherry, sheep laurel, and blueberries. Views are in all directions: the Mahoosucs to the north, the Baldface and Carter ranges to the west, Kezar Lake to the south, and the rest of Maine to the east. The view of the thickly forested and roadless Caribou-Speckled Mountain Wilderness Area to the south is particularly impressive. From the summit, follow the Mud Brook Trail, which drops down to the south for several yards before turning right and traversing the open west ridge of the mountain.

The trail descends steeply into spruce and fir for about fifteen minutes before providing one last good viewpoint from an open ledge looking south. The trail continues a steep descent through boreal forest before the grade eases and you reach the first of several brook crossings. By this time, you are once again in a storm-damaged northern hardwood forest. While unsightly at first, extensive storm damage in a well-protected wilderness area can actually benefit the forest by knocking down weaker trees, creating habitat for a variety of wildlife, and giving surviving trees the opportunity to grow bigger and stronger than they would have in a forest thick with competing trees. The remainder of the hike becomes easier as the trail flattens out on its way back to the parking area.

Federally Designated Wilderness

In 1964 Congress passed the Wilderness Act, which protected 54 wilderness areas across the country and provided a process for creating additional wilderness areas in the future. In 1975 Congress passed the Eastern Wilderness Act, which recognized both the need for and unique aspects of wilderness in the eastern part of the country. Unlike western wilderness, most eastern wilderness areas have a history of logging and other human uses and are in the process of recovering their natural wild character. As of 2008 there were 704 areas in the National Wilderness Preservation System, protecting approximately 108 million acres. Wilderness areas are generally roadless portions of national forests, parks, or wildlife refuges that are off-limits to motorized or mechanized vehicles (including mountain bikes), logging, and mining. In the 780,000-acre White Mountain National Forest there are currently six wilderness areas, comprising 153,052 acres:

- Great Gulf Wilderness—5,552 acres, established in 1964
- Presidential Range–Dry River Wilderness—29,000 acres, established in 1975
- Sandwich Range Wilderness—35,800 acres, established in 1984 and expanded in 2006
- Pemigewasset Wilderness—45,000 acres, established in 1984
- Caribou–Speckled Mountain Wilderness—14,000 acres, established in 1990
- Wild River Wilderness—23,700 acres, established in 2006

In addition to restrictions on vehicle use in White Mountain National Forest wilderness areas, the Forest Service has dismantled most of the shelters and cabins built in these areas before they were designated wilderness. Because of this, backpacking in the wilderness areas of the White Mountains is often a more rugged experience than in other parts of the national forest; it is also a more satisfying experience as few signs exist of human interference. When planning a hike or backpack into designated wilderness, you should be aware of the following restrictions:

- Hiking and camping groups may contain no more than ten people.
- No camping or wood or charcoal fires are allowed within 200 feet of any trail, except at designated campsites.

You can learn more about the federally designated wilderness areas in the White Mountains, including current regulations regarding their use, by visiting the White Mountain National Forest website:

www.fs.fed.us/r9/forests/white_mountain/recreation/wilderness/.

The Great Gulf headwall in the Great Gulf Wilderness surrounds the biggest cirque in the White Mountains.

TRIP 17
THOREAU FALLS

Rating: Moderate
Distance: 9.2 miles up and back
Elevation Gain: 500 feet
Estimated Time: 5 hours
Maps: AMC White Mountain Trail Map #2: G7, USGS Crawford
  Notch Quadrangle

This relatively flat hike passes through good wildlife habitat to mountain views and Thoreau Falls.

Directions

From the intersection of US 3 and US 302 in Twin Mountain, follow US 302 south for 2.2 miles and turn right onto Zealand Road. The parking area is at the end of Zealand Road, 3.5 miles from US 302.

Trip Description

With its sunny rock ledges and excellent views of Mount Bond, Thoreau Falls is a popular destination on hot summer days, but its relatively long distance from the nearest road keeps the number of visitors down to a tolerable level. It can be reached from either Crawford Notch or the end of Zealand Road, and both routes have their highlights. We prefer the trip in from Zealand Road—the walk along the rockslide on Whitewall Mountain is one of the most scenic valley hikes in the White Mountains. This trip shares its beginning with the Zealand Falls/Zeacliff hike, and in fact a long day hike combining the two trips is possible (see the description of trip 18 for more details). There is not much climbing on this trip (only 500 feet of elevation gain), but the hike is rated as moderate due to its 9.2-mile length.

You begin your hike on the Zealand Trail, which starts at the end of Zealand Road. The trail begins as a wide path that climbs gradually through a mixed forest of spruce, fir, maple, and birch. After about 0.4 mile you cross a wooden bridge and climb through a grove of spruce trees over a heavily eroded trailbed. (Please try to stay on the trail here by following the blue

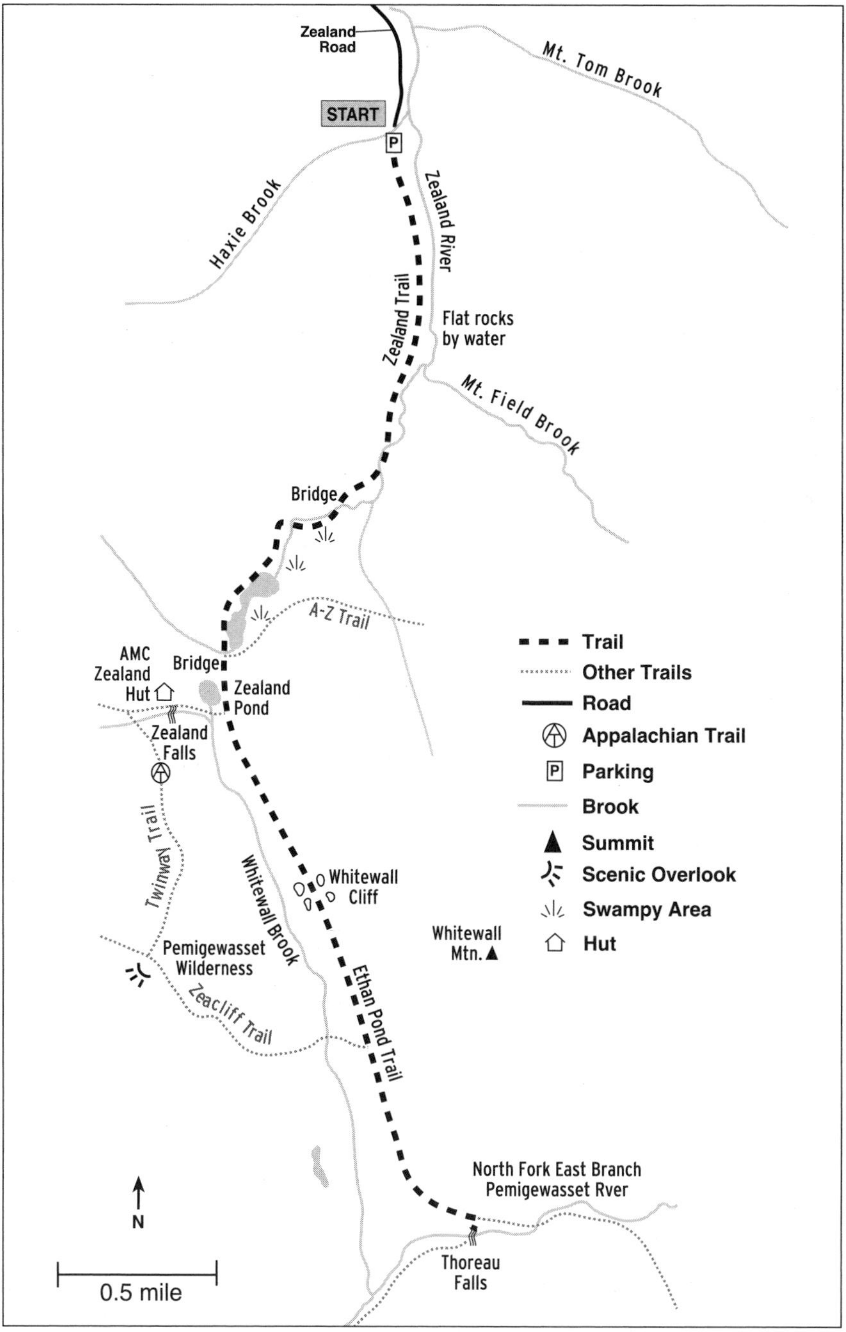
Zealand Road
START
Mt. Tom Brook
Haxie Brook
Zealand River
Zealand Trail
Flat rocks by water
Mt. Field Brook
Bridge
A-Z Trail
AMC Zealand Hut
Bridge
Zealand Pond
Zealand Falls
Twinway Trail
Whitewall Brook
Whitewall Cliff
Whitewall Mtn.
Pemigewasset Wilderness
Zeacliff Trail
Ethan Pond Trail
North Fork East Branch Pemigewasset Rver
Thoreau Falls
N
0.5 mile
Trail
Other Trails
Road
Appalachian Trail
Parking
Brook
Summit
Scenic Overlook
Swampy Area
Hut

Thoreau Falls from the top.

blazes). You will soon hear the Zealand River on your left. After making a close approach to the river at 0.8 mile, the trail turns to the right and continues a gradual climb. After crossing the river on a wooden bridge, you begin to walk through an area of beaver activity that lasts for almost 1.0 mile. The trail passes alder thickets and over wooden bridges and occasionally you will have good views of Zealand Mountain and Zeacliff to the southwest.

Just before reaching a junction with the A-Z Trail at 2.3 miles, you pass the largest of the beaver ponds, where there are at least two large beaver lodges and frog song is common. Various species of flycatchers and swallows can be seen feeding on insects above the ponds, and warblers and vireos are common in the surrounding forest. With a little luck, you might even see a moose in this area. Continue straight on the Zealand Trail and you will soon come to Zealand Pond on your right. After crossing the outlet of the pond on a wooden bridge, the trail follows the eastern shore of the pond before ending at its intersection with the Ethan Pond Trail and the Twinway, 2.5 miles from the parking area.

To go to Thoreau Falls, take the left fork, which is the Ethan Pond Trail. The Ethan Pond Trail, part of the Appalachian Trail, follows a straight course through a forest of paper birch with a few spruce and fir trees. Signs of moose are common on this section of trail. The trail is built on an old railroad bed, which was constructed in the 1880s in order to transport lumber out of the heart of what is now the Pemigewasset Wilderness Area. At one point the railroad tracks went as far as Shoal Pond and Ethan Pond. Today the wide, level hiking trail is all that is left of the railroad, although you might run across an occasional railroad spike.

About 1.0 mile past the Zealand Trail, the Ethan Pond Trail emerges from the forest and passes under a huge rockslide on the side of Whitewall Mountain. Large white boulders are piled up on either side of the trail. Excellent views can be seen here through Zealand Notch to Mount Carrigain and Mount Hancock, as well as up to the cliffs on Whitewall Mountain and Zea-cliff. Looking back, you can just make out Zealand Falls Hut, about 1.5 miles away. Continue straight past the junction with the Zeacliff Trail, 3.8 miles from the parking area. About 0.3 mile after the trail reenters the woods, turn right onto the Thoreau Falls Trail for a 150-yard walk to the falls.

The falls are in a beautiful wilderness setting, with the water tumbling away from you in a graceful S-curve toward the East Branch of the Pemigewasset River. Rising into view across the valley are the thickly forested slopes of Mount Bond and Mount Guyot. The ledges at the top of the falls are a comfortable place to soak in the scenery, but they are well worn and slippery and care should be taken, especially with children. Although the falls are named after Henry David Thoreau, no evidence exists to suggest that he ever visited this part of the White Mountains. To complete your hike, walk back to the Ethan Pond Trail and turn left, following it and the Zealand Trail back to the parking area.

TRIP 18
ZEALAND FALLS AND ZEACLIFF

Rating: Moderate
Distance: 8.2 miles up and back
Elevation Gain: 1,750 feet
Estimated Time: 5 hours, 30 minutes
Maps: AMC White Mountain Trail Map #2: G7, USGS Crawford
Notch Quadrangle

This moderate day hike reaches wildlife-rich beaver ponds, Zealand Falls, and excellent views of the Pemigewasset Wilderness Area.

Directions
From the intersection of US 3 and US 302 in Twin Mountain, follow US 302 south for 2.2 miles and turn right onto Zealand Road. The parking area is at the end of Zealand Road, 3.5 miles from US 302.

Trip Description
This was our first hike in the White Mountains, and we return time and time again to take in the incredible beauty of the Zealand valley. All kinds of wildlife habitat can be seen on this hike, including a hardwood forest, beaver swamps, a mountain pond, a thick boreal forest, and a high-elevation bog. Signs of moose are common and the birdlife is extremely varied. You can see multitudes of warblers and flycatchers as well as grouse, woodcock, and ducks, and migrating birds of prey such as osprey and merlin in the fall. This trip also visits the AMC Zealand Falls Hut, which is situated next to the ledges of Zealand Falls—a great place to sit and take in the views of the Zealand valley. The hike from the hut to Zeacliff is a steep one, but the views from the top of the cliff are some of the best in the White Mountains.

You begin your hike on the Zealand Trail, which starts at the end of Zealand Road. The trail begins as a wide path that climbs gradually through a mixed forest of spruce, fir, maple, and birch. After about 0.4 mile you cross a wooden bridge and climb through a grove of spruce trees over a heavily

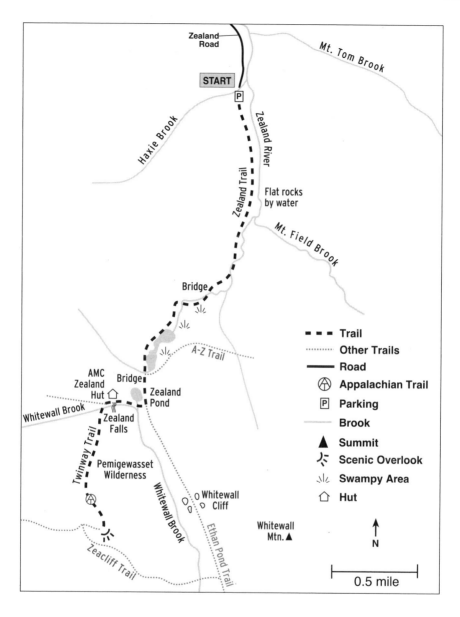

eroded trailbed. (Please try to stay on the trail here by following the blue blazes.) You will soon hear the Zealand River on your left. After making a close approach to the river at 0.8 mile, the trail turns to the right and continues a gradual climb. After crossing the river on a wooden bridge, you begin to walk through an area of beaver activity that lasts for almost 1.0 mile. The trail passes alder thickets and over wooden bridges and occasionally you will have good views of Zealand Mountain and Zeacliff to the southwest.

Just before reaching a junction with the A-Z Trail at 2.3 miles, you pass the largest of the beaver ponds, where there are at least two large beaver lodges and frog song is common. With a little luck, you might even see a moose in this area. Continue straight on the Zealand Trail and you will soon come to Zealand Pond, which will be on your right. Beaver dams are on either side of the bridge that spans the outlet of the pond, and a quiet hiker visiting the pond at dawn or dusk can most likely spot a beaver swimming. After the bridge, the trail follows the eastern shore of the pond before ending at its intersection with the Ethan Pond Trail and the Twinway. To make your way to the hut and the falls, follow the Twinway to the right for a short but steep climb.

Zealand Falls Hut is one of three AMC huts open year-round (the others are Lonesome Lake and Carter Notch huts; in winter, they are self service—visit www.outdoors.org for more information), and it makes a great destination during any season. The ledges of Zealand Falls provide excellent views across Zealand Pond to Mount Tom, across Whitewall Brook to Whitewall Mountain, and through Zealand Notch to the heart of the Pemigewasset Wilderness. This is definitely one of the best views for the effort in the White Mountains. The falls itself is more than picture-worthy, whether in spring with blooming shadbush and pin cherry, during fall foliage season, or in winter when the falls freezes and the spruce lining the brook are covered in fluffy snow. If the sun is out, you will have a hard time picking yourself up off the granite to begin the climb up to Zeacliff.

To reach Zeacliff, follow the Twinway as it passes the left side of the hut and crosses the brook (twice) before beginning a moderate, and sometimes steep, climb up the north side of Zeacliff. Most of the forest on this leg of the hike is filled with paper birch and balsam fir. In fall, the woods have a yellow glow as the sun filters through the leaves of the birch trees. In spring, you will find the understory filled with false hellebore, hobblebush, clintonia, wild lily of the valley, and a variety of ferns. Sometimes the footing is rough, but it is never difficult. As you hike higher up, the fir start to push out the birch, and by the time you near the top of the cliff, you are in a boreal forest of fir and spruce.

Zeacliff provides a striking view of Mount Carrigain.

Soon after the trail levels out, about 1.1 miles above the hut, follow a side path on the left marked "View." Here you will find the ledges of Zeacliff and their spectacular views down into Zealand Notch and across to the Willey Range, with Mount Washington visible in the distance. Most of the wide expanse of the 45,000-acre Pemigewasset Wilderness Area lies below you. One of the largest roadless areas in the eastern United States, this wilderness area was once one of the most heavily logged and burnt-over forests in New Hampshire. The destruction that occurred in this area at the end of the nineteenth century inspired groups like the AMC and the Society for the Protection of New Hampshire Forests to lobby Congress for the creation of the White Mountain National Forest. In 1911 they succeeded when Congress passed the Weeks Act, preserving the White Mountains as a national forest.

Once you have taken in the views from the cliff, you can begin your trip back down to the hut or spend some time looking at the plants living in the high-elevation bog, which can be found on the Twinway just past the side trail to the cliff. Here you will find rhodora, sheep laurel, Labrador tea, and cotton grass, growing through a thick mat of sphagnum moss. Since this is an up-and-back trip, complete your hike by retracing your steps back to the parking area.

Alternate trip: This trip can easily be combined with the trip to Thoreau Falls (trip 17) to make a long day hike. From the summit of Zeacliff, continue on the Twinway away from the hut for about 0.25 mile and turn left onto the Zeacliff Trail. Follow the Zeacliff Trail for 1.4 miles to the Ethan Pond Trail and turn right to head toward Thoreau Falls (from this point on, follow the description in trip 17). *A word of caution: The Zeacliff Trail is extremely steep and can be dangerous to descend in wet or icy weather or with a heavy pack.*

American Indians in the White Mountains

The White Mountains probably became suitable for human habitation around 12,000 years ago, but there is very little evidence that humans lived in the region then. The only artifacts currently known are from seven sites, which date from about 8,000 to 10,000 years ago. At that time, the area was similar to the Arctic in climate, and it is impossible to determine whether people lived year-round in the White Mountains or just passed through at certain times of year. As the climate warmed, American Indians eventually settled in the more hospitable climes of river valleys like the Saco, Pemigewasset, and Ammonoosuc.

By the time Europeans arrived in the area, various bands of Abenaki Indians lived in the White Mountains, cultivating corn to supplement a diet of wild game, fish, and native plants. The names of some of these Abenaki tribes and their chiefs are now names used for various places in the area—Penacook, Pequawket, Pemigewasset, Kancamagus, Passaconaway, and Chocorua. Most of these chiefs had contact with European settlers, but it was Chocorua who became the best known. The tragic story of his young son's untimely death and the events that followed became the stuff of legend.

When visiting other members of his Penacook tribe who had fled to Quebec, Chocorua's son accidentally died while in the care of a local white family, the Campbells. Hearing of his son's death, Chocorua killed Cornelius Campbell's wife and children. Campbell and several other men then chased Chocorua to the summit of the mountain. Trapped, Chocorua leapt to his death while uttering a

American Indians settled along the Saco River, seen here rushing over rocks.

curse upon the white men that was blamed for years for the mysterious death of cattle in local towns. While probably very little of this story is true, Mount Choco-rua does bear the name of the Penacook chief, similar to several other peaks in the Sandwich Range: Paugus, Wonalancet, Passaconaway, and Kancamagus.

Although American colonists did not settle the White Mountains in great numbers until the late eighteenth century, most Abenakis in the region died of diseases from early European contact. Most of the remaining American Indians fled to Quebec in the early eighteenth century as a result of persecution by white settlers, the most notable example of which was a massacre along the Baker River in 1712. Today the largest communities of Abenakis are in eastern Maine and Quebec.

TRIP 19
MOUNT MOOSILAUKE

Rating: Moderate
Distance: 7.4 miles up and back
Elevation Gain: 2,450 feet
Estimated Time: 6 hours
Maps: AMC White Mountain Trail Map #4: I3, J3, USGS Mount
   Moosilauke and Mount Kineo Quadrangles

Cascading streams lead the way to New Hampshire's western-most alpine peak.

Directions
From I-93 take Exit 32, following NH 112 west for 2.9 miles and turn left on NH 118. In 7.0 miles, turn right on Ravine Lodge Road. Park at the end of Ravine Lodge Road, 1.6 miles from NH 118.

Trip Description
"Moosilauke" is the Algonquin Indian word for bald place. It is a fitting name for this open, rounded peak, which is the westernmost above-treeline summit in the White Mountains. Mount Moosilauke is a significant landmark for northbound hikers of the Appalachian Trail, as it is the first bald peak they encounter north of Virginia. The mountain is also important to Dartmouth College, which owns about half of the mountain and maintains most of its trails. This hike begins next to the college's Ravine Lodge at the southeastern base of the mountain, and climbs to the summit via the Gorge Brook Trail. The moderate grades and scenic qualities of this trail make it popular, and heavy traffic has created some rough footing at the beginning of the hike; however, the trailbed is smoother after the first mile. An option exists to make this a loop hike, by walking down Mount Moosilauke's south ridge and returning via the Moosilauke Carriage Road and Snapper Trail.

Walk along the old gravel roadbed that extends from the end of Ravine Lodge Road to reach the Gorge Brook Trail. In about 50 yards, turn left onto a trail that leads down to the Baker River. Cross the river on the bridge and

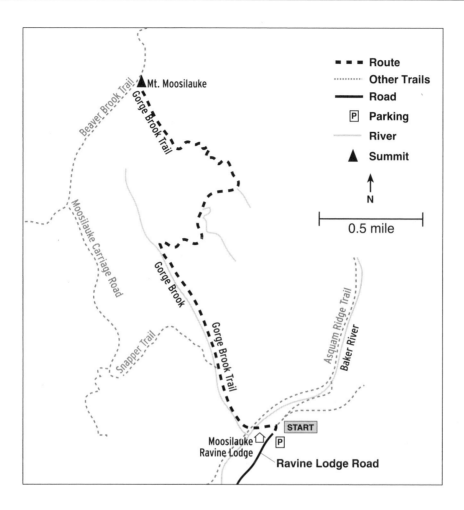

turn left onto the Gorge Brook Trail on the other side of the river. The Baker River, which flows into the Pemigewasset River, was used extensively for logging operations in the late nineteenth century. Logs harvested on Mount Moosilauke were floated down the river to mills in Plymouth. The last old-growth spruce logs harvested from the mountain were used to build the Ravine Lodge in 1937 and 1938. The remaining old-growth forest on the mountain was destroyed soon after by the 1938 hurricane.

The Gorge Brook Trail soon reaches a junction with the Hurricane Trail; turn right to stay on the Gorge Brook Trail. The trail climbs steadily over rocks and roots as it parallels Gorge Brook. After crossing the brook on a

A hiker pauses in front of a cairn at the summit of Mount Moosilauke.

wooden bridge at 0.6 mile, the Gorge Brook Trail turns right while the Snapper Trail goes to the left. Stay on the Gorge Brook Trail, which continues to parallel the brook, climbing moderately. During this part of the hike, you are treated to the constant sounds of rushing water as Gorge Brook flows from cascade to cascade. At 1.3 miles the trail crosses the brook for the last time and heads due west for a while before turning north and climbing the southeastern ridge of the mountain.

Following the moderate grade of an old logging road, the trail soon brings you to an outlook with good views to the southeast. The forest changes to spruce-fir, indicating you are one habitat zone below the alpine world of Mount Moosilauke's summit. The trail continues to climb via switchbacks that show off the excellent trail-building skills of the Dartmouth Outing Club. As the trees get shorter, the views get better and better and begin to include Franconia Ridge to the northeast and other mountains to the south and east. You reach the plateau below the summit after making one last right-hand switchback. The trail teases as you hike in and out of the trees with the bare summit in view. Shortly before reaching the summit, you break out of the trees for good and are surrounded by a meadow of rocks, grasses, and sedges, with blueberries, cranberries, and three-toothed cinquefoil adding splashes of color.

The alpine summit of Mount Moosilauke is somewhat separated from the rest of the White Mountains to the east, giving you a unique view of the national forest from Kinsman Ridge to Franconia Ridge to the Presidential Range. Immediately to the west is the low, flat Connecticut River valley. Rising up to the west of the river are the Green Mountains of Vermont, and on clear days you can see all the way to New York's Adirondack Park. Scattered about the summit are the foundations of various structures that are part of the mountain's history. The most notable building was a hotel built in 1860 called the Prospect House and later known as the Tip Top House and Summit House. During the winter of 1869–1870, Joshua Huntington and Amos Clough became the first people to spend a winter on one of the summits in the White Mountains. They used Prospect House as a base to study the weather, and in February of 1870 measured winds in excess of 100 MPH— the strongest winds ever recorded at that time. They remained on the mountain from January 1 through February 26 and their success inspired them to begin the weather observatory on Mount Washington the following winter.

To finish your hike, you can either return via the Gorge Brook Trail or make a loop using the Carriage Road (Appalachian Trail) and Snapper Trail. While the Gorge Brook Trail is a much more scenic hike than the wide, rock-filled Carriage Road (it really looks like a road), the lure of hiking the Appalachian Trail down the narrow ridge connecting Mount Moosilauke with its south summit is hard to pass up. To complete this optional loop, which only adds 0.1 mile to the hike, follow the Carriage Road south from the summit, making sure to turn left at its junction with the Glencliff Trail. When you reach the Snapper Trail, turn left again and then take a right onto the Gorge Brook Trail when you reach Gorge Brook.

The Appalachian Trail

Many of the hikes in this book follow the Appalachian Trail (AT) for at least part of the trip, as it traverses most of the major ridges through the White Mountains. The AT is more than a path through the White Mountains—it is a 2,167-mile trail from Springer Mountain in northern Georgia to Katahdin in Maine. It supports a community of its own during the warmer months of the year as thousands of hikers attempt to complete the entire length of the trail. The AMC maintains approximately 122 miles of the AT in New Hampshire and Maine. Other hiking clubs also maintain the trail, with much of the trail work being completed by volunteers.

The AT was the vision of Benton MacKaye, who in 1921 wrote an article for the *Journal of American Architects* titled "An Appalachian Trail, A Project in Regional Planning." MacKaye believed that an increasingly urban America was in need of wilderness camps that would provide workers a respite from their jobs in factories and offices. He envisioned the Appalachian Trail as a footpath from Mount Mitchell in North Carolina to Mount Washington in New Hampshire. Along the way would be farms, work camps, and study camps, where hikers could spend time communing with nature and other hikers. Within a couple of years his idea took root and eager volunteers blazed the AT's first miles. Now a National Scenic Trail administered by the National Park Service and extending from Georgia to Maine, the AT has become a national treasure.

In 1948 Earl Shaffer became the first person to complete an end-to-end hike of the trail. Known as thru-hikers, people attempting to hike the entire length of the trail in one season are now a common sight. About 2,500 people a year attempt a thru-hike, most of them starting in Georgia and walking north. Other hikers complete the trail over the course of several years and are known as section hikers. Only about one in ten complete a thru-hike, with physical and/or mental fatigue causing most people to pack it up and head home. It takes most thru-hikers five or six months to complete the trail, averaging 12 to 15 miles a day. The trail passes near towns every few days, allowing hikers the chance to resupply at local stores or at the post office, where friends back home mail carefully planned boxes of food. Whether a hiker completes a thru-hike or not, he or she is guaranteed to be rewarded with awe-inspiring views, quiet thought-provoking moments, and new friendships.

This unmistakable white blaze identifies the Appalachian Trail along its route from Georgia to Maine.

While you can now read books or take classes on how to complete a hike on the Appalachian Trail, the act of actually following the trail is rather simple. The AT is marked by rectangular, white-paint blazes (2 inches wide and 6 inches tall) on trees and rocks from its beginnings in Georgia to the summit of Katahdin. The hiking itself varies considerably, from flat valley walks in thick oak-hickory forests to the long above-treeline trek across the Presidentials. Passing over the Smoky Mountains, the Blue Ridge Mountains, and the Green Mountains before hitting the Whites and western Maine, the Appalachian Trail explores the most rugged, scenic terrain in the eastern United States.

To learn about how to protect the trail or how to hike it, contact the Appalachian Trail Conservancy (ATC) at 799 Washington Street, P.O. Box 807, Harpers Ferry, WV 25425-0807; 304-535-6331. Plenty of good information is also available on the ATC's website, www.appalachiantrail.org.

TRIP 20
MOUNT CHOCORUA

Rating: Strenuous
Distance: 7.5 miles round-trip
Elevation Gain: 2,600 feet
Estimated Time: 6 hours
Maps: AMC White Mountain Trail Map #3: J9, USGS Mount
   Chocorua Quadrangle

This scenic loop hike leads to one of the most photographed mountains in New England.

Directions

From the intersection of NH 16 and NH 113 in Chocorua, New Hampshire, drive west on NH 113. In 2.9 miles turn right on NH 113A. In another 3.3 miles turn right on Fowlers Mill Road. In another 1.2 miles turn left on Paugus Road, following the sign for the Liberty and Brook Trails. The parking area for both trails is at the end of Paugus Road, 0.7 mile from Fowlers Mill Road.

Trip Description

Mount Chocorua (pronounced Chu-CORE-ooh-a) is a popular peak at the eastern end of the Sandwich Range, south of the Kancamagus Highway. Often photographed from the shores of Chocorua Lake in Tamworth, this peak is the first large mountain seen by travelers approaching the White Mountains from the south on NH 16. You can reach the 3,500-foot-high summit from just about any direction, but any hike of Chocorua involves significant elevation gain. It is worth the climb, though, as the bare summit dome of Chocorua provides excellent 360-degree views. This trip makes a loop up over the summit via the Brook and Liberty Trails on the southwest side of the mountain. These trails are a good alternative to the more popular Piper Trail on NH 16, and the very crowded Champney Falls Trail on the Kancamagus Highway.

   This loop is completed in a clockwise direction and begins on the Brook Trail, which is found by walking past the gate at the end of Paugus Road. Fol-

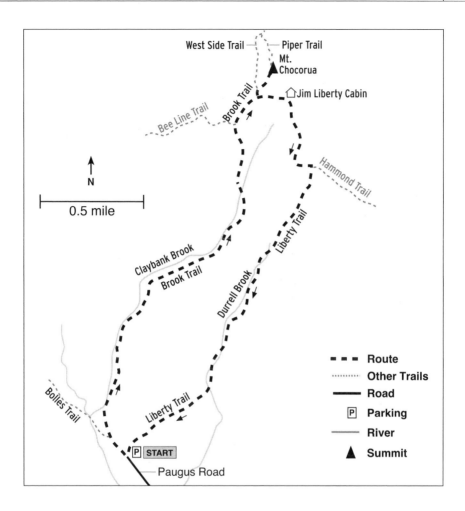

low the dirt road for about 100 yards, turn right at the fork, and follow signs for the Brook Trail. Just before a bridge over Claybank Brook, the Brook Trail leads into the woods on the right and parallels the brook. As is common throughout the northern hardwood forests of the White Mountains, the cool microclimate of the brook provides the perfect habitat for eastern hemlock. The trail climbs gradually, passing the Bickford Trail at 0.9 mile and crossing the brook at 2.5 miles. After crossing the brook, you pass through a forest of beech and birch that was heavily damaged during the 1998 ice storm. From here to the summit the trail climbs steeply, reaching the first open ledges after 3.0 miles with views opening up to the south and west. The trail makes

Mount Chocorua reflecting off Chocorua Lake.

several difficult rock scrambles (be very careful in wet or icy conditions), and at 3.4 miles the Liberty Trail enters from the right.

 At the junction with the Liberty Trail, turn left to complete the last 0.2 mile of climbing to the summit, making sure to stay to the right at a junction with the Piper Trail. *Though well below treeline, the summit of Chocorua is completely exposed and can be a dangerous place to be in a thunderstorm.* Of course, this exposure is what makes the views from the summit so spectacular, taking in Lake Winnipesaukee, the Sandwich Range Wilderness, the mountains that rise above the Pemigewasset Valley, and Mount Washington.

To complete this trip, follow the Brook Trail back down from the summit, turning left at its junction with the Piper Trail. Turn left again onto the Liberty Trail, 0.2 mile below the summit. The Liberty Trail makes a very steep descent over bare rock ledges at first, but soon you will find the hike down very easy. At 0.3 mile below the Brook Trail you will pass the Jim Liberty Cabin, and at 0.9 mile you pass a trail junction with the Hammond Trail (stay to the right). When you cross Durrell Brook it is only 1.1 miles to the parking area on Paugus Road.

TRIP 21
MAHOOSUCS ADVENTURE:
GOOSE EYE AND MOUNT CARLO

Rating: Strenuous
Distance: 7.7 miles round-trip
Elevation Gain: 2,700 feet
Estimated Time: 6 hours
Maps: AMC White Mountain Trail Map #6: C12, C13, D12, D13,
    USGS Shelburne and Success Pond Quadrangles

A rugged hike that will take you to spectacular views in the wild and woolly Mahoosuc Range.

Directions

From the western junction of NH 16 and US 2 in Gorham, New Hampshire, follow NH 16 north for 4.5 miles and turn right onto the Cleveland Bridge. In another 0.7 mile, continue straight through a set of lights. After the lights, the road bears right, crosses a set of railroad tracks, and then bears to the left and becomes Hutchins Street. At 1.3 miles beyond the traffic light, turn right onto Success Pond Road, a dirt logging road often marked only by a sign saying "OHRV Parking, 1 mile." The Goose Eye and Carlo Col Trails will be on the right, 7.8 miles from Hutchins Street. Take care driving on Success Pond Road as it is an active logging road. Always yield to working logging vehicles for your own safety. The road is usually passable for most vehicles, except in early spring when it can be deeply rutted and missing some culverts.

Trip Description

Straddling the Maine-New Hampshire border northeast of Gorham, the Mahoosucs is a rugged range of peaks that runs southwest to northeast. Although only one peak breaks the 4,000-foot barrier (Old Speck at 4,170 feet), the remote and rocky nature of the range makes the hiking both challenging and rewarding. The Appalachian Trail runs the entire length of the Mahoosucs, crossing all the major summits and traversing the Mahoosuc Notch, a 1-mile stretch of house-sized boulders that is often described as

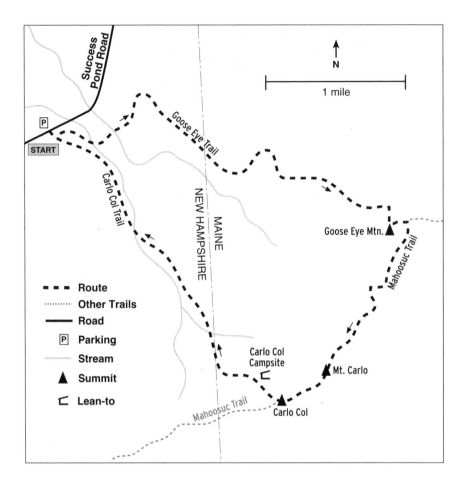

the most difficult mile on the entire Appalachian Trail. This hike up Mount Carlo and Goose Eye Mountain avoids the notch, but nonetheless contains some rough hiking over steep sections of exposed rocks. The effort is worth it, though, as the views from the bald summit of Goose Eye Mountain are some of the best in the White Mountains.

This trip leaves Success Pond Road on the Goose Eye and Carlo Col Trails, which follow an old logging road. After about 100 yards, turn left onto the Goose Eye Trail, which immediately descends the steep road bank and crosses a stream. The trail soon turns right, heading over muddy ground through a second- or third-growth forest of spruce, fir, and birch. There is not much elevation gain as the trail crosses two fairly wide streams that can be difficult to cross in high water. Soon after the second large stream crossing, the Goose Eye Trail joins a logging road for about 100 yards before leaving the road, passing through a set of cairns on the right.

After leaving the road, you will notice the trail begins to climb, gradually at first. The forest is in various stages of growth, as most of the northwestern slopes of the Mahoosucs are owned by paper and forest management companies that manage the land for wood products. The trail gets steeper as you enter a forest of hardwoods filled with the typical wildflowers of the area—trout lilies, mayflowers, early yellow violets, red trilliums—as well as forest birds such as ovenbirds, hermit thrushes, and ruffed grouse. As the trail angles up and around the northwestern side of Goose Eye Mountain, the footing gets rougher and the climbing steeper. As you climb, you will enter the familiar spruce-fir/paper birch forest that is common at higher elevations in New England.

You get a short break from the steep climbing as you attain the ridgeline and catch a glimpse of the rocky, pointed summit of Goose Eye through the trees. Of course, the trail soon gets steep again as you climb the summit cone, with the last 300 yards being very steep with some scrambling over bare rock. Shortly before reaching the summit, you emerge above treeline into a world of krummholz. Sheep laurel, Labrador tea, mountain cranberries, and diapensia grow through a mat of sphagnum moss and reindeer lichens. After 3.2 miles and 2,250 feet of elevation gain, you reach the summit and are treated to excellent views in all directions, with the Presidential Range to the southwest and the wild, undeveloped Northern Forest to the north and east. You can also see the Appalachian Trail as it winds its way across the treeless ridge to the north.

From the summit, follow the Goose Eye Trail 0.1 mile to the Mahoosuc Trail (Appalachian Trail) and turn right to head toward Mount Carlo. The Mahoosuc Trail immediately makes a steep and difficult descent over rocky ledges to a flat area below the summit containing an alpine bog. After the bog the trail continues a steep descent to the col between Goose Eye and Mount Carlo, then begins a steep climb through spruce-fir forest. The trail passes through another boggy area and makes a series of small climbs and descents before reaching the actual summit of Mount Carlo, about 1.5 miles from Goose Eye. Despite some small trees on and around the summit, good views can be seen in all directions.

These signs on Goose Eye Mountain point hikers toward their destination.

Continue south on the Mahoosuc Trail for a 0.4-mile descent to the Carlo Col Trail and turn right. The Carlo Col Trail descends steeply to the Carlo Col Campsite, 0.3 mile below the Mahoosuc Trail. (This is the first reliable source of water since the stream crossings on the Goose Eye Trail.) After leaving the campsite, the Carlo Col Trail continues a steep descent following the banks of a stream, crossing it often, and sometimes following the stream course itself—just keep your eyes open for trail blazes and a worn footpath. After leaving the stream, the trail descends more moderately, crossing several small brooks. As the trail begins to level out, it follows a large brook (on the left) for about 0.3 mile. The trail then crosses the brook, turns right, and follows an old woods road for the final 0.8 mile, ending back at the parking area on Success Pond Road.

AMC and the Mahoosucs

Tucked in the upper northeast corner of the White Mountain National Forest is one of the area's most ecologically and recreationally significant places. The Mahoosucs region, which straddles the New Hampshire-Maine border, is home to the "toughest mile" on the Appalachian Trail and offers a great range of outdoor opportunities. The Androscoggin River, with everything from flatwater to whitewater paddling, bounds the region to the west, the south, and partially to the east. The Grafton Loop Trail, completed in 2007, offers both overnight backpacking and scenic day hikes, and wildlife watching is popular throughout the region, especially along the Androscoggin and at Lake Umbagog National Wildlife Refuge. The refuge also offers flatwater paddling, including overnight canoe and kayak camping at remote campsite locations, as well as fishing, hunting, and whitewater paddling. Cross-country and downhill skiing are popular activities in the winter, while road and mountain biking are popular in the summer and fall.

The Appalachian Mountain Club has a long history of exploration, trail construction and maintenance, and conservation in the Mahoosucs. The AMC began construction of the 27-mile Mahoosuc Trail in 1918, and completed it in 1925. It is now part of the Appalachian Trail. AMC maintains this section of the AT as well as five tentsites and four shelters. To celebrate its 100th anniversary, AMC built the Centennial Trail to Mount Hayes in 1976. More recently, working with the Maine Appalachian Trail Club, AMC and other partners completed the 34-mile Grafton Loop Trail, a multi-day backpacking loop that connects to the Appalachian Trail in Grafton Notch. The trail project continues to be a cooperative effort between landowners, nonprofit organizations, community interests, and the state of Maine.

Today, the AMC is working with a diverse group of local, regional, and national organizations, including the Androscoggin River Watershed Council, Bethel Area and Northern White Mountain Chambers of Commerce, the Northern Forest Alliance, Appalachian Trail Conservancy, and The Wilderness Society, on the Mahoosucs Initiative. This cooperative effort is addressing conservation, community, and economic needs in the region, recognizing that land use and conservation are closely intertwined with the local and regional economy. The

Initiative is focused on providing new opportunities for community members and others who care deeply about the region to identify economic and conservation priorities, setting the stage for collaborative and cooperative thinking. Partners in the Mahoosuc Initiative helped the Trust for Public Land and the state of Maine to gain $2 million in federal Forest Legacy Program funding to acquire 3,688 acres in Grafton Notch for addition to the Maine Bureau of Public Lands' Mahoosuc Unit.

Resources:

Mahoosucs Initiative (www.mahoosucinfo.org)

Scenic Touring Map of the Mahoosucs (includes parks, campgrounds, guide services, natural and cultural features), available free of charge at local chambers of commerce and many area businesses.

The view from Puzzle Mountain on the Grafton Loop Trail.

Rating: Strenuous
Distance: 9.7 miles round-trip
Elevation Gain: 3,600 feet
Estimated Time: 7 hours
Maps: AMC White Mountain Trail Map #5: G12, USGS Wild River
  and Chatham Quadrangles

**This spectacular day hike includes more than 3 miles of hiking
above treeline.**

Directions
From the junction of ME 113 and US 302 in Fryeburg, Maine, head north
on ME 113. Park in the lot on the right side of ME 113, which is 17.1 miles
north of Fryeburg and just past the AMC Cold River Camp. The trail is across
the road from the parking area.

Trip Description
While both North and South Baldface top out at less than 4,000 feet, this
hike near Evans Notch contains a long stretch of hiking over open ledges.
It is somewhat removed from the traditional hiking centers in the White
Mountains and thus receives far less foot traffic than trails in the Presidential Range, Pemigewasset Wilderness Area, and Franconia Notch. It does
attract some hikers, though, because the views over the Wild River valley
to the Carter Range and Mount Washington are spectacular. This is a difficult hike with substantial exposure that creates dangerous conditions in bad
weather. The crossing of Charles Brook can be treacherous in high water. In
good weather, however, this is one of the best loop hikes in New England.

Begin your hike on the Baldface Circle Trail, which leaves the west side of
ME 113 across from the parking lot just north of the AMC Cold River Camp.
The scent of pine immediately overtakes you as you enter a mixed forest of
white pine, spruce, and various hardwoods. The trail parallels a stone wall
for a while as it climbs gradually and then passes through a cool, dark grove

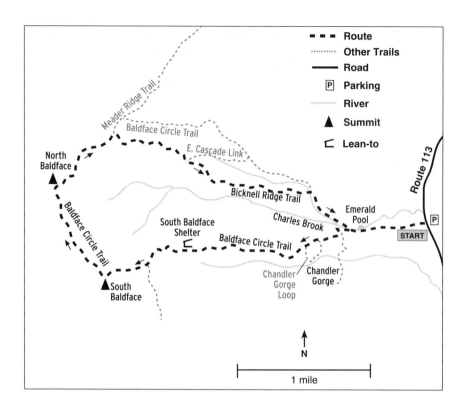

of hemlock as you near Charles Brook. At 0.7 mile you reach a fork in the trail known as Circle Junction. A side trail leads left 0.1 mile to Emerald Pool, a deep swimming hole that sits below a rocky gorge and a steep bank topped by hemlock trees. This is a great place to cool down at the end of your hike. For now, follow the Baldface Circle Trail to the left, heading toward South Baldface. The trail soon begins to climb moderately through a northern hardwood forest that becomes increasingly dominated by American beech trees. The trail gets steeper shortly before it reaches the South Baldface Shelter at 2.5 miles.

After the shelter, you will climb very steeply over rock ledges as you begin to reap the rewards of this trip with good views to the east and south. This is the most difficult section of the hike with many steep scrambles over exposed

 rock. *In wet or icy conditions this is a dangerous undertaking.* This portion of the trail is marked by paint blazes on rock, as it is impossible to build cairns on the steep rock face. Vegetation is restricted to small shrubs such as pin cherry,

The hike along Baldface Circle Trail provides about 4 miles of unobstructed views.

blueberries, and rhodora. At 3.0 miles you reach the east ridge of South Baldface and the hiking becomes much easier, although it is still a steep climb the rest of the way to the summit—3.7 miles from ME 113. The 360-degree views from this 3,570-foot peak are spectacular and include Mount Washington, the Mahoosucs, and the Caribou-Speckled Mountain Wilderness.

The trail turns to the northwest to make the traverse of the ridge between the two Baldface summits. The trail descends back into the trees for a short distance, but you will spend most of your time hiking in the open for the 1.2 miles between the two peaks. About 200 feet of steep climbing is needed in order to reach the summit of North Baldface, but it is much less difficult than the climb up South Baldface. The summit of North Baldface has more of the excellent views you saw while on the south peak. The Carter Range is about 7 miles to the west, separated from the Baldface Range by the thick forests of the Wild River valley (the Spruce Brook Campsite and Perkins Notch Shelter make excellent backpacking destinations for those who want to explore the wilderness along the Wild River). The nearby peaks in the Evans Notch area are Mount Meader, Royce Mountain, Caribou Mountain, and Speckled Mountain.

The trail leaves North Baldface heading northeast as it descends steeply through spruce and fir before breaking out into the open again. Warm air rising above the open ridges of the Baldfaces makes this a great place to watch for hawks and geese during the fall migration. It is also a good spot for sampling wild blueberries in late summer. The trail travels in and out of the trees until its junction with the Bicknell Ridge Trail (5.8 miles from ME 113) in a flat area thickly populated with sheep laurel, blueberries, and mountain cranberries. At this point you can either stay on the Baldface Circle Trail or turn right onto the Bicknell Ridge Trail. We suggest taking the Bicknell Ridge Trail, which stays out in the open a little longer.

Bicknell Ridge is a rocky outcropping of schist flecked with shiny mica and lined with veins of quartz and basalt dikes. It also provides an excellent view of North and South Baldface and the circular ridge connecting the two. The trail makes a steep descent, finally entering the forest for good as the trees change from conifers to hardwoods. Shortly before its lower junction with the Baldface Circle Trail, the trail crosses Charles Brook (in high water cross about 20 yards upstream). Once you are back at the Baldface Circle Trail, turn right. You will soon cross Charles Brook again. This crossing can be very difficult in high water—try downstream this time. Shortly after crossing the brook, you complete the loop and have a flat 0.7-mile walk back to the car.

Camping and Hiking in Bear Country

Black bears are common in the White Mountains, although hikers rarely see them. More timid than their larger cousins the grizzly bears (which do *not* live in the White Mountains), black bears are mostly vegetarians, feeding on nuts, fruits, grasses, and insects. Black bears can grow to be 6 feet long and weigh as much as 450 pounds, though they average around 300 pounds. Though not true hibernators, black bears do experience a significant slowdown in their metabolism during the winter. In general, they sleep for five to seven months, denning in caves, burrows, or even the hollowed-out trunks of large trees. Females give birth to their cubs during this winter downtime. While rare, it is possible to encounter a bear in winter.

While you are unlikely to encounter bears while hiking, you may see signs of them. Beech trees often have scars in their bark made by the claws of bears that climb the trees for their nuts in the fall. A bear's footprints are large and exciting to find, measuring up to 7 inches long and 4 inches across, with five distinct toes and claws visible above a rounded, triangular-shaped foot.

If you do see a bear while hiking, do *not* approach it—not to get a better look, not to take a picture, not for anything. Slowly back away and find another route to where you are going. Most likely the bear will run at the sight of you. Sometimes black bears can be frightened away by making a lot of noise and throwing rocks in their vicinity, but don't throw rocks *at* the bear or you will risk making him angry.

Seeing more than the hind end of a black bear while hiking in the White Mountains is extremely rare. More common are bear visits to campgrounds, both in the backcountry and next to roads. Follow these precautions when camping in bear country to ensure your safety, the safety of future campers, and the safety of the bears. (Once bears get a taste of human food, they can rarely resist sampling it again and often end up being relocated or killed because they lose their fear of humans.)

- Hang food from a high branch that will not support a bear's weight, at least 12 feet off the ground and 6 feet from the tree's trunk.
- Wrap trash and odorous foods in sealed plastic bags or other sealed containers to conceal smells. Hang *all* trash and food as well as other items such as sunscreen, insect repellent, and toiletries that can attract animals.
- Keep a clean cooking area and fire pit. Grease and food scraps will attract bears. If you can, cook at least 100 yards from your tent.
- Remove the clothes you've worn while cooking; they hold food odors and attract bears. Hang such clothing with your pack.
- Never store food in your tent. This will keep rodents out of your tent as well as bears.
- If a bear gets your stuff, don't attempt to get it back.
- Report any bear encounters to the nearest forest ranger or ranger station.

We have never had a bear encounter in the White Mountains, and if you follow these precautions you will most likely enjoy sleep-filled, bear-free camping.

TRIP 23
FRANCONIA RIDGE

Rating: Strenuous
Distance: 8.9 miles round-trip
Elevation Gain: 4,000 feet
Estimated Time: 8 hours
Maps: AMC White Mountain Trail Map #2: H4, H5, USGS Franconia
Quadrangle

This spectacular loop over Mount Lafayette and Mount Lincoln includes the longest above-treeline hike in the White Mountains outside of the Presidential Range.

Directions
From the Franconia Notch Parkway (I-93), follow signs to Lafayette Campground, 7.6 miles north of NH 112. Park in the hiker parking area at the Lafayette Campground in Franconia Notch State Park. The exit for the campground is on the southbound side of the parkway, but hiker parking is also on the northbound side. The Old Bridle Path leaves the parking area on the northbound side of the highway.

Trip Description
This trip is easily near the top of the list of best hikes in New England. Of course, Franconia Ridge also can be a very busy place during any weekend with good weather; however, early risers and weekday hikers stand a good chance to have at least part of the ridge all to themselves. The reward for climbing 4,000 feet in a day is spending several hours above treeline, soaking in views from well above the surrounding mountains and forests. Below treeline is exciting as well, as you pass several waterfalls and hike through all of the major forest types found in the White Mountains. You will also pass the AMC Greenleaf Hut, which at 4,220 feet is the highest hut outside of the Presidentials and offers an excellent base for those who would prefer to make this a two-day trip. (See Appendix D for contact information.)

⚠ *Caution: Franconia Ridge is extremely exposed to the weather. Its knife-edge ridgeline is susceptible to lightning strikes and very strong winds. Check the weather*

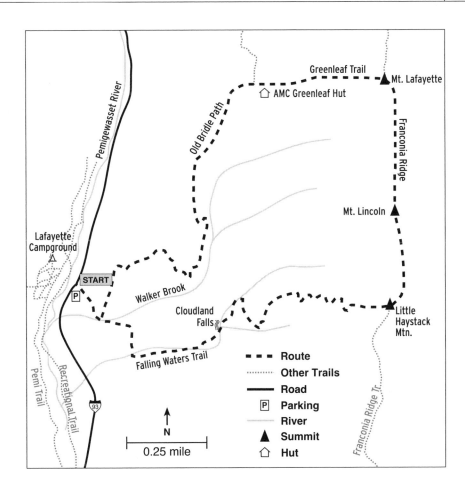

forecast before undertaking this hike, and realize that, even in good weather, the summits can experience suddenly dangerous weather conditions. Plan ahead and pack appropriate clothing and equipment. (See Safety and Etiquette on page 2.)

This trip makes a loop by utilizing four trails: the Old Bridle Path, the Greenleaf Trail, the Franconia Ridge Trail, and the Falling Waters Trail. The loop can be hiked in either direction. By following the Falling Waters Trail first, you attack the steepest climbing on the way up and get to Franconia Ridge a little quicker. This is the preferred route for those who tend to get sore knees on steep descents. However, this description follows the Old Bridle Path up Mount Lafayette at the beginning, saving the waterfalls (and their feet-soaking pools) for the end of the trip. The Old Bridle Path leaves from a parking area on the east side of the Franconia Notch Parkway. (You can also park at Lafayette Campground on the west side of the parkway and walk through the tunnel under the highway to the trailhead.)

The hike begins in a typical northern hardwood forest, soon passing the Falling Waters Trail on the right at Walker Brook. The hiking is easy as you climb at a moderate grade for about 1.0 mile. The trail gets steeper and at 1.6 miles makes a sharp left turn at an obstructed view of Mount Lincoln through what is now a spruce-fir forest. In the spring, hobblebush, trilliums, rose twisted stalk, and star flowers add splashes of white, red, and pink to an otherwise green and brown forest. At 1.9 miles you walk out of the forest onto open ledges, which have excellent views of Mount Lafayette and Mount Lincoln. In good weather you may be able to see very small figures making their way across the top of the ridge between the peaks. That is your destination and you should be there in about two more hours.

After making your way across the ledges, you once again enter the boreal forest and make a steep climb up to Greenleaf Hut (2.9 miles), which sits above Eagle Lake, a small but scenic pond surrounded by a bog filled with interesting flora such as sundew, mountain cranberries, and pitcher plants. Eagle Lake itself is colored yellow by blooming water lilies in June and July. In late spring, summer, and early fall, Greenleaf Hut is a good place to fill up on potable water and chocolate bars. If you think you want to spend the night and experience the pleasure of eating a home-cooked meal at 4,200 feet, be sure to make reservations well ahead of time. The hut marks the end of the Old Bridle Path. To continue this trip, follow the Greenleaf Trail down to Eagle Lake and then 1.1 miles up to the summit of Mount Lafayette.

Much of the hike up Mount Lafayette from the hut is above treeline and the views to the west are excellent. However, the true visual prize is the view from the summit, where you stare across the vast, roadless forests and peaks of the Pemigewasset Wilderness Area. You also will find the stone foundation of an old shelter, which once gave refuge to early visitors to Mount Lafayette who climbed the summit via horseback on both the Old Bridle Path and the Greenleaf Trail beginning in the 1850s. Originally called Great Haystack, Mount Lafayette was named after the French general the Marquis de Lafayette during his visit to New Hampshire in the 1820s.

From the summit, take a right and follow the Franconia Ridge Trail south. Except for one brief section between Lafayette and Lincoln, your entire hike on the Franconia Ridge Trail will be above the trees in one of the few true alpine environments in the eastern United States. Just above treeline you will

Although the hike along Franconia Ridge is strenuous, the rewards make the trip worth your while.

find the short, twisted, bonsai-like balsam fir known as krummholz. Soon, even these little trees disappear and you will find only alpine plants such as diapensia, mountain aven, deer's-hair sedge, and bearberry willows. You reach the excellent views from the summit of Mount Lincoln about 1.0 mile from Mount Lafayette. About 300 feet of elevation gain is between the two summits, but after climbing 3,600 feet to the summit of Mount Lafayette, you won't even notice the climb up Mount Lincoln.

From Mount Lincoln, continue south on the Franconia Ridge Trail. The knife-edge nature of the trail between Mount Lincoln and Little Haystack Mountain is perhaps the most exciting section of this hike; the mountain drops off steeply on both sides of the trail, giving you the feeling of being on top of the world. The hike to Little Haystack is all above treeline with one short section of climbing. From the summit of Little Haystack (5.7 miles), the Franconia Ridge Trail continues south to Mount Liberty, but to complete this hike, turn right onto the Falling Waters Trail and begin a very steep descent.

From Little Haystack, the Falling Waters Trail drops 3,000 feet in just 3.2 miles. It is a steep trail, but there is no scrambling. The trail enters the boreal forest almost immediately after leaving the ridge, and at 1.4 miles below the ridge it reaches a short spur trail that leads 100 yards to Shining Rock, which has excellent views of Franconia Notch, Cannon Mountain, and Kinsman Ridge.

The Falling Waters Trail continues its steep descent and reaches Dry Brook 1.6 miles below the Franconia Ridge. You soon begin to encounter the waterfalls that give this trail its name. First you will see two 25-foot cascades that face each other and fall together to form the pool above Cloudland Falls. From the top of Cloudland Falls—one of the most beautiful waterfalls in the White Mountains—you get an impressive view to Mount Moosilauke. The trail continues its steep descent and passes Swiftwater Falls and finally Stairs Falls where it begins to flatten out.

With 0.7 mile left to go, you will cross Dry Brook and have a relatively easy hike the rest of the way. After crossing Walker Brook on a wooden bridge, turn left onto the Old Bridle Path for the final 0.2 mile of the loop.

The Alpine Zone

Although alpine habitat is rare in the eastern United States, it is fairly common in the White Mountains, which boasts the most extensive areas of alpine habitat in the east (8 square miles), most of it occurring on Mount Washington, the Presidential Range, and the Franconia Range. Generally occurring above 4,500 feet in the White Mountains, the alpine zone is a world without trees that provides hikers with the spectacular views they spend hours of effort trying to achieve. More importantly, this treeless habitat is an environment that contains a unique mix of plants and animals, some of which are found nowhere else in the world. Immersing yourself in the miniature world of diapensia and alpine azalea, plants more commonly found in the Arctic, can be a fascinating experience.

The alpine habitat in the White Mountains has a growing season of only 60 to 70 days, making it impossible for annuals to sprout, which is why you will find only perennials growing above treeline. Plants include not only herbaceous (nonwoody) plants like mountain sandwort, but also dwarf shrubs and trees, ferns and mosses, lichens, sedges, grasses, and rushes. Each species employs

One of the two Lakes of the Clouds sits in the col between Mount Washington and Mount Monroe in the White Mountains' alpine zone.

different strategies for survival, but they all hug the ground in order to survive the cold and strong winds (which regularly reach hurricane force) that are a fact of life above treeline. The fight for survival is so difficult for these plants that a misplaced step by a hiker can kill a plant that took decades to grow. When above treeline, please make an extra effort to stay on the trail or on the rocks.

Several different alpine communities are within the alpine zone, each with its own habitat characteristics and species composition. Diapensia communities consist of hummock-shaped mats of white- and yellow-flowered diapensia scattered among bare patches of rocks and, sometimes, mats of pink alpine azalea and Lapland rosebay. Bigelow's sedge communities consist mostly of Bigelow's sedge and look like grassy meadows. Other communities include the dwarf shrub and heath, snowbank, alpine bog, and streamside communities. In snowbank, streamside, or bog communities you may find the beautiful yellow mountain aven, which lives only in the White Mountains and a few islands in Nova Scotia. The rarest plant in New England is the federally endangered dwarf cinquefoil, which has small yellow flowers (1/4 inch across), and is found only on Mount Washington and in the Franconia Range.

New England's alpine communities are a remnant from the tundra environments that recolonized the area after the last ice age. As the climate warmed and trees began spreading northward, the arctic plants that thrived in the tundra were pushed farther north and higher up the mountains until approximately 10,000 years ago when the distribution of plant species reached its current makeup in New Hampshire. The harsh conditions in the alpine zone support far less animal life than the comfy confines of the forests below. Birds you might encounter include ravens, dark-eyed juncos, white-throated sparrows, yellow-rumped and blackpoll warblers, American pipits, and the increasingly rare Bicknell's thrush. Mammals like moose, fox, and coyote are rare visitors to the alpine zone. You are likely to encounter snowshoe hares near the treeline and even woodchucks high on the slopes of Mount Washington. Cold-blooded amphibians and reptiles cannot survive for long above treeline, although in the summer you might find red efts and American toads at higher elevations. We have even seen wood frogs in the stream next to the AMC Madison Hut.

If you would like a great reference to the alpine zone of the White Mountains, check out the *AMC Field Guide to the New England Alpine Summits* by Nancy G. Slack and Allison W. Bell.

TRIP 24
MOUNT WASHINGTON VIA BOOTT SPUR

Rating: Very strenuous
Distance: 9.5 miles round-trip
Elevation Gain: 4,300 feet
Estimated Time: 8 hours
Maps: AMC White Mountain Trail Map #1: F9, USGS Mount
Washington Quadrangle

This climb up New England's tallest peak provides plenty of above-treeline hiking and awesome views.

Directions
This hike begins behind the AMC Pinkham Notch Visitor Center on the Tuckerman Ravine Trail. The visitor center is about 12.0 miles north of US 302 in Glen and 11.0 miles south of US 2 in Gorham.

Trip Description
At 6,288 feet, Mount Washington is the highest point in New England, and its weather is considered the worst in the world. It is easily one of New Hampshire's most popular attractions, with an auto road and cog railway transporting visitors who are unwilling or unable to use one of the various hiking trails that approach the summit from every direction. This hike uses the Boott Spur Trail for the ascent, taking you away from the almost certain crowds on the Tuckerman Ravine Trail. Views are spectacular of the glacial cirque known as Tuckerman Ravine from the Boott Spur Trail and the Lion Head Trail on the way down.

Caution: This is a very strenuous hike, gaining 4,300 feet in elevation over *sometimes rough terrain. Attempt this hike only if you are in excellent physical shape, well-equipped for a day above treeline, and the weather forecast looks favorable; people die almost every year on Mount Washington due to falls, hypothermia, avalanches, and rock slides. All of the above-treeline portion of this hike is extremely exposed to the weather and is susceptible to lightning strikes and very strong winds. Check the weather forecast before undertaking this hike and realize that, even in good weather, this area can experience suddenly dangerous weather conditions. Be prepared to seek shelter or turn around if the weather changes for the worse.*

This hike begins behind the AMC Pinkham Notch Visitor Center on the Tuckerman Ravine Trail. The trail is wide and rocky and climbs moderately, reaching the Cutler River and Crystal Cascade in just 0.3 mile. At 0.4 mile turn left onto the Boott Spur Trail where the Tuckerman Ravine Trail makes a sharp right. The Boott Spur Trail climbs very steeply at times, reaching an outlook with views of Wildcat Mountain and the Carter Range about 45 minutes above Pinkham. At 1.4 miles a short spur path leads left to a good view of Huntington Ravine, Lion Head, and Boott Spur. The trail continues to climb steeply through spruce and fir, and at 2.1 miles another side trail leads right to Harvard Rock, which has excellent views of Tuckerman Ravine. Shortly after Harvard Rock, the trail climbs above treeline, makes a brief southward turn, and levels out (catch your breath here) before turning right at a large boulder known as Split Rock and resuming its steep climb.

At 2.6 miles the trail reaches the Boott Spur Link, which leads 0.6 mile down to the Hermit Lake Shelters in Tuckerman Ravine. From this junction it is another 0.7 mile and 800 feet up to the end of the Boott Spur Trail. Along the way you will have spectacular views into Tuckerman Ravine, at times being more than 1,500 feet above the floor of the ravine. During your rest breaks, look at the alpine flora next to the trail. Depending on the time of year, you may see berries of various colors—red, blue, white, and black. The red ones are mountain cranberries, also known as lingonberries. Blueberries are either dwarf alpine blueberries or bog bilberries. The white ones are creeping snowberries and the black are black crowberries. All of these plants are common in arctic and subarctic environments in eastern North America.

The Boott Spur Trail ends at the Davis Path, 3.4 miles from Pinkham Notch. The summit of Boott Spur is the large jumble of rocks to the left. While 5,500 feet tall, from here Boott Spur looks like just a resting spot on the way to Mount Washington, which looks close enough to touch. Looks can be deceiving, however, as you are still 2.0 miles and 900 feet below the summit. To reach the summit turn right onto the Davis Path. At 0.6 mile from the Boott Spur Trail the Davis Path passes the Lawn Cutoff (if you are too tired to continue to the summit, follow the Lawn Cutoff to Tuckerman Junction and take the Tuckerman Ravine Trail back to Pinkham Notch). It

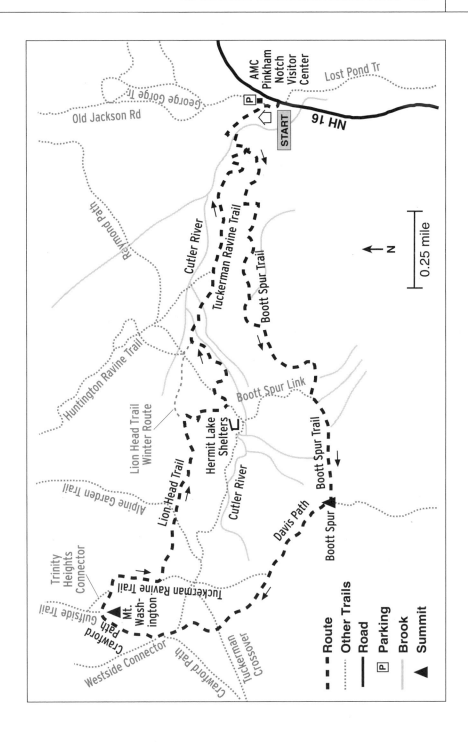

A hiker takes a break on Lion Head to take in the view of Tuckerman Ravine.

soon crosses the Camel Trail and Tuckerman Crossover on its way to the Crawford Path, 1.4 miles below Boott Spur. Turn right onto the Crawford Path for the final 0.6 mile to the summit.

The summit of Mount Washington is a bustling place, with hikers mixing with tourists who either rode the Cog Railway or drove their cars up the Mount Washington Auto Road. A building also houses the Mount Washington Observatory (www.mountwashington.org) and its scientists who observe the weather and subarctic environment on Mount Washington year-round. The views from the summit are, of course, spectacular in every direction, although Mount Washington averages only 65 clear days a year. The craggy peaks and cirques of the nearby Northern Presidentials provide the most dramatic scenery. To the west the Southern Presidentials gradually slope down toward Crawford Notch. On clear, smog-free days you can see the sun reflecting off the Atlantic Ocean, about 80 miles to the southeast.

To return to Pinkham Notch find the Tuckerman Ravine Trail, which leaves the auto road just below the lower parking lot on the summit. Follow the trail from boulder to boulder as it makes a steep descent from the summit cone. At 0.4 mile below the summit turn left onto the Lion Head Trail, which continues the steep descent over lichen-covered boulders. At 0.9 mile below the summit you cross the Alpine Garden Trail, which leads across an alpine plateau well known for its early summer wildflower displays. Soon you reach the Lion Head, a craggy overhang with spectacular views into Tuckerman Ravine.

From Lion Head the Lion Head Trail continues a steep, rocky descent to the Hermit Lake Shelters and the Tuckerman Ravine Trail, which you reach 2.0 miles below the summit. By the time you reach the shelters (Hermit Lake is a short walk to the right up the Tuckerman Ravine Trail), you have completed the above-treeline portion of your hike. Turn left on the Tuckerman Ravine Trail for 2.3 miles of hiking over rocks with sore feet and tired legs during your moderate descent back to Pinkham Notch.

Mount Washington: Tallest, Stormiest, Deadliest

Mount Washington, previously called Agiochook—meaning "home of the great sprit"—by the local Abenaki people, is the tallest mountain in the northeast, rising 6,288 feet above sea level. The first recorded climb of the mountain was by Darby Field in 1642. Field moved to New Hampshire from England to escape religious persecution. He left his home in Durham with several Native Americans as guides and made his way to the Mount Washington area by following the coast to Saco, Maine, where he followed the Saco River north and west. Once he was near the mountain, local Native Americans showed him the route to the summit, where he went in search of jewels. What he found was "terrible freesing weather" and views all the way to the Atlantic Ocean. His route to the summit is still debated, with some historians believing he attained the summit via Boott Spur, first going up either the Ellis River or the Rocky Branch. However, there are those who believe he ascended via the Southern Presidentials. In any event, Field convinced a few others to climb the mountain later that year, but it was not until the 1720s that reports of other people climbing the mountain began to appear.

As the highest peak north of the Smokies and east of the Rockies, Mount Washington now draws several hundred thousand visitors a year, who arrive at the summit by foot, car, or cog railroad. Awaiting those visitors are incredible views and a collection of structures that house a visitor center and cafeteria, the Mount Washington Observatory, and various TV and radio antennas. Nicknamed "the rock pile," the summit cone is strewn with acres and acres of boulders and talus created by the freezing and thawing of ice over thousands of years.

Mount Washington is famous for having the "worst weather in the world," and for being the deadliest mountain in the eastern United States. The mountain lies in an area of North America that is at the confluence of three major storm tracks. This confluence, combined with the mountain's height and north-south orientation, creates optimal conditions for extended periods of extremely high winds. The highest wind speed ever recorded on the planet was 231 MPH on Mount Washington on April 12, 1934. Stronger wind gusts have most likely occurred elsewhere that were not recorded, but this does not diminish the fact that Mount Washington's weather can be deadly as it is consistently cold, wet, and windy with low visibility.

In the winter the average high temperature on the summit is 15 degrees and the wind regularly reaches hurricane strength. When it's not snowing, the summit is often covered in a thick fog that freezes on contact, creating a layer of rime ice on rocks, buildings, and plants. In the summer the temperature rarely rises above the low 50s, and rain, fog, and high winds are common. It snows on the summit every month of the year. To learn more about the weather on Mount Washington, visit the Mount Washington Observatory on the summit or at its Weather Discovery Center, 2936 White Mountain Highway, NH 16 in North Conway. You can also visit the observatory online at www.mountwashington.org.

It is usually the weather that causes problems for visitors to the mountain. With mountains twice as high regularly hiked in shorts and T-shirts in the western United States, it is easy for people to get lulled into thinking that Mount Washington must not be a dangerous place. Winter, of course, has proven to be the deadliest season on the mountain, but people have died of hypothermia in all seasons on Mount Washington; they are not prepared for windy, wet weather that can come unexpectedly and chill to the bone. More than 120 people have died here since it became a regular tourist destination in the late 1840s. Several have died within just a few hundred yards of the summit buildings or one of the huts, and some have merely disappeared, presumably getting lost and dying of exposure. *Not Without Peril* by Nicholas Howe is an excellent read for those interested in the more compelling stories of those who have lost their lives on Mount Washington. Don't fall victim to Mount Washington's weather. Plan ahead and pack appropriate clothing and equipment. (See Safety and Etiquette on page 2.)

This ice-coated sign provides a sense of how brutal the weather can be on Mount Washington.

TRIP 25
HUT TO HUT PRESIDENTIAL TRAVERSE

Rating: Very strenuous

Distance: 23.2 miles one-way without summits, 25.5 miles
including all summits

Elevation Gain: 6,500 feet without summits, 9,600 feet including
all summits

Estimated Time: 3–4 days

Maps: AMC White Mountain Trail Map #1: E9, F9, G8, USGS Mount
Washington, Carter Dome, Stairs Mountain, and Crawford Notch
Quadrangles

**Over three days, this hike will offer you spectacular views on
the largest piece of alpine real estate in the eastern United
States.**

Directions

This hike begins on the Great Gulf Trail, which starts on the west side of NH
16, 6.7 miles south of US 2 in Gorham and 16.2 miles north of US 302 in
Glen. The trail ends in Crawford Notch at the parking area for the Webster-
Jackson Trail, at the hostel at the AMC Highland Center. The hostel is 8.5
miles south of the intersection of US 3 and US 302 in Twin Mountain, and
21.0 miles north of the intersection of NH 16 and US 302 in Glen.

Trip Description

Hiking the Presidential Range from end to end is one of the classic treks
in the United States. Of course, numerous trails can be used to accomplish
this trip, although the main route between Madison Hut and Mizpah Spring
Hut via Lakes of the Clouds Hut is fairly standard. Perhaps the most al-
luring aspect of this hike is that it offers hikers the opportunity to bag as
many as eight 4,000-footers. Even if you choose to skip the summits, you
will have an incredible hike above treeline, peering into glacial cirques, taking in views that stretch from horizon to horizon, and encountering alpine
plant species that are more common on the tundra of northern Canada than

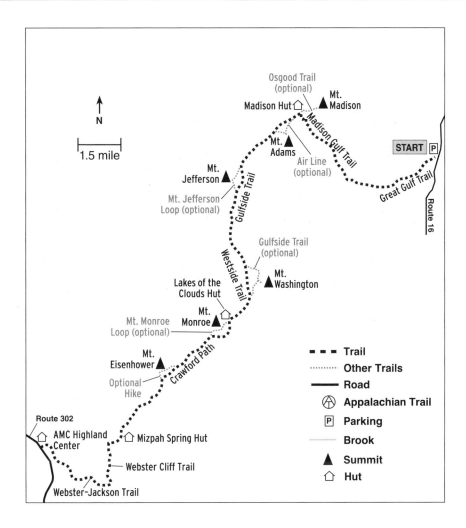

in New England. Most people need three or four days in order to enjoy this experience. By staying at AMC huts, you can lighten your load and have an easier time of it while scaling the heights.

Caution: A large portion of this hike, from Madison Spring Hut (reached on Day 1) to the summit of Mount Pierce (Day 3), is extremely exposed to the weather. The entire Mount Washington area is susceptible to lightning strikes and very strong winds. It can snow any month of the year, but any kind of wet weather above treeline can create the potential for hypothermia, especially when it is windy. Bring extra clothing regardless of the forecast, and study the maps

Staying hydrated is essential when taking a multi-day hike in the Whites.

ahead of time in case you need to make an emergency trip below treeline to escape unsafe weather. Check the weather forecast before each day's hike (a forecast is read at breakfast and posted at each hut at 8 A.M.) and realize that, even in good weather, you may experience suddenly dangerous weather conditions.

This is a one-way hike that starts in the Pinkham Notch area and concludes in Crawford Notch. If you are hiking in a group, you can leave cars at either end. You can also choose to take advantage of the daily hiker shuttle that the AMC runs during the summer. To reserve a spot on the shuttle and at the huts call 603-466-2727. Space fills up quickly, especially in July and August, so try to reserve your space as far in advance as possible.

This hike begins with an approach of Madison Hut from Madison Gulf. The headwall of Madison Gulf is very steep and dangerous in bad weather. If someone in your group has a fear of heights or if there is an unfavorable weather forecast, you should consider hiking the Valley Way Trail as an alternative. The Valley Way begins at the Appalachia parking area on US 2 west of Gorham and remains safely below treeline for most of its 3.8 miles to the hut.

Day 1: NH 16 to Madison Hut

5.9 miles, 3,600-foot elevation gain, 5 hours

From the parking area on NH 16, begin your hike on the Great Gulf Trail, which parallels the Peabody River for much of the way between the parking area and the Madison Gulf Trail. The Peabody River drains the Great Gulf, which is the largest glacial cirque in the White Mountains. At 1.8 miles you will pass the Osgood Trail, an alternate route to Mount Madison. At 2.7 miles the Osgood Cutoff continues straight and you will need to turn left to remain on the Great Gulf Trail, which crosses Parapet Brook and soon reaches the Madison Gulf Trail. Turn right onto the Madison Gulf Trail, which soon has you climbing steeply through a dense boreal forest. The next 3.0 miles will be the most difficult of your trip.

The Madison Gulf Trail lies within the Great Gulf Wilderness Area, 5,552 acres of roadless wilderness. The trail is well marked, but makes numerous stream crossings where care must be taken to remain on the trail by following the blue-paint blazes. In high water some of these stream crossings can be difficult, but they are usually passable. Two miles from the Great Gulf Trail you will reach Sylvan Cascade, an attractive waterfall that falls 30 feet over a moss-covered wall of rock. Sylvan Cascade marks the entrance to Madison Gulf, an attractive glacial cirque. After a moderate climb across the floor of the gulf, you begin the very steep climb up the headwall. Make no mistake about it: this is one of the most difficult sections of trail in the White Mountains, with steep scrambles over rocky ledges that can be slippery and dangerous when wet. Expect to spend a lot of time on the headwall, particularly if you have a heavy pack.

As you climb the headwall, you will begin to have good views to the south and east, but you do not emerge from treeline until you crest the ridge and reach the Parapet Trail 5.5 miles after leaving the parking area. Turn left on the Parapet Trail for a short walk to Star Lake, a small alpine lake that sits in the col between Mount Madison and Mount Adams. Star Lake seems a world apart from the thick forests you just spent the day hiking through. Its shallow waters reflect the treeless, rock-strewn upper slopes of Mount Adams and Mount Madison, while alpine plants like cotton grass, mountain aven, and pale laurel grow in the thin soils filling the spaces between boulders covered with map and target lichens. At Star Lake turn right onto the Star Lake Trail for a short, mostly flat walk to Madison Hut.

Optional Mount Madison Summit Hike. 0.5 mile, 550-foot elevation gain, 35 minutes. Once at Madison Hut it is easy to add the 5,366-foot summit of Mount Madison to your list of 4,000-footers. Just take the Osgood Trail from the hut to the summit. It is a steep hike from boulder to boulder. The summit has great views in all directions, especially to the north and east where the towns of Gorham and Berlin give way to the wild expanse of the Northern Forest.

Day 2: Madison Hut to Lakes of the Clouds Hut
6.9 miles, 2,050-foot elevation gain, 4 hours, 40 minutes
(not including summits)

After getting your fill of an expertly cooked AMC hut breakfast, start your day on the Gulfside Trail. Your entire day will be spent above treeline on what may be the most beautiful stretch of hiking in the White Mountains. In just 0.3 mile you reach the Air Line Trail, which coincides with the Gulfside Trail for about 100 yards before branching to the left and heading to the summit of Mount Adams—the second highest mountain in the Northeast. To bypass the summit continue straight on the Gulfside Trail, which rises moderately on the way to Thunderstorm Junction, 0.9 mile from the hut. Along the way you will have spectacular views into King Ravine on the right as you hike over piles of rocks.

Optional Mount Adams Summit Hike. 0.9 mile, 650-foot elevation gain, 55 minutes. From the Gulfside Trail turn left onto the Air Line Trail, which reaches the conical summit of Mount Adams about 0.6 mile above the Gulfside Trail. At 5,799 feet you are standing on the highest mountain in the Northeast without a road, and the views are truly spectacular. On a clear day, Mount Washington looks close enough to touch. To continue your hike toward Lakes of the Clouds, take Lowe's Path west to Thunderstorm Junction, where you turn left onto the Gulfside Trail.

From Thunderstorm Junction, continue straight on the Gulfside Trail, enjoying an easy hike amongst the boulders and alpine flora of the Presidentials. Shortly after Thunderstorm Junction, the Israel Ridge Path joins the Gulfside Trail. At 1.5 miles from Madison Hut the Israel Ridge Path turns right. Continue straight on the Gulfside Trail and you will soon see Jefferson Ravine to the left. At 2.2 miles from the hut you reach Edmands Col, and in another 0.2 mile you reach the Mount Jefferson Loop. If the weather is good

Be prepared for rugged terrain when hiking above treeline.

and your legs are up for it, turn right here to add Mount Jefferson to your day; otherwise, continue straight on the Gulfside Trail.

Optional Mount Jefferson Summit Hike. 0.7 mile, 600-foot elevation gain, 40 minutes. To reach the summit of Mount Jefferson just turn right onto the Mount Jefferson Loop Trail, which reaches the 5,716-foot summit of Mount Jefferson in 0.4 mile. More great views—you will come to expect them by this point in the hike. From the summit follow the Mount Jefferson Loop Trail southeast for a 0.3-mile descent back to the Gulfside Trail. Turn right to continue to Lakes of the Clouds Hut.

After Mount Jefferson, the Gulfside Trail descends Sphinx Col before beginning the climb around Mount Clay on its way to Mount Washington. At 3.8 miles from Madison Hut you will reach the Mount Clay Loop. Turn left onto the Mount Clay Loop (if you are low on water, continue straight on the Gulfside Trail, where in 0.2 mile a side trail leads to Greenough Spring). About 0.5 mile above the Gulfside Trail, you reach the summit of Mount Clay, which has spectacular views of the Northern Presidentials and the Great Gulf. You can easily imagine a glacier carving out the gulf, being joined by glaciers flowing from Jefferson Ravine and Madison Gulf. Continuing south from the summit, the Mount Clay Loop Trail rejoins the Gulfside Trail in another 0.7 mile.

Turn left on the Gulfside Trail and follow it for a few hundred yards to its junction with the Westside Trail. To reach Lakes of the Clouds Hut turn right onto the Westside Trail and follow it for 0.9 mile to the Crawford Path. Turn right onto the Crawford Path for the final 0.9 mile to the hut.

Optional Mount Washington Summit Hike. 1.6 miles, 800-foot elevation gain, 1 hour, 15 minutes. Instead of turning right onto the Westside Trail, continue straight on the Gulfside Trail, which begins a steady climb up the northwest summit ridge of Mount Washington. As you climb from boulder to lichen-encrusted boulder, you will understand why Mount Washington is nicknamed "the rock pile." At 1.0 mile above the Westside Trail turn right onto the Crawford Path for the final 0.2 mile to the summit. The views from Mount Washington, the tallest mountain in the Northeast, are of course spectacular. On its summit you also are treated to the highest snack bar in the Northeast. From the summit follow the Crawford Path 1.5 miles to Lakes of the Clouds Hut.

Optional Mount Monroe Summit Hike. 0.8 mile, 350-foot elevation gain, 30 minutes. Mount Monroe is so close to Lakes of the Clouds Hut that an after-dinner summit hike is almost irresistible. From the hut follow the Crawford Path for about 100 yards, where you should turn right onto the Mount Monroe Loop Trail. A short, steep climb takes you to the summit (5,372 feet) in about twenty minutes.

Day 3: Lakes of the Clouds Hut to Mizpah Spring Hut
4.8 miles, 350-foot elevation gain, 3 hours

You have the option of finishing your trip on Day 3 by hiking the Crawford Path from Lakes of the Clouds Hut for 7.0 miles down to Crawford Notch. However, you can extend your stay in the mountains by spending the night at Mizpah Spring Hut and spending Day 4 bagging a few more peaks. Either way, from Lakes of the Clouds Hut take a right on the Crawford Path, which skirts around the summit of Mount Monroe and passes through an area rich in alpine flowers like pale laurel, mountain aven, diapensia, and alpine azalea. This area is also one of only two places on the planet (Franconia Range is the other) where the tiny dwarf cinquefoil lives. Take care to stay on the trail, as all of these plants are extremely fragile. With the Dry River valley below you on the left, you will have about 2.0 miles of hiking before reaching the Mount Eisenhower Trail. Shortly beyond this trail, you reach the Mount Eisenhower Loop Trail, which leads right to the summit of Mount Eisenhower.

Optional Mount Eisenhower Summit Hike. 0.8 miles, 300-foot elevation gain, 35 minutes. Turn right off the Crawford Path onto the Mount Eisenhower Loop Trail and make the short, steep climb to the bald summit of Mount Eisenhower (4,760 feet), which takes about 30 minutes. To return to the Crawford Path, continue over the summit on the Mount Eisenhower Loop Trail, which reaches the Crawford Path in 0.4 mile.

Continuing on the Crawford Path, you will make a moderate descent to the col between Mount Eisenhower and Mount Pierce, where you will find a small stream if you are in need of water. The trail then climbs moderately to the Webster Cliff Trail, 3.9 miles from Lakes of the Clouds Hut. If you plan to skip Mizpah Spring Hut and Day 4 of this trip, continue straight on the Crawford Path for the final 2.9 miles to Crawford Notch. Otherwise, turn left onto the Webster Cliff Trail and follow it for the short 0.1-mile climb to the summit of Mount Pierce (4,312 feet), which offers good views back toward Mount Washington. From the summit of Mount Pierce, follow the Webster Cliff Trail for a steep, 0.8-mile climb down to Mizpah Spring Hut.

Day 4: Mizpah Spring Hut to Crawford Notch
via Mount Jackson and Mount Webster
5.6 miles, 500-foot elevation gain, 4 hours

Day 4 is divided fairly evenly between a wooded ridge walk to Mount Jackson and Mount Webster, and a steep climb down through the woods to your final destination, Crawford Notch. From the hut, follow the Webster Cliff Trail to the left for a walk through high-elevation forest on your way to Mount Jackson. Here you'll be able to watch for spruce grouse, an increasingly rare bird in New Hampshire that can survive only in spruce-fir forests. Once you find them, they are easy to keep an eye on, as they are very tame—tame enough to earn them the nickname "fool's hen" because they are so easy to catch.

You reach the summit of Mount Jackson 1.7 miles after leaving Mizpah Spring Hut. Mount Jackson (4,052 feet) provides dramatic views of the Presidentials as seen across the expanse of the Presidential Range–Dry River Wilderness. From the summit, walk south on the Webster Cliff Trail for a 1.4-mile ridge walk to Mount Webster (3,910 feet). Mount Webster sits atop a cliff with impressive views that look straight down into Crawford Notch. To complete your hike, walk back toward Mount Jackson on the Webster Cliff Trail for 0.1 mile and turn left onto the Webster-Jackson Trail. At this point you have nowhere to go but down, and this trail takes you 2.4 miles and 2,050 feet down to the floor of Crawford Notch. About 1.0 mile below Mount Webster you will need to turn left after a beautiful waterfall on Silver Cascade Brook. At the end of the trail turn right on US 302 for a short walk to Crawford Notch Depot Visitor Center where you can catch the hiker shuttle. You will also find lodging at the Highland Center here.

2

Biking in the White Mountains

BIKING IN THE WHITE MOUNTAINS can range from epic 50-mile road trips to quiet rides on pastoral dirt roads to technically challenging mountain bike excursions. The majority of bike trips described in this guide use a combination of dirt roads and quiet paved roads, though a few delve into more technical terrain. The Forest Service is currently developing management plans for sites that are appropriate for mountain biking, so this guide mentions only the few areas that are currently considered appropriate for this use. For the most part, biking in the White Mountains is confined to the lower elevations, which means you will not find the spectacular views that you might encounter on a hike in the Presidentials. However, a bike ride in the Whites can take you through beautiful northern hardwood forests, past rushing trout streams and waterfalls, and to verdant valleys with views of distant peaks.

Trip Times

The times listed for the bike rides in this chapter are fairly conservative and based on what we feel it would take a rider in average physical condition to complete the trip. We do assume that you have been on a bike ride recently and that your heart and leg muscles are in riding shape. Infrequent bikers may need more time. Those who ride consistently from week to week will probably need less time. You should add extra time when trails are wet or when rain is expected.

Trip Ratings

We list two ratings for each trip: aerobic level and technical difficulty. Aerobic level is based on changes in elevation and the number of miles. Trips with few ups and downs are generally listed as *easy*, though longer-mileage trips on gently rolling terrain may be listed as moderate. *Moderate* trips usually contain a fair amount of elevation gain, which is broken up into shorter sections of climbing. On a *strenuous* trip expect significant elevation gain via either steep climbs or long, drawn-out climbs of 2 or more miles.

Technically, an *easy* trip usually means that most of the riding is on a paved or dirt road, or rail trail with an easily rideable surface. *Moderate* trips include single-track (a narrow trail usually used for hiking) or double-track (usually an old logging road or snowmobile trail) trails that have a varying amount of roots and rocks requiring some maneuvering on the part of the bike-rider. Most intermediate riders can handle these trails. A trip rated as technically *difficult* usually involves a consistently difficult ride over roots and rocks, often on steep terrain. All but the best riders will end up walking sections of these trails.

Etiquette

Most of the bike trips in this book follow roads, paved or dirt, and rail trails, where erosion caused by bicycles is not a problem. Hikers rarely use these roads or trails, so the incidence of hiker-biker conflict is low. Biking is allowed on any trail in the White Mountain National Forest (except for a few posted high-traffic areas) that is not in federally designated wilderness. For this reason, it is important that all mountain bikers use good judgment when riding in order to protect the environment and to allow others to enjoy their wilderness experience. To practice responsible riding, follow the "rules of the trail" as suggested by the International Mountain Biking Association (www.imba.com):

- Ride on open trails only. Respect trail and road closures (ask if uncertain), avoid trespassing on private land, and obtain permits or other authorization as may be required. Federal and state wilderness areas are closed to cycling. Remember: the way you ride will influence trail management decisions and policies.
- Leave No Trace. Be sensitive to the dirt beneath you. Recognize different types of soils and trail construction and practice low-impact cycling. Wet and muddy trails are more vulnerable to damage. When the trailbed

is soft, consider other riding options. This also means staying on existing trails and not creating new ones. Do not cut switchbacks. Be sure to pack out at least as much as you pack in. (Also follow the Leave No Trace guidelines set forth in this book's introduction.)

- Control your bicycle. Inattention for even a second can cause problems. Obey all bicycle speed regulations and recommendations.
- Yield to others. Do your utmost to let your fellow trail users know you're coming—a friendly greeting or a ring of a bell is a good method. Try to anticipate other trail users as you ride around corners. In general, bicyclists yield to other trail users, though this may vary by region and by trail. Another common convention is that bicyclists traveling downhill yield to ones headed uphill. In general, riders should strive to make each pass a safe and courteous one.
- Never scare animals. Animals are startled by an unannounced approach, a sudden movement, or a loud noise. This can be dangerous for you, others, and the animals. Give animals extra room and time to adjust to you. When passing horses use special care and follow directions from the horseback riders (ask if uncertain). Running cattle and disturbing wildlife is a serious offense. Leave gates as you found them or as marked.
- Plan ahead. Know your equipment, your ability, and the area in which you are riding—and prepare accordingly. Be self-sufficient at all times, keep your equipment in good repair, and carry necessary supplies for changes in weather or other conditions. A well-executed trip is a satisfaction to you and not a burden to others. Always wear a helmet and appropriate safety gear.

Most trail erosion in the White Mountains occurs during spring and after heavy rains. Try to avoid riding on single-track trails at these times. In the Whites, trails are pretty muddy from the time the snow melts until at least mid-June. We usually wait until mid-July to avoid the mud and the hordes of black flies.

Safety and Comfort

Since bike trips in the White Mountains are usually completed at lower elevations, the above-treeline, weather-related risks associated with hiking are not generally a problem. Of course, rain and wet leaves can make descending on rocky trails a more dangerous proposition, and long rides on a cold, rainy day can lead to hypothermia. Most biking accidents occur on technical trails, where riders get going too fast for their abilities. For a safe and comfortable biking experience, keep your bike under control at all times and consider the following tips:

- Select a trip that is appropriate for everyone in the group. Match the ride to the abilities of the least capable person in the group.
- Plan to be back at the trailhead before dark. Determine a turn-around time and stick to it even if you have not reached your goal for the day.
- Check the weather forecast. Avoid riding during or immediately after heavy rains. Give yourself more time to stop in the rain, as wet brakes do not work as well as dry ones.
- Bring a pack or pannier with the following items:
  - ✓ Water: Bring two or more quarts per person depending on the weather and length of the trip
  - ✓ Food: Even for a short, one-hour trip, it is a good idea to bring some high-energy snacks like nuts, dried fruit, or snack bars. Bring a lunch for longer trips.
  - ✓ Map and compass
  - ✓ Extra clothing: Rain gear, wool sweater or fleece, hat and mittens
  - ✓ Headlamp or flashlight, with spare batteries and lightbulb
  - ✓ Sunscreen
  - ✓ First-aid kit: Adhesive bandages, gauze, nonprescription painkiller
  - ✓ Pocketknife
  - ✓ A trash bag
  - ✓ Waterproof matches and a lighter
  - ✓ Basic bike-maintenance tools and a spare inner tube and/or tire-repair kit
- Wear appropriate footwear and clothing. Consider wearing hiking boots, since having to push or carry your bike over rough trails is a real possibility. Legwear should be tight-fitting; loose pants can get stuck on pedals and in the gears of a bike, causing nasty accidents. Bring rain gear even in sunny weather, since unexpected rain, fog, and wind is possible at any time in the White Mountains. Avoid wearing cotton clothing, which absorbs sweat and rain, making for cold, damp riding. Polypropylene, fleece, silk, and wool are all good materials for keeping moisture away from your body and keeping you warm in wet or cold conditions.

Maps

Most of the routes in this guide are shown on the AMC series of White Mountain maps, although the names of some of the Forest Service roads do not appear on the maps. The Forest Service also offers maps of mountain biking routes in the Pemigewasset and Conway areas that can be purchased at one of the ranger stations listed at the beginning of this book

The trips in this chapter range from an easy, flat ride along the banks of the Pemigewasset River, to the thigh-burning, epic ride from Shelburne to Evans Notch. If you were to ride all of these trips, you would experience New Hampshire's forests at their best: fresh mountain air, waterfalls and wildlife, and secluded mountain ponds reflecting rounded and craggy peaks. During your rides you might encounter deer, moose, coyote, and bears—you will definitely see signs of their presence. You will also enjoy the thrills of careening down a trail or road as fast as you can safely stand it. All in all, biking in the White Mountains is as diverse and rewarding as any other outdoor adventure.

TRIP 26
BARTLETT EXPERIMENTAL FOREST

Aerobic Level: Easy

Technical Difficulty: Easy on gravel roads; Moderate on single-track

Distance: 4.8 miles round-trip

Elevation Gain: 400 feet

Estimated Time: 1 hour

Maps: AMC White Mountain Trail Map #3: I9, USGS Bartlett Quadrangle

This smooth ride will take you through beautiful forest followed by a fun and bumpy stretch of single-track.

Directions
From the intersection of US 302 and Bear Notch Road in Bartlett, head south on Bear Notch Road for 0.8 mile and turn right onto a gravel road. Park in the pullout on the left.

Trip Description
The Bartlett Experimental Forest is a 2,600-acre tract in the White Mountain National Forest used by Forest Service scientists to study various aspects of forest ecology and the effects of forest management on the forest and the wildlife that lives there. Established in 1931, this experimental forest was chosen because its elevation, soils, climate, and tree composition were typical of northern New England and New York (for more information, visit the Forest Service's Bartlett Experimental Forest website at www.fs.fed.us/ne/durham/4155/bartlett.htm). For the mountain biker, this area provides a few miles of smooth gravel roads as well as some fun single-track. A little bit of elevation gain is on this trip, but for the most part it is an aerobically easy ride. Experienced riders will find the single-track to be a fun test of their abilities; beginner and intermediate riders will also enjoy it, although they may need to walk a few short difficult sections.

Begin your trip by riding up the gravel road, heading away from Bear Notch Road. (While you are on this side of Bear Notch Road, feel free to explore the

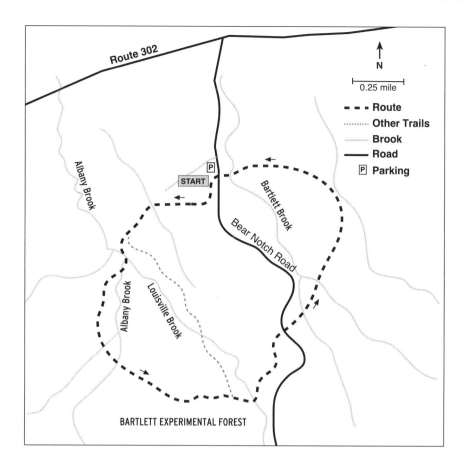

gravel roads, but please stay off of the single-track, as it has recently been posted as off-limits to bikes.) At 0.7 mile bear right at a fork in the road and ride past a large water tank on the left. You then cross Albany Brook, which cascades over a long and picturesque stretch of rock ledges culminating in a deep swimming hole. A mix of hardwoods and hemlock shades the banks of the brook. You will turn left at 1.0 mile onto another dirt road. Reaching a fork in the road at 1.5 miles, you will stay to the left. At 2.4 miles continue straight as a road comes in from the left. Up until this point you have climbed about 300 feet in elevation over a series of gentle ups and downs.

At 2.5 miles you will cross a stream on a wooden bridge and then enjoy a nice downhill cruise through a beautiful northern hardwood forest. At 3.1 miles turn right onto Bear Notch Road and follow it for about 0.1 mile before turning left back into the woods onto the Reservoir Brook Trail. This is the

Be prepared to encounter roots when riding along Reservoir Brook Trail.

single-track portion of the ride, as the trail is narrow with occasional rocks and roots. At 3.4 miles you make the first of two stream crossings, both of which can be difficult to ride due to the steep banks. After the second stream, you enter an old clearcut with some obstructed mountain views before making a moderate descent over rough trail to another stream crossing and a trail junction at 3.6 miles.

At this junction turn right for a short, steep climb to another trail junction at 3.7 miles, where you should turn left. You now make a sometimes steep and technical descent on a narrow and windy trail. At 4.0 miles continue straight at a trail junction as the trail eases in steepness and difficulty. At 4.3 miles stay to the right at a trail junction and continue the downhill ride over a wider trail. The trail levels off at 4.7 miles, where you should turn left, cross the stream, and take the left fork up the steep hill. At 4.8 miles you return to Bear Notch Road; turn left for a short ride back to the starting point, which will be on your right at 4.9 miles.

TRIP 27
CONWAY RECREATION TRAIL

Aerobic Level: Easy
Technical Difficulty: Easy
Distance: 6.0 miles up and back
Elevation Gain: 200 feet
Estimated Time: 1 hour, 30 minutes
Maps: AMC White Mountain Trail Map #5: I11, J11, USGS North
  Conway East and Conway Quadrangles

Take this easy ride through tall pines next to the Saco River.

Directions

From the intersection of NH 16 and US 302 in Conway, head east on US 302. In 1.5 miles, turn left onto East Conway Road. Take your first right onto Meeting House Hill Road and follow it 0.4 mile until it ends in the parking lot for Conway's Smith-Eastman Recreation Area.

Trip Description

Close to Conway Center, the Conway Recreation Trail is a great ride for those in need of an early morning leg-stretcher. It is also a fun and easy ride for kids, with the trail paralleling the Saco River for about half of the trip. You also can visit an old mineral spring, where water from under the ground still bubbles up through the pool. This trail, which is located in Conway's Smith-Eastman Recreation Area, is a popular place for runners and walkers, so you will want to watch your speed on tight corners in order to avoid unexpected collisions. Some of the trails on this ride are adjacent to private property; please make an extra effort to adhere to Leave No Trace rules in order to ensure these trails will remain open to bike-riders in the future.

From the parking area follow the trail to the right and cross the narrow footbridge (you will need to walk across). With the Saco River on your left, you will be riding over a thick bed of pine needles, which provide a soft ride except for the occasional tree root. As you breathe in the scent of pine and listen to the rushing waters of the Saco, you will soon understand why this level trail is a favorite with local residents. The Saco is also a popular river for

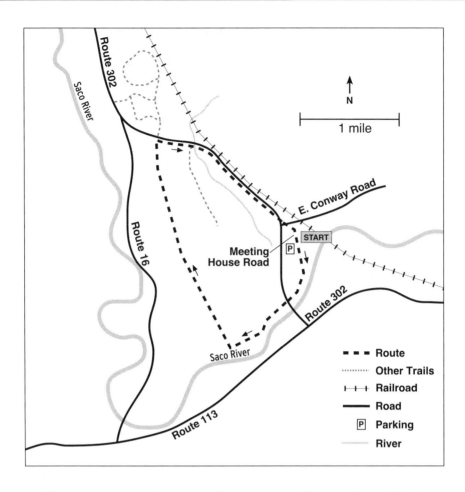

paddlers, as it contains long stretches of easy paddling and sandy beaches. At 0.4 mile the trail drops down to river level in order to pass under a bridge carrying US 302. At this point you will experience the sands of the Saco firsthand. Beginner riders may need to walk their bikes for a few yards to get through this section.

After the bridge the trail climbs back up to the level ground above the river and continues its ride through the pines. At 0.75 mile stay left where a side trail comes in from the right. At 0.9 mile turn right, following the arrow. The trail leaves the river, but riders who enjoy riding on a twisting, rolling trail will find the change enjoyable. Yellow "caution" signs precede the few rocks, roots, and water bars that add a slight challenge to the ride, but begin-

Bike riders can enjoy the rushing waters of the Saco River on the Conway Recreation Trail.

ner riders should have no problem tackling these relatively minor obstacles. You will see a few unmarked, narrow side trails on this stretch of trail; just stay on the obviously well-traveled, wide path.

At 2.2 miles you enter a grassy field. An old building at the edge of the field on the left houses a pool that collects water from a mineral spring. The water from this spring was bottled during the late 1800s and sold to tourists visiting the White Mountains. Water continues to bubble up through the pool, but as with any water source in the White Mountains, filter or chemically treat the water before drinking it. To continue the trip, ride through the field. As the trail enters the woods a side trail leads to the right. Stay to the left on what becomes a wide dirt road that passes through a mixed forest of pine, oak, maple, and birch. At 2.9 miles you pass under some power lines, and at 3.0 miles you reach US 302 and the end of the Conway Recreation Trail.

To complete your trip, you have two options. The first is to turn around and return the way you came. The second option is to make a loop of this trip by turning right on US 302, left on East Conway Road, and then right on Meeting House Hill Road. However, the return ride through the woods is much more worthwhile.

TRIP 28
LINCOLN WOODS

Aerobic Level: Easy

Technical Difficulty: Easy except for the crossing of Pemigewasset River

Distance: 6.4 miles round-trip

Elevation Gain: 300 feet

Estimated Time: 1 hour, 30 minutes

Maps: AMC White Mountain Trail Map #2: H5, H6, I5, I6, USGS Mount Osceola Quadrangle

This easy ride will take you along the rushing waters of the Pemigewasset River.

Directions

Take Exit 32 off of I-93 in Lincoln. Drive east on the Kancamagus Highway (NH 112) for 5.0 miles. The Lincoln Woods parking area will be on the left, immediately after crossing the East Branch of the Pemigewasset River.

Trip Description

This is an excellent choice for families and people just growing accustomed to riding bikes over rocks and through mud. Experienced riders in the mood for an easy ride next to one of the most beautiful rivers in the White Mountains will also enjoy this trip. This trip begins at the Lincoln Woods parking area on the Kancamagus Highway just east of Lincoln, N.H. It follows an old woods road up the east side of the Pemigewasset River, crosses the river over a series of large boulders, and returns via the Lincoln Woods Trail above the west bank of the river. It is also possible to make a side trip to Franconia Falls, where you can swim in the cold waters of Franconia Brook. (Please note that the Forest Service now limits the number of visitors it allows at the falls, so check with the ranger station at the Lincoln Woods parking area about obtaining a Franconia Falls visitor permit. A permit is not required to ride on the Lincoln Woods Trail.)

Beginning from the Lincoln Woods parking area, ride north on the old road that begins just beyond the Forest Service information building. The

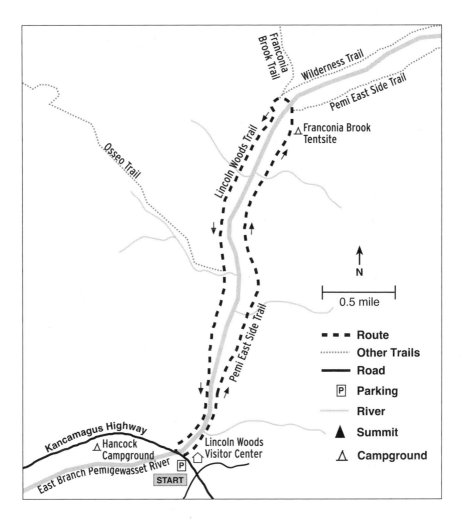

road surface is good gravel, with only a few larger rocks to avoid. At 0.2 mile a spur path leads 0.1 mile to a clearing filled with raspberries and aspen that provides obstructed views toward the Bonds. At 0.6 mile the Pine Island Trail leaves to the left. Continue straight on the road, which makes a short climb before resuming a relatively level grade. After crossing a stream and passing another side trail at 1.1 miles, the road begins a moderate climb and at 2.5 miles reaches an overlook high above the Pemigewasset River. From here you get a good look at the rushing waters of the Pemigewasset, where it is wide and filled with granite boulders. The banks are lined with sugar maple, yellow birch, and white pine, and in fall the foliage is truly spectacular.

The Pemigewasset River begins in Franconia Notch and flows 65 miles until it merges with the Winnipesaukee River to form the Merrimack River.

Good views also can be seen of Owl's Head, Mount Flume, and Whaleback Mountain.

At 2.7 miles you reach the ranger headquarters for the Franconia Brook Campsites, which have replaced the tent sites that used to be on the western side of the river. Twenty-four campsites spread out on both sides of the road and outhouses are on the left. At 2.9 miles you reach a gate that marks the boundary of the Pemigewasset Wilderness Area (bikes are not allowed in the wilderness area). The road turns left and descends a hill; to reach the river, turn right at the bottom of the hill. Here you are faced with the task of crossing the Pemigewasset. The Forest Service has placed a series of large boulders across the river at a wide spot in order to make the crossing easier. You still need to be able to carry your bike while balancing on these boulders. If this is too difficult (or the water level is too high), you can just return the way you came.

Once across the Pemigewasset, you will need to cross Franconia Brook, make a steep climb up the bank to the Lincoln Woods Trail, and turn left. (The Lincoln Woods Trail was formerly called the Wilderness Trail and remains the Wilderness Trail north of Franconia Brook.) At 3.4 miles and immediately after recrossing Franconia Brook on a wooden bridge, a side trail leads 0.4 mile right to the falls, which form a natural granite waterslide that can provide hours of entertainment for hardy swimmers (or interested spectators). This side trail is not appropriate for bikes and, as mentioned before, you must obtain a permit from the Forest Service to visit the falls.

The Lincoln Woods Trail follows the bed of an old logging railroad, making a gradual descent over partially buried railroad ties. This was one of the last logging railroads in operation in the White Mountains, finally closing down in the 1940s. At 3.8 miles you pass the Black Pond Trail, and at 5.0 miles you pass the Osseo Trail, which backpackers use to hike to Mount Flume and Franconia Ridge. The trip ends at 6.4 miles, where you should turn left, cross the river on the large suspension bridge, and follow the trail up to the information center.

Grand Hotels and Lumber Barons

Prior to the 1850s, the White Mountains region was primarily populated by homesteaders and a few small business proprietors (most notably the Crawford family in Crawford Notch), who provided room and board for the few travelers who ventured into the Whites on their way between Portland, Maine, and the Connecticut River valley. However, the second half of the century brought rail travel to Gorham, N.H., and publicity created by the literature of writers like Thoreau, Emerson, and Hawthorne, as well as the art of Thomas Cole and Benjamin Champney. Soon, tourists from cities like Boston and New York visited the Whites for extended vacations—sometimes all summer—in order to breathe the purifying air and absorb the "sublime" views.

During the next 50 years, the Whites became one of the premier tourist destinations in the world. More than 200 hotels were built in the region, which eventually could accommodate up to 12,000 guests. Grand hotels, accommodating up to 400 guests each, provided visitors with luxurious amenities such as gas lighting and lawn tennis. These hotels also provided guided hiking services, and hiking trails began to proliferate. It was during this time that the AMC and other hiking clubs were formed, providing the impetus to develop a comprehensive system of trails. However, most tourists at that time spent their days playing tennis, riding horses, and enjoying the social scene. The few hardy souls who ventured into the backcountry found a much different scene than we enjoy today, as the forests were valued more for their timber than their wilderness.

The railroads brought not only tourists to the area, but timber barons who saw the potential of the forest. In 1850 there were 376 miles of railroad in the entire state of New Hampshire, and while the state as a whole was at its lowest percentage of forest coverage, most of the unsettled, rugged peaks of the White Mountains were still covered by virgin boreal and northern hardwood forests. In 1867, with hopes of jump-starting the post-Civil War economy, Governor Walter Harriman sold all of the state's land in the White Mountains to timber speculators for $27,000. By 1880 there were 1,200 miles of railroads in the state and the race to cut trees in the Whites was under way. It is ironic that the first wave of nature appreciation and tourism in the Whites coincided with the virtual destruction of most of the area's forest, but that is exactly what happened.

Mount Jefferson is the backdrop for the Mount Washington Hotel.

During the next 50 years, railroads were built into most of the remote valleys of the White Mountains and, except for a very few small pockets of old growth, all of the forest was cut. Lumber barons such as George Van Dyke and J.E. Henry showed no mercy to the forest. Clear-cutting was the method of choice, though in less accessible areas only the largest, most valuable trees were removed. In addition, large accidental fires—started primarily by the sparks from logging railroad engines and fueled by massive amounts of logging debris—consumed tens of thousands of acres of cutover and uncut land. By 1900 New Hampshire was the most intensively lumbered state in the country, with as much as 750 million board feet a year harvested. As a comparison, recent annual timber harvests across the state average 300 million board feet, with the White Mountain National Forest supplying about 8 percent of this total.

All this timber harvesting did create a boom in the economies of surrounding towns as saw mills and paper mills were established in large numbers. The populations of places like Berlin, Lincoln, and Conway grew considerably during the timber era. However, the unsustainable practices of the lumber barons caused the forest to be played out, and, while harvesting continues to this day, most of the logging railroads ceased operations by the end of World War I. The last railroad, which penetrated deep into what is now the Pemigewasset Wilderness Area and supplied timber to the mills in Lincoln, completed its last run in 1948. Today you can still find the railroad ties for this line if you hike or bike the Wilderness Trail (a.k.a. Lincoln Woods Trail) along the East Branch of the Pemigewasset River.

The clear-cutting and extensive forest fires (more than 200,000 acres burned in 1903 alone) of the late nineteenth and early twentieth centuries had a direct influence on the way forests are managed in the eastern U.S. today. In 1901, the Society for Protection of New Hampshire Forests (SPNHF) formed with the specific purpose of saving the White Mountains from further exploitation. A decade of lobbying by SPNHF and other groups, including the AMC, resulted in the passage of the Weeks Act in 1911. This law allowed the federal government to purchase private land east of the Mississippi for purposes of establishing national forests, and by 1912 more than 70,000 acres of New Hampshire had been set aside as the White Mountain National Forest.

Just as logging waned after the virgin timber was cut, the grand hotels also declined in popularity. With the advent of the automobile, people began taking shorter vacations and these grand hotels fell out of favor. Most eventually burned to the ground. Two remain: The Mount Washington Hotel in Bretton Woods and The Balsams in Dixville Notch.

TRIP 29
SAWYER RIVER ROAD

Aerobic Level: Moderate
Technical Difficulty: Easy
Distance: 8.0 miles out and back
Elevation Gain: 750 feet
Estimated Time: 1 to 2 hours
Maps: AMC White Mountain Trail Map #3: I8, USGS Mount
    Carrigain and Bartlett Quadrangles

This easy ride on a dirt road takes you through beautiful forests and follows the rushing waters of the Sawyer River.

Directions
From the junction of NH 16 and US 302 in Glen, drive west on US 302 for 10 miles to the parking area on the left, just before Sawyer River Road.

Trip Description
This is a relatively easy ride on a quiet gravel road in the heart of the White Mountains. You can start at either end of Sawyer River Road, but by beginning the ride at the US 302 end, you get all of the climbing done on the first half of the ride. Besides paralleling the beautiful Sawyer River for its entire length, this ride also passes by the remnants of the abandoned logging town of Livermore, which has been melting back into the forest for the last 70-plus years. You also have the option of taking a break from riding in the middle of the trip to make the 3-mile round-trip hike into Sawyer Pond.

From the parking area on US 302, the ride on Sawyer River Road begins to climb immediately at a moderate pace. The road works its way through hardwoods on both sides of the road and there is a steep bank down to the Sawyer River on the left. The sounds of the river may entice you to scramble down the bank to get a look or to cool your feet, but hold off on that for now—there is easier access farther upstream. The climb continues at a moderate pace until about the 1.0-mile mark, where it levels out to a very gradual climb for the remainder of the ride.

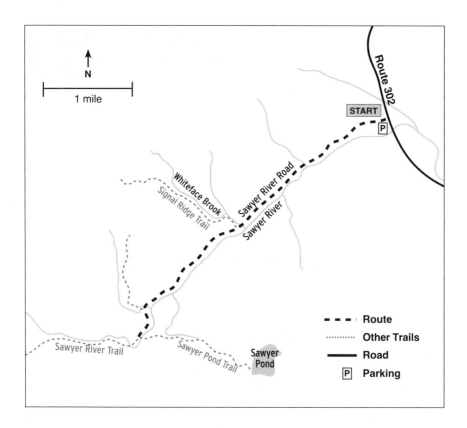

About 1.5 miles from US 302, you will pass a clearing on the left with an old camp. This is the site of Livermore, which in the 1880s was a small logging town with a school, store, offices, two sawmills, and a row of houses. In 1928, the mills in Livermore were closed for good as most of the accessible timber nearby had already been harvested, and the residents started moving elsewhere. In 1936, the land that had been the town was added to the White Mountain National Forest. If you explore the woods here today, you will still find evidence of the town—cellar holes, brick chimneys, bridge abutments, and a large concrete foundation that must have been one of the sawmills. You can also easily access the river here.

Continuing up the road from Livermore, the ride is an easy one with just the slightest uphill grade. The road stays near the river so you are constantly treated to the sounds of rushing water as you pedal through the forest. At 2.1 miles, you will cross a tributary and pass the Signal Ridge Trail. At 3.5 miles, you cross another stream and then reach a gate across the road 3.9

A fir tree grows on the brick ruins of a mill in the old logging town of Livermore.

miles from US 302. Continue past the gate for an additional 0.1 mile to a bridge over the Sawyer River. This is a great spot on a sunny day to rest up, eat some lunch, and cool off in the river. You can continue on from here, but the road gets rougher and eventually turns into a rough and wet hiking trail that is not appropriate for casual biking, so we recommend turning around here and making the 4.0-mile downhill ride back to your car.

However, if you are up for a side trip, you can hike into Sawyer Pond on the Sawyer Pond Trail, which leaves Sawyer River Road about 100 yards past the gate at the end of the road and leads 1.5 miles and up 350 feet to the pond. The pond is a good place to go for a swim or fish for brook trout under the cliffs of Mount Tremont and Owls Cliff. The hike into the pond and back takes about two hours.

Aerobic Level: Easy
Technical Difficulty: Easy
Distance: 7.2 miles out and back
Elevation Gain: Minimal
Estimated Time: 1 to 2 hours
Maps: AMC White Mountain Trail Map #2: E6, E7, USGS Twin
   Mountain, Mount Dartmouth, and Lancaster Quadrangles

**This easy ride provides great views of the Presidentials and
excellent wildlife viewing.**

Directions

From the junction of US 3 and NH 115 in Twin Mountain, drive 4.3 miles
east on NH 115. Turn left (west) on Airport Road, also called Hazen Road.
The parking area is on the right in 1.4 miles.

Trip Description

Pondicherry Wildlife Refuge is one of those rare places that has abundant
wildlife, spectacular views, and relatively easy access, but is practically unknown outside of the local community and some birding enthusiasts. The
refuge, which is owned by New Hampshire Audubon, U.S. Fish and Wildlife, and the state of New Hampshire, encompasses the wetlands and forests
surrounding Big and Little Cherry Ponds in Jefferson, N.H. More than 200
species of birds have been recorded here (120 breeding species) and it is also
home to big game like moose and bear, so pack a pair of binoculars. The site
was once home to a grand hotel, whose visitors arrived by train at Waumbek
Junction, which is still visible today near the inlet of Big Cherry Pond. Today,
most signs of the hotel are gone, and the refuge is accessible only on foot or
by bike via the rail trail.

The ride in from the parking area near the White Mountain Regional
Airport in Whitefield is about as easy as it gets—flat and straight on the
well-packed former railway. In summer, there are often plentiful raspberries

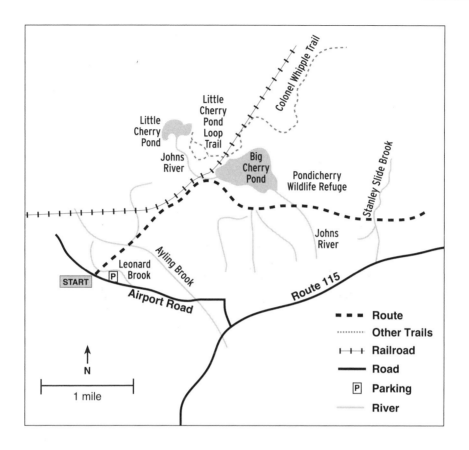

ripe for the picking on the side of the trail, and you will be treated with a view of Mount Waumbek for most of the way. At 0.9 mile, the trail crosses under a set of power lines with views of the Presidential Range to the east. At 1.6 miles, you will come to a junction with the Presidential Rail Trail on the right. For now, continue straight ahead, where you will reach the inlet (the Johns River) to Big Cherry Pond in another 0.1 mile at Waumbek Junction. Stop here, grab a snack, and drink in the expansive views of Cherry Mountain and the Presidential Range over Big Cherry Pond.

From this point, you have several choices. First, you can explore the shoreline of Big Cherry Pond on foot, by walking up the rail line for about 50 yards and following the path into the woods on the right. This path is only several hundred yards long, but it offers an up-close view of the pond, its wildlife, and its extensive views. Second, you can make the 1.5-mile loop

The Presidential Range rises above Big Cherry Pond in the Pondicherry National Wildlife Refuge.

hike to Little Cherry Pond via the Little Cherry Pond Trail. To find the trail, continue north on the rail line from Waumbek Junction for about 0.25 mile and look for the trail on the left. The Little Cherry Pond Trail was designated a National Recreation Trail in 2006, and works its way through boreal forest and traverses forested wetlands via bog bridges. It is a popular place for birders, as it is home to a great blue heron rookery, osprey, and boreal species such as spruce grouse, boreal chickadees, black-backed woodpeckers, and gray jays. A variety of duck species also use the pond, including wood ducks, hooded mergansers, and ring-necked ducks.

If you would rather stay on your bike, head back south to the junction with the Presidential Rail Trail and follow it east (left). You'll soon see a viewing platform on the left that juts out into Big Cherry Pond. Continuing east, the trail passes a very interesting wetland complex of beaver ponds and bogs filled with larch trees. In high water, the beaver ponds may spill over the trail, making for some wet riding, so you may want to consider wearing hiking boots in the spring or after heavy rains. Two miles from the Pondicherry Rail Trail, you will come to a bridge that crosses a stream and beaver pond complex with views of the Kilkenny Range and Cherry Mountain. This is the end of the good views and wildlife viewing, so it makes a good place to turn around and head back to the parking area. If you are up for more riding, the trail keeps going all the way to Gorham and beyond, hooking up with the Presidential Rail Trail described in trip 34 in another 2.2 miles.

Missing Predators: Wolves, Mountain Lions, and Lynx

The White Mountains contain hundreds of thousands of acres of wilderness that are relatively healthy—rich forests teeming with wildlife such as otters, black bears, and moose. However, the ecological balance is drastically different now than before people settled New Hampshire and systematically extirpated the forest's largest predators. Most heavily persecuted were gray wolves and mountain lions, which were both feared as human-killers and blamed for the killing of livestock and for competing with people for game animals. While the smaller lynx were not as despised, they most likely have been extirpated from the White Mountains, due largely to habitat loss and trapping. The forest has, of course, found a new balance. Coyote have moved in from the west and taken over as top predators. People also are part of the mix, taking part in annual deer, moose, and bird hunts. Still, the lack of the historically present predators—wolves, mountain lions, and lynx—does create a sense that something is missing, that we have lost some of the region's wildness.

The Canada lynx, which resembles a large, long-haired tabby that weighs 20 to 40 pounds, was recently added to the federal list of threatened species by the U.S. Fish and Wildlife Service. Outside of Alaska and Canada, only Maine, Washington, and Montana have breeding populations of lynx. Of the large predators, the lynx survived for the longest in New Hampshire, with the last known lynx sighting reported in the state in 1993. Lynx are long-distance travelers, often covering a few hundred miles, and most likely last bred in the state in the 1960s. Lynx have large, snowshoe-like paws that allow them to successfully hunt for their primary food: snowshoe hares. With a breeding population in neighboring Maine, any lynx recovery efforts will most likely include the White Mountain National Forest.

Mountain lions, also known as pumas, cougars, catamounts, or panthers, are large cats that can grow to be 8 feet long and weigh as much as 150 pounds. They are also the widest-ranging predator in the New World, populating the forests and deserts of both North and South America from western Canada to Patagonia. As a species, mountain lions are not considered endangered, but the Florida panther and eastern subspecies are federally endangered. The eastern subspecies, which roamed all of New England until the early 1900s, is most likely extinct; however, mountain lion sightings in New England have persisted until the present, and some of these sightings have been confirmed by DNA analysis of the hair in lion droppings. The big debate is whether these are lions that were illegally released into the wild by exotic pet owners, or remnants of the eastern subspecies that have somehow managed to reproduce successfully, unknown to scientists, for more than 100 years.

The gray wolf is perhaps the most heavily persecuted animal on the planet. Feared and reviled throughout European history, wolves have been systematically hunted and eliminated from most of the United States. Wolves prey on small mammals such as mice and rabbits, as well as larger animals such as deer, moose, and musk ox. The last known wolf in New Hampshire was killed in 1887 and the closest viable populations that exist today are in Quebec. At least two wolves have been killed in Maine in recent years, although these animals most likely were lone wolves that came to Maine from Canada. In the lower 48 states, the gray wolf is listed as a federally endangered species, with the largest and most stable population living in the forests of northern Minnesota.

The recent successful reintroduction of wolves to Yellowstone National Park has encouraged environmental groups and wolf lovers to push for the reintroduction of gray wolves to other parts of their historic range in North America. Biologists have identified the Northern Forest in Maine and New Hampshire as suitable habitat for wolf reintroduction, and the U.S. Fish and Wildlife Service is considering developing a reintroduction plan for the area. Who knows—maybe someday a night in the backcountry of the White Mountains will once again be accompanied by the sound of wolves howling.

TRIP 31
CHOCORUA–TAMWORTH LOOP

Aerobic Level: Moderate

Technical Difficulty: Easy

Distance: 11.4 miles round-trip

Elevation Gain: 600 feet

Estimated Time: 1 hour, 30 minutes

Maps: AMC White Mountain Trail Map #3: K9, K10, USGS Mount
Chocorua and Silver Lake Quadrangles

This easy ride takes you on gravel roads through the tranquil forests of Tamworth.

Directions
From the intersection of NH 16 and NH 113 in Tamworth, drive north on NH 16. Turn left in 1.6 miles onto Chocorua Lake Road and park in the lot on the left. This lot has a small picnic area on the lake as well as a portable toilet.

Trip Description
These back roads in the town of Tamworth are little traveled and you will rarely, if ever, need to yield to motorized vehicles. The best views on this trip are actually from the parking lot, which has the classic view of Mount Chocorua as it rises above Chocorua Lake, but riding these roads that gently rise and fall through quiet northern hardwood forests is a great way to spend a summer or fall afternoon. Some climbs occur during this trip, but for the most part they are moderate and short and followed by relaxing downhills. Most of the ride travels through private property, so you will want to use the facilities in the parking area before getting under way. Please be respectful of private property.

Start your trip by riding over the bridge on Chocorua Lake Road, which becomes Fowler's Mill Road. As you leave the mountain views of the lake behind, you enter a different scenic New England, one of rolling dirt roads, stone fences, and tall white pine. At 0.6 mile you reach an intersection with

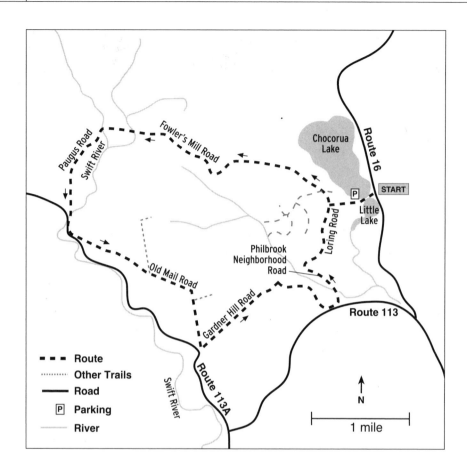

Loring Road. Stay to the right on Fowler's Mill Road, and then bear left at another fork at 0.9 mile, following a sign for "Mountain Trails." From here you will climb moderately until you reach another intersection at 1.8 miles. Continue straight, staying on Fowler's Mill Road, which eventually begins a 1.0-mile-long descent at 2.3 miles. At 3.3 miles you pass Paugus Road on the left. After two stream crossings and a bumpy section of road, you reach NH 113A at 4.5 miles.

Turn left onto the pavement of NH 113A and make a quick left onto Old Mail Road at 4.6 miles. After making a steep but short climb, you will enjoy the packed dirt surface of Old Mail Road as it passes through the northern hardwoods of the Hemenway State Forest. At about 6.0 miles you begin a gradual descent that takes you all the way to Gardner Hill Road at 6.8 miles. Turn left onto the pavement of Gardner Hill Road (unmarked) and make a

The beginning of your ride will offer beautiful views of Chocorua Lake and the mountains beyond it.

gradual climb until 7.6 miles. You are then treated to another downhill ride that lasts until NH 113 at 8.6 miles where you should turn left. Make a quick left onto Philbrick Neighborhood Road at 8.7 miles.

Philbrick Neighborhood Road is a dirt road that sometimes gets a little bumpy, but takes you past a good view of Mount Chocorua on its way to Loring Road at 10.0 miles. Turn right onto Loring Road, which is marked by a hard-to-spot, small green sign (if you cross a wooden bridge, you've gone past it). At 10.8 miles you come back to Fowler's Mill Road, where you should turn right for the ride back to the parking area at 11.4 miles.

TRIP 32
FRANCONIA NOTCH BICYCLE PATH

Aerobic Level: Moderate

Technical Difficulty: Easy

Distance: 18.4 miles out and back

Elevation Gain: 600 feet

Estimated Time: 2 hours, 30 minutes

Maps: AMC White Mountain Trail Map #2: G4, H4, USGS Franconia
and Lincoln Quadrangles

**This easy ride on a paved bike path through Franconia Notch
is one of the most scenic places in the White Mountains.**

Directions

Take Exit 35 on I-93 following US 3 north. The Skookumchuck Trail parking area will be in 0.6 mile on the right. The bike path leaves from the south end of the parking lot.

Trip Description

Franconia Notch—home to Echo Lake, the former Old Man of the Mountain, the Basin, and the Flume Gorge—is one of the main attractions of the White Mountains. The huge cliffs of Cannon Mountain and the high, alpine ridgeline of Mount Lafayette and Mount Lincoln create the walls of the notch, which were formed by glaciers during the last ice age. The bike path was created in the 1980s when the road through the notch was being redesigned as an interstate highway. The AMC and other environmental organizations advocated successfully to preserve the integrity of the notch and the road was built as the only segment of an interstate highway to be designed as a parkway. Instead of a high-speed, four-lane highway, the parkway is a two-lane road with a maximum speed of 45 mph, which is not much different than the old US 3, which the new parkway replaced. The wide, paved bike path is easy to ride and can be accessed from several parking areas. This trip describes the path from its northern end at a parking area on US 3, just north of the notch, to its southern terminus at the Flume Gorge Visitor Center. However, by parking a car at the terminus or planning shorter out-and-back trips it is easy to come up with your own variation of this trip.

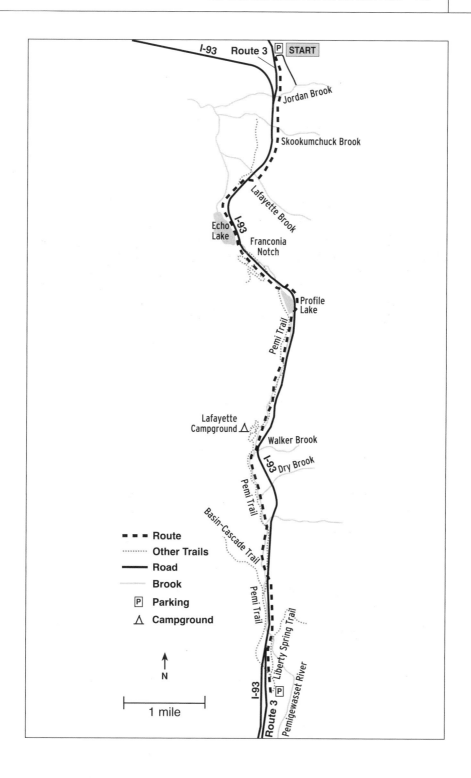

I-93 Route 3 P START

Jordan Brook

Skookumchuck Brook

Lafayette Brook

I-93

Echo Lake

Franconia Notch

Pemi Trail

Profile Lake

Lafayette Campground △

Walker Brook

I-93 Dry Brook

Pemi Trail

Basin-Cascade Trail

Pemi Trail

Liberty Spring Trail

Pemigewasset River

I-93

Route 3

P

- - - Route
.... Other Trails
—— Road
—— Brook
P   Parking
△   Campground

↑
N

1 mile

The paved nature of the Franconia Notch Bike Path makes this a pleasurable ride.

From the Skookumchuck Trail parking area, ride south on the paved path. This is actually not part of the Franconia Notch Bicycle Path but the remnants of an older version of US 3. The path makes a gradual climb, parallel to the current US 3, up to the Lafayette Brook Overlook at 1.5 miles. From the overlook excellent views can be seen to the west over the Connecticut River into Vermont, and to the east up to Mount Lafayette. On the other side of the bridge is a cul-de-sac and parking area. Be sure to follow the bike path to the right, where it drops down under I-93 before turning left and making a long but gradual climb. At 2.25 miles you pass under NH 18 and reach Echo Lake and good views of Cannon Mountain and the cliffs on the eastern side of the notch. As you look at Cannon keep your eyes open for black bears, which are known to frequent the ski slopes in search of raspberries.

Cannon Mountain was one of the earliest downhill ski areas in the United States, and was home to the country's first aerial tramway built in 1938. This fact is memorialized at the ski museum, which you will pass at 2.7 miles. The path continues through the notch, alternating between flat sections, gentle downhill sections, and short uphill sections. At 3.7 miles you pass through the Old Man Viewing parking area where you will see a sign that says "Bike Walk"; you should get off of your bike and walk for the next 0.4 mile, as required by the park. During your walk you pass the north end of Profile Lake and its view of the remnants of the Old Man of the Mountain. Profile and Echo Lakes, as well as Franconia Notch itself, were all formed 12,000 to 15,000 years ago during the last ice age as a huge river of ice flowed through the notch—much as I-93 does today. In the second half of the nineteenth century the notch was home to two huge hotels, the Flume House and the Profile House, both of which accommodated visitors lured by the writings of Wordsworth and Thomas Starr King, as well as paintings by Thomas Cole.

After crossing under the highway the bike path reaches a parking area at 4.2 miles, and then once again crosses under the highway and begins to parallel the Pemigewasset River. At 4.5 miles you will pass a 300-ton boulder that recently fell from Cannon Cliffs, tumbling 0.5 mile down the mountain and knocking down 60-foot tall trees in its path. At 5.5 miles you reach Lafayette Campground, which has bathroom facilities, fresh water, and a small store. Continuing past the campground, the bike path winds its way along the banks of the river, often crossing it on small wooden bridges. A gradual downhill continues from here to the end of the path. At 7.1 miles you will reach a side path that leads to the Basin, a 30-foot diameter pothole that is well worth checking out. You will need to walk your bike on this short trail, as it is usually very crowded with sightseers. If you'd like, you can lock your bike to one of the trees. Formed by melting glacier ice as well as the rushing waters of the Pemigewasset, the Basin was visited by Henry David Thoreau during his first visit to Franconia Notch in 1846.

After the Basin the side trail brings you back to the bike path, which crosses under the highway one last time, passes through a parking area, and then continues its gradual descent along the banks of the Pemigewasset River. At 8.2 miles you pass the Liberty Spring Trail and ride over a bridge that spans the widening river. The deep shade of hemlock keeps you cool as you make a short but steep climb after the bridge. At 9.2 miles you reach the end of the bike path and the Flume Gorge Visitor Center, which has restrooms, a restaurant, and a gift shop. The Flume Gorge is an impressive 800-foot-long gorge, with rock walls that are 70 to 90 feet tall and only 12 to 20 feet apart. It is a short hike to the gorge, but you will have to pay a $12 entrance fee at the visitor center. If you spotted a car at the visitor center, this is the end of your trip. If not, turn around and follow the bike path back through the notch to your car.

The Great Stone Face

During the early morning hours of May 3, 2003, five giant slabs of Conway granite peeled off of the side of Cannon Mountain and tumbled hundreds of feet to the base of the cliff. The rock slide was relatively minor from a geology perspective and caused little physical damage to the forest below. Though no one was there to witness this event, it was noticed soon after dawn by travelers in Franconia Notch expecting to catch a glimpse of the rock formation known as the Old Man of the Mountain—the Old Man's 40-foot-tall face had fallen off the mountainside. This little rock slide soon made national news, prompted people to leave flowers at the base of the mountain, and caused the governor of New Hampshire to create a task force to determine how to best remember the Old Man. The state was in mourning.

For some, it may be hard to understand why a natural geologic event like this would lead to an entire state grieving, but the Old Man of the Mountain was much more than a quirky feature on a cliff that happened to look like an old man's face. The Old Man, first noticed by American settlers in 1804, had come to symbolize the "Live Free or Die" spirit of New Hampshire and is proudly displayed on the state's license plate and on the back of New Hampshire's statehood quarter. Its fame was solidified early in the nineteenth century by Daniel Webster who wrote about the Old Man this way: "Men hang out their signs indicative of their respective trades; shoe makers hang out a gigantic shoe; jewelers a monster watch, and the dentist hangs out a gold tooth; but up in the Mountains of New Hampshire, God Almighty has hung out a sign to show that there He makes men." It was further immortalized by Nathaniel Hawthorne's short story, "The Great Stone Face," in which he writes, "With the clouds and glorified vapor of the mountains clustering above it, The Great Stone Face seemed positively to be alive."

Though not alive, the rocks that comprised the Old Man were definitely active. The cliffs on the east side of Cannon Mountain were formed during and after the last ice age. Layers of rock peeled off the side of the cliffs as water seeped into cracks in the rock, freezing and expanding, and over time causing the rock to fracture further until chunks fell off. This process is still happening today and it is what led to the Old Man's ultimate demise. As early as 1906, people recog-

The Old Man of the Mountain before it collapsed on May 3, 2008.

nized the fragility of the profile and in 1916, New Hampshire Governor Rolland H. Spaulding began state efforts to shore up the cliffs with cables and waterproofing. These efforts continued until the Old Man's collapse. In the 1980s, during public hearings discussing the construction of I-93 through Franconia Notch, geologists warned that vibrations from the highway could put the Old Man at further risk of falling, but there is no evidence that the highway caused the collapse.

Today, the former Old Man viewing area at Profile Lake has a pair of coin-operated viewfinders that show how the Old Man looked before his collapse. In 2007, the Old Man of the Mountain Legacy Fund announced plans for a memorial at Profile Lake that will include five huge stones that will re-create the Old Man's visage. No installation date for the memorial has been announced as of this writing, but you can learn more about the memorial at www.oldmanofthemountainlegacyfund.org/.

TRIP 33
KILKENNY ROAD TRIP

Aerobic Level: Moderate

Technical Difficulty: Easy

Distance: 17.5 miles round-trip

Elevation Gain: 1,150 feet

Estimated Time: 2 to 3 hours

Maps: AMC White Mountain Trail Map #6: C9, D9, D10, USGS West Milan and Mount Crescent Quadrangles

This long ride follows dirt roads through beautiful, undeveloped forests in the North Country.

Directions

From the intersection of NH 110 and NH 110A in Milan, head east on NH 110 for 4.0 miles, then turn right on York Pond Road. In 1.6 miles, turn left as the road forks and park in one of the pull-outs on either side of the road.

Trip Description

This ride north and west of Berlin takes you through an area of the White Mountain National Forest that sees far fewer visitors than the hot spots to the south. It follows a dirt forest service road for most of its length, sometimes paralleling the Upper Ammonoosuc River as it meanders through the valley to the east of the Kilkenny Range, which tops out on Mount Cabot, the northernmost of New Hampshire's 4,000-footers. The ride has the occasional view of the nearby peaks, but its real appeal is the solitude afforded by the remoteness of the roads and the quiet beauty of the forests. Though this ride gains 1,150 feet in elevation, the hardest climbing is done in one 5-mile stretch near the beginning, making the rest of this 17.5-mile trip a relatively easy ride in the woods.

From the parking area, ride on the left fork of the road (which soon becomes Forest Road 15), and pass the Forest Service gate that blocks the road in winter. The road follows the rushing waters of the Upper Ammonoosuc River on the left for about a mile before beginning to climb at a moderate pace. The road is packed dirt and gravel, making the ride an easy one from

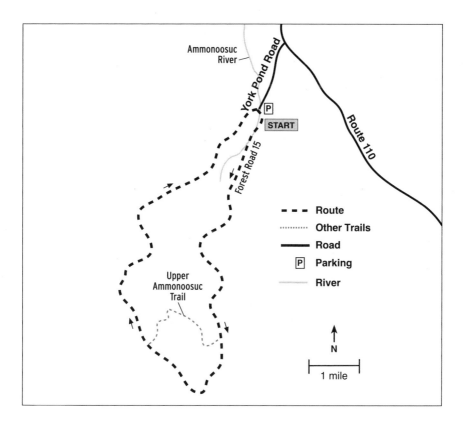

a technical perspective, but this is the beginning of a 5-mile climb where you will gain 700 feet in elevation. As you ride uphill, you will see the forest change from a mosaic of hardwoods and softwoods to a hardwood forest consisting primarily of beech, sugar maple, and paper birch trees. With bright green ferns lining the roadway, the challenge of the climb will be somewhat tempered by the beauty of the scenery.

Four-and-a-half miles from the car, the climb eases somewhat, as you continue to ride through a beautiful hardwood forest. By now you will probably feel the solitude, as you have left most signs of civilization far behind. Keep an eye out for moose, which are common throughout this valley. At 7.0 miles, the road crosses a brook with some interesting cascades on the left that are definitely worth a picture break in high water. You will soon be rewarded with a downhill coast to another brook crossing at 7.9 miles, where the road turns sharply to the right and begins a 3-mile stretch of alternating climbs and descents. At 11.0 miles, the ride turns into a primarily

Dirt paths such as this one make the Kilkenny Road Trip a technically easy one.

downhill one, cruising down the eastern slope of Mount Weeks to a clearing with an excellent view to the east at 12.6 miles. Mount Weeks is named for John Wingate Weeks, the U.S. Congressman who fought to pass the Weeks Act, which established the White Mountain National Forest in 1911. Mount Weeks can be accessed by hikers via the Kilkenny Ridge Trail, a 20-plus-mile-long trail that traverses the entire ridge crest of the Kilkenny Range.

From the clearing, it is a mostly downhill ride to 15.2 miles, where you'll reach a stop sign and a paved road. Turn right, following the pavement for an easy 1-mile uphill ride to a series of wetlands on the right with views of Jericho and Sugar Mountains in Berlin and the Crescent Range to the south. At 17.5 miles you cross the Upper Ammonoosuc River and reach the end of the loop. After your ride, you can drive (or ride if you still have energy) the right fork of the road about 5 miles to the Berlin Fish Hatchery. If you're into fish, you might find touring the fish pens an interesting diversion. The hatchery is open Monday through Friday, 8 A.M. to 4 P.M.

TRIP 34
PRESIDENTIAL RAIL TRAIL

Aerobic Level: Moderate
Technical Difficulty: Moderate
Distance: 13.75 miles one-way
Elevation Gain: 500 feet
Estimated Time: 2 to 3 hours
Maps: AMC White Mountain Trail Map #6: E7, E8, E9, E10, USGS
Mount Dartmouth, Mount Washington, Carter Dome, and Berlin
Quadrangles

**This is a long but rewarding ride through rich wildlife habitat
and past views of the Northeast's tallest peaks.**

Directions
From NH 16 and US 2 in Gorham (the northern intersection), head west on
US 2 for 0.9 mile and park in the parking area on the right. To spot a car on
the western end of the trail, continue on US 2 for 12.0 miles and turn left
on NH 115. In 4.4 miles, you will see Valley Road on the left. The rail trail
crosses NH 115 in another 20 yards or so, where there is room to park a
couple of cars on the west side of the road.

Trip Description
US 2 from Gorham to Jefferson is one of the most scenic drives in the White
Mountains, with the Northern Presidentials towering above the road to the
south. For bike riders who prefer not to battle 18-wheelers on a narrow two-
lane highway with no shoulders, there is the very convenient option of riding the nearby Presidential Rail Trail, which follows an abandoned Boston &
Maine rail line from the Maine border in Shelburne to Pondicherry National
Wildlife Refuge in Jefferson. This trip follows the rail trail from a parking
area just west of downtown Gorham to its intersection with NH 115 in Jefferson. The trail's surface is in good shape, with occasional bumps and loose
gravel, and overall, the trail passes through good scenery, wildlife habitat,
and occasional views of the mountains. You can do this ride as an out-and-
back ride of 27.5 miles if your legs are in good riding shape, or you can spot
a car at either end and make it a one-way ride of 13.75 miles.

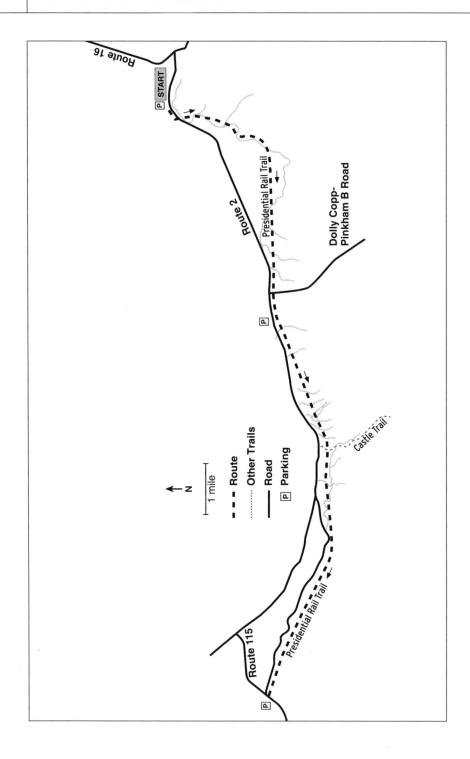

Lupine flowers grow in a field near the Presidential Range.

From the parking area in Gorham, follow the rail trail west through a small residential area. In 0.3 mile, the trail crosses Jimtown Road (which leads to Moose Brook State Park), and then passes under US 2 at 0.75 mile, where you will have to ride around an orange gate. The trail soon parallels the Moose River, which provides a sweet soundtrack for the next several miles, as its rushing waters drown out the sounds of US 2. At this point you will notice that the ride begins climbing. It climbs for most of the next 8 miles, but the elevation gain is so subtle, it is quite possibly the easiest 8-mile climb in all of the White Mountains. The trail crosses the river at 1.8 miles and again at 2.8 miles, where you can see an old abandoned two-story concrete building giving way to nature's forces. By the size of trees growing inside the building, it has probably been abandoned for 30 or 40 years.

You will cross the river one more time before reaching a series of beaver ponds at 4.0 miles. These ponds show extensive beaver activity, with several lodges and dams that are 4 to 6 feet in height. The ponds also afford good views of the mountains and are frequented by moose that leave their tracks and scat right on the trail. We have also seen bear sign in this area. In another 0.5 mile, you will need to cross Pinkham B Road—just remember to watch for traffic. At 5.5 miles, you cross a tributary of the Moose River and then pass the Appalachia trailhead on the right (you could also spot a car here if you wanted a shorter ride).

The trail continues to climb gradually through both hardwood and mixed forests, until reaching another series of beaver ponds shortly after passing the trail to Lowe's Store at 8.0 miles. These ponds also provide good wildlife habitat as well as nice views of the Northern Presidentials. This is the height of land that forms the boundary between the Moose River and Israel River watersheds. From a bigger perspective, it divides the Androscoggin and Connecticut river watersheds, with the Moose flowing into the Androscoggin, which eventually reaches the Atlantic in midcoast Maine, and the Israel flowing into the Connecticut, which empties into Long Island Sound at Old Lyme, Conn.

From here the trail descends just as gradually as it climbed the first 8 miles, reaching the Castle Trail at 8.6 miles and a bridge over the Israel River at 9.8 miles. At 10.8 miles the trail crosses Jefferson Notch Road, then parallels Valley Road and the Israel River, passing the occasional house, on its way to NH 115 and the end of the trip at 13.75 miles. If you've got the energy you can continue past NH 115 for another 4.0 miles to Pondicherry Wildlife Refuge (see trip 30)

Climate Change and the White Mountains

Though scientists and activists have been warning about the effects of climate change (or global warming) for more than two decades, it didn't attract wide media coverage and become a political issue until around 2006. Most scientists now agree that human acts are responsible for the warming of our climate during the last century, with the primary factor being the emission of large

Climate change could have an impact on the amount of snow coverage in the White Mountains.

amounts of carbon dioxide into the atmosphere. Most also agree that unless we dramatically curb carbon dioxide emissions, this warming will continue during the twenty-first century, warming the earth from 4 to 10 degrees Fahrenheit.

What does this mean for New England and the White Mountains? From an ecological perspective, the plant and animal species are likely to be different than they are now, with the rarest species possibly becoming extinct. As our climate warms, the make-up of White Mountain forests is likely to change, with southern species such as oak and hickory eventually becoming more prominent at lower elevations. The spectacular fall foliage displays may become duller as the sugar maples that provide some of our most vibrant color displays may not be able to compete with the species that advance from warmer climates and will likely die out. In addition to losing sugar maples, the White Mountains may also lose significant boreal habitat—those spruce-fir forests typically found above 3,000 feet. In turn, boreal animal species like pine martins, spruce grouse, and Bicknell's thrush are at risk of declining numbers as their habitat slowly dies off.

Higher up the mountains, alpine plant species are at great risk of being squeezed out as well. Rare plants such as the federally endangered Robbins' cinquefoil (found only on Mount Washington and Mount Lafayette) can withstand the extreme winds and cold atop Mount Washington but will not survive if the climate warms to the point where more aggressive plants will move upslope into their habitat. These plants are relics of the last ice age, having moved upslope over thousands of years as the ice retreated to the north. This time, though, there is no room for them to move higher and they may just die out. If temperatures increase at the projected rate, it is likely (depending on local wind and weather cycles) that the treeline could move upslope as well, possibly covering many alpine areas in the White Mountains with trees over time.

The loss of alpine habitat would certainly mean fewer of those cherished 360-degree views that hikers currently enjoy, and there will be other impacts on recreation. Ice climbers are already contending with less-reliable ice conditions, as increased freeze-thaw activity is reducing snowpack and regular ice formation in the mountains. This decade, ski areas are experiencing volatile changes in snow conditions from year to year and by the end of the century, it could be much worse. In the summer, more hot days would lead to an increase of hazardous ozone and other atmospheric particulates, making hiking potentially bad for your health (especially for people with asthma and other respiratory conditions) on the worst days. In addition, insect-borne diseases such as Lyme disease and West Nile Virus, already common in southern New England, will likely become more common in northern New England, including the White Mountains.

This is a somewhat frightening future to contemplate, but these changes are already occurring. Nations and individuals need to take action now to reduce carbon emissions if we are to have any hope at slowing and eventually stopping the rapid pace of climate change. The AMC's website, www.outdoors.org/conservation/energy/index.cfm, is a great resource for climate change information and gives you the opportunity to join its Conservation Action Network. Another good source of information is available at the Clean Air-Cool Planet website, cleanair-coolplanet.org/.

TRIP 35
LOWER NANAMOCOMUCK SKI TRAIL

Aerobic Level: Moderate

Technical Difficulty: Moderate

Distance: 8.4 miles up and back

Elevation Gain: 800 feet

Estimated Time: 2 hours, 30 minutes

Maps: AMC White Mountain Trail Map #3: I9, J9, USGS Bartlett
and Mount Chocorua Quadrangles

**This is one of the more scenic backcountry rides in the White
Mountains.**

Directions

The Nanamocomuck Ski Trail parking area is on the west side of Bear Notch
Road, 8.0 miles south of US 302 in Bartlett and 0.8 mile north of the Kancamagus Highway.

Trip Description

The Lower Nanamocomuck Ski Trail winds its way along the scenic Swift
River for several miles. This trip utilizes about 3.0 of those miles and includes a short hike to Rocky Gorge, where the waters of the Swift River are
squeezed through a narrow chasm in the granite bedrock. This trail tends
to collect a lot of water during the wet seasons, so you may encounter some
muddy conditions, although the wettest part of the trail is skipped in this
trip by beginning on a Forest Service road. The trail alternates between a
relatively smooth, gentle footpath and a rough, tree-root-ridden rut with
frequent stream crossings. In spring the Swift River has some of the wildest
and most dangerous whitewater in the White Mountains, but this ride also
takes you past calm meandering oxbows, where big trees lean out over the
water and heron wait patiently for their chance at a meal.

From the parking area on Bear Notch Road, ride north for 0.2 mile and
turn right onto Forest Service Road 209, a smooth gravel road. You make a
long gradual climb on the service road before descending to the Paugus Link
Trail at 1.0 mile. Keep an eye out for moose in here, as they often forage

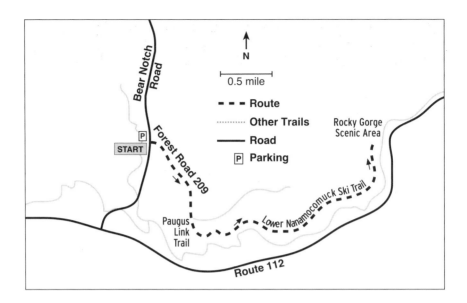

along the road. Turn right onto the Paugus Link Trail, which makes a rocky but passable descent on its way to the Nanamocomuck Ski Trail at 1.2 miles; turn left onto the ski trail. The trail makes several short ascents and descents on its way to the banks of the Swift River, which will appear on your right at 1.6 miles. The river curves gently with a slow current through a mixed forest of spruce, fir, pine, larch, and maple. This is one of the most enjoyable sections of mountain biking trail in the White Mountains.

The trail parallels the river and crosses a small stream on a wooden bridge at 2.0 miles; stay to the right at a junction with the Paugus Ski Trail. The trail begins to get rougher as stream crossings and tree roots proliferate after the 2.5-mile mark. Soon you enter a grove of hemlock trees, where the temperature drops a few degrees and the forest floor is covered with checkerberry plants, small evergreens with scarlet berries. If you crush the thick, shiny oval leaf of a checkerberry plant in your hands and inhale, you will know why it is also called wintergreen.

As the trail gets rougher, so does the river. The calm, lazy oxbows are replaced by rushing whitewater as the river drops steadily toward Rocky Gorge. At 3.6 miles you make a very close approach to the river and will most likely pause to stare at the giant white pine that somehow survived the logging that took place in this area 100 years ago. A 0.1-mile stretch of trail here is very rough and will make some riders dismount and push their bikes. The ups and downs continue and you pass through a curious stand of red pine

The Swift River flows through granite of Rocky Gorge.

planted in neat rows just prior to reaching the Wenonah Trail at 4.2 miles. This is the end of the bike-riding part of this trip. From here, turn right and walk the 0.3 mile through a grove of tall spruce trees to the Rocky Gorge Scenic Area, which is next to the Kancamagus Highway and about 3.5 miles east of Bear Notch Road.

At Rocky Gorge the Swift River is forced through a cleft in the granite, about 20 feet wide, 100 yards long, and 30 feet tall. The water falls with incredible force through the gorge, constantly polishing the dark gray rock. From here the Swift River provides some of the most difficult, uninterrupted whitewater boating runs in New England. For a more mellow experience you can also hike the Lovequist Loop, an easy 1.0-mile walk around Falls Pond. To complete this trip, you can either ride back the way you came or take a right on the Kancamagus and follow it to Bear Notch Road and the Nanamocomuck trailhead. If you decide to ride the Kancamagus, be prepared for a road with a small shoulder and car drivers who may be paying more attention to the scenery than the road.

TRIP 36
MINERAL SITE AND MOAT MOUNTAIN

Aerobic Level: Moderate

Technical Difficulty: Easy on gravel roads; difficult on single-track
(with an easy alternative)

Distance: 8.6 miles round-trip

Elevation Gain: 1,000 feet

Estimated Time: 2 to 3 hours

Maps: AMC White Mountain Trail Map #5: I10, I11, USGS North
Conway West Quadrangle

**This trip begins as a fast downhill run over rocky single-track
and is followed by miles of riding on quiet forest roads.**

Directions

From the intersection of NH 16 and River Road in North Conway (near the
Eastern Slope Inn), head west on River Road. After 1.0 mile turn left onto
West Side Road. In another 5.4 miles turn right onto Passaconaway Road,
and in another 1.2 miles bear right onto an unmarked gravel road known as
High Street. In 1.8 miles bear left at a Forest Service gate (FR 380), following signs for the Moat Mountain Mineral Site. Park at the end of the road in
another 0.8 mile.

Trip Description

Good views of Moat Mountain greet riders who make it to the end of this
ride, which combines a swift descent on technical single-track with 7.0 miles
of mellow forest roads. The single-track that begins this trip is difficult,
but can be avoided by making this an up-and-back trip—see alternate trip
description. Whether or not you skip the single-track, you will get a good
workout, as about 1,000 feet of elevation gain is on this ride. Rock hounds
can make a side trip to the Moat Mountain Smoky Quartz Area, and ambitious multisport athletes can combine this trip with a hike up North Moat
Mountain via the strenuous Red Ridge Trail. Please note that while this trip
is completely within the White Mountain National Forest, it abuts private
land and many unofficial side trails lead to private houses; it is important

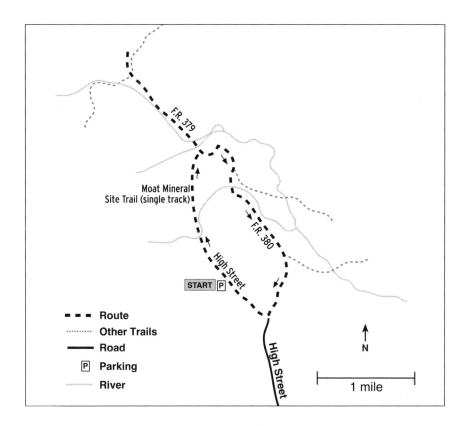

to stay on the official Forest Service trails and roads. Mountain bikers have recently lost access to some trails in this area because of inappropriate behavior on private property.

From the parking area ride through the boulders onto the trail marked "Moat Mountain Mineral Site." At 0.1 mile bear right onto a wide single-track trail that makes a moderate descent over rocks and roots. At 0.4 mile cross a pair of streams with steep banks and follow the moderately technical trail over rolling terrain. At 0.7 mile continue straight at a trail junction and at 1.0 mile you reach the Moat Mountain Smoky Quartz Area, a part of the White Mountain National Forest set aside for visitors who want to look for quartz crystals. At the intersection with the mineral site trail, continue straight for a downhill ride to a clearcut with views of Cranmore Mountain and North Conway at 1.4 miles. From just above the clearcut to an intersection with Forest Road 379 at 1.6 miles, the trail makes a steep, difficult descent over loose rocks and gravel.

This mountain biker is enjoying his ride on a quiet forest road.

Turn left onto Forest Road 379 (unmarked), which soon crosses a stream in a grove of hemlock and makes a steady climb for about 0.5 mile. Technically, the ride is much easier, as the road has a good packed dirt and gravel surface. Just before the 2.4-mile mark, you begin to get views of Moat Mountain as you enter an old clearcut. At 2.6 miles the road gets rougher and you may need to walk your bike as you cross a stream filled with white, volleyball-sized boulders. Like all the streams on this side of Moat Mountain, this stream eventually flows to the Saco River.

After crossing another stream on a bridge, the road becomes a narrow single-track trail and crosses the Red Ridge Trail. If you are up for a strenuous hike up to incredible views, stash your bike here and turn left on the Red Ridge Trail. To complete this trip, continue straight at this intersection and enjoy the smooth surface of the single-track as it makes a few easy climbs and descents on its way to more views of Moat Mountain in a clearing at 3.5 miles. Moat Mountain is actually a long ridge with three distinct peaks: North Moat, Middle Moat, and South Moat. North Moat, at 3,196 feet, is the tallest, but good views (and many blueberries) are available from many points along the ridge. While the trail does appear to continue beyond the clearing, it soon ends on posted private property.

Turn around and follow the single-track and then Forest Road 379 back for a well-deserved, long downhill run. Ride past the mineral site trail you rode in on at 5.4 miles, and ride around the Forest Service gate at 5.5 miles. Continue the downhill ride until you reach a fork in the road at 6.1 miles; bear right onto Forest Road 380 (unmarked). At first FR 380 rolls gently along through a fragrant forest of red and white pine and crosses a stream on a wooden bridge at 6.3 miles. At 7.1 miles you will begin an uphill ride that lasts for more than 1.0 mile, which will probably feel steeper than it is since you are at the end of the ride. At 7.9 miles ride around the Forest Service gate and turn right onto the gravel road (High Street). At 8.3 miles the road levels out and you can coast most of the way back to your car, which should be at the 8.7-mile mark.

Alternate trip: It is easy to avoid the difficult single-track portion of this trip if you would rather go for a relaxing ride through the woods on gravel roads. From the parking area just ride back down High Street until 0.8 mile; turn left and pass the Forest Service gate onto Forest Road 380. From here just follow FR 380 to FR 379 and turn left, riding it to the end.

TRIP 37
SANDWICH NOTCH ROAD

Aerobic Level: Strenuous
Technical Difficulty: Moderate
Distance: 8.0 miles one-way
Elevation Gain: 1,270 feet
Estimated Time: 2 to 3 hours
Maps: AMC White Mountain Trail Map #3: K6, L6, L7, USGS
 Waterville Valley, Squam Mountains, and Center Sandwich
 Quadrangles

A historic road with big elevation gain and a great downhill thrill.

Directions
From the intersection of NH 49 and NH 175 in Campton (about a mile east of I-93 Exit 28), head east on NH 49. In 3.3 miles, you will see Sandwich Notch Road on the right. Continue past Sandwich Notch Road and park in the lot on the right in about 30 yards. To spot a car at the other end of the ride, drive south on Sandwich Notch Road for 8.0 miles until it ends at Diamond Ledge Road, where there is parking on the left (2.4 miles north of Main Street, NH 113, in Sandwich).

Trip Description
Built in 1801, Sandwich Notch Road is a historic route that connected the Waterville Valley region with the Lakes Region in the early nineteenth century. Today, the road is a little-maintained, rough gravel road that passes though beautiful woodlands that are, for the most part, devoid of houses or other development. This ride will test your strength, as it gains almost 1,300 feet in elevation, but you are rewarded with a spectacular downhill thrill on the back end of the ride. Most riders opt to spot a car and do this ride one-way, but if you're in the mood to repeat that uphill climb on the return route and that burning feeling in your quads, go for it.

 The ride starts right off with a steep climb up pavement (you did carbo-load, didn't you?) for about half a mile. The road then turns to the dirt and

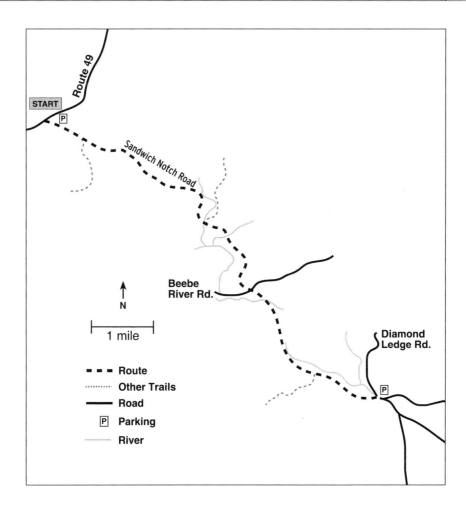

gravel surface that you'll ride on for the remainder of the trip. Though the road is well packed and easy to ride on, it does get bumpy in places so you'll need to watch your speed on the downhills. At 0.8 mile you pass a Forest Service road and then West Meadow Road, as you get a short reprieve from the climb and ride past some hay fields with nice views. The climb soon resumes, and you will ride mostly uphill through hardwoods and a smattering of spruce until you reach the height of land at 2.7 miles, and 850 feet higher than where you started.

Time to hold on for a fast and fun downhill ride. You'll soon pass a beautiful old farm house, complete with a stone wall and a field with a few views. Then the road crosses a stream and continues mostly downhill, passing the

A stone wall hints at the agricultural past of the region.

Algonquin Trail at 3.6 miles, and then bottoming out at 5.0 miles. Here the road passes under some power lines and then Beebe River Road comes in from the right. An alternative to continuing on Sandwich Notch Road is to take a detour on the Beebe River Road, following the Beebe River (see trip 39). Beyond Beebe River Road, Sandwich Notch Road crosses the river, passes the Guinea Pond Trail on the left, and then begins the second major climb of the ride. Though not as long as the initial climb, the road here does gain 280 feet in a little more than half a mile.

At 5.6 miles, the climb ends and begins a wonderful 2.4-mile downhill run. Along the way you'll cross several streams in a forest of mixed hard-woods and softwoods, which show signs of beaver activity. At 7.3 miles you will pass Sandwich Notch Park on the left. If you are up for a side trip, you can leave your bike in the parking lot here and make the short walk to Beebe Falls and the nice swimming hole at their base. From here it is a fairly level ride to Diamond Ledge Road and the end of the ride.

Aerobic Level: Moderate

Technical Difficulty: Moderate

Distance: 12.5 miles round-trip; 15.8 miles with optional single-track

Elevation Gain: 200 feet; 500 feet with optional single-track

Estimated Time: 3 to 4 hours

Maps: AMC White Mountain Trail Map #3: I8, I9, J8, J9, USGS Mount Carrigain, Bartlett, Mount Chocorua, and Mount Tripyramid Quadrangles

This is an easy woods ride on a gravel road with the option for some adventurous single-track.

Directions

From the intersection of NH 16 and NH 112 (Kancamagus Highway) in Conway, drive west on NH 112 for 12.3 miles and turn right onto Bear Notch Road. Rob Brook Road will be on the left in 1.0 mile. Parking is allowed on the southbound side of the road. From Bartlett, Rob Brook Road is 8.0 miles south of US 302.

Trip Description

Rob Brook Road is a gated Forest Service road that provides excellent access to the forest south of Sawyer Pond, Green's Cliff, and Owls Cliff. While riding this road's packed dirt and gravel surface you might encounter a logging vehicle or two, but usually the road is free of traffic, making it a great place for those seeking a long but fairly easy ride through quiet White Mountain scenery. This trip also includes an option for a few miles of exciting single-track up and around Birch Hill, as well as an option for a few miles of hiking to Sawyer Pond—one of the more scenic spots in the White Mountains (due to heavy hiker traffic, bikes are not allowed on the Sawyer Pond Trail). As a loop trip this ride ends up with 3.0 miles of riding on the Kancamagus Highway and Bear Notch Road. However, the crossing of the Swift River just prior

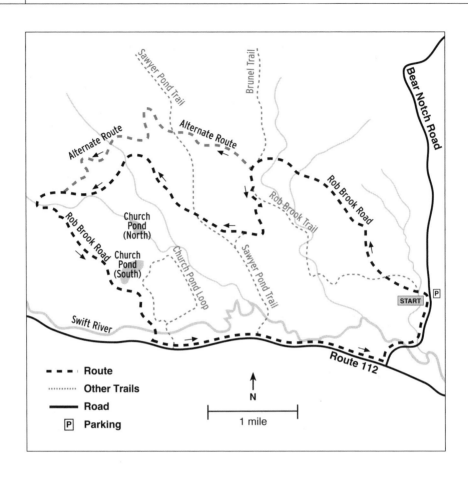

Route

Other Trails

Road

P Parking

N

1 mile

to reaching the Kancamagus can be impossible in high water, necessitating a return trip on Rob Brook Road, which would make the trip 17.4 miles long.

To begin your trip, pedal around the Forest Service gate onto Rob Brook Road. The road has an excellent riding surface for almost all of its 8.7 miles, occasionally climbing and descending gradually, with the downhills serendipitously feeling longer than the uphills. At 0.6 mile you pass the first of several intersections with the Rob Brook Trail—just stick to the road at all of these intersections. The ride takes you through a mixed forest where there are signs of recent logging such as log yards and overgrown skidder roads. At 1.5 miles and 1.8 miles you will pass unmarked trails on the right, and at 2.1 miles you will pass some large boulders and an unmarked trail on the left; continue straight. At 2.5 miles you pass the Brunel Trail on the right and then a pair of unmarked trails, the second of which at 2.8 miles is the beginning of the Birch Hill loop (see alternate description at the end of this trip).

The road continues its gently rolling nature as the forest becomes consistently populated by northern hardwoods with the occasional grove of hemlock. At 4.3 miles you cross the Sawyer Pond Trail. (If you feel like taking a hike, stash your bike and turn right on the Sawyer Pond Trail; it is 2.8 miles up to the pond.) The road provides occasional views of Green's Cliff and the chance to see wildlife such as moose and white-tailed deer. In summer you are likely to encounter American toads and garter snakes soaking in the warmth of the sun on the road. You also will find wildflowers that tend to populate disturbed areas like roadsides and clearcuts. These flowers include nonnative invaders like black-eyed Susans, daisies, and orange hawkweed, as well as native plants like milkweed, fireweed, and asters.

At 6.3 miles the Birch Hill loop (unmarked) rejoins Rob Brook Road. At 6.6 miles you pass an unmarked logging road in a clearing where a stream passes through a boggy area, providing more views of the cliffs as well as some bird-watching opportunities. You will come to an intersection at 8.2 miles where the main road bends to the right and up a hill, while a grassy logging road is straight ahead. Continue straight on this logging road, which immediately passes an intersection with the Church Pond Loop Trail and Nanamocomuck Ski Trail. Following a sign for the Kancamagus Highway you reach the Swift River at 8.7 miles. The Swift River makes a great lunch spot and is a good place to cool off on a hot summer day. The river is usually easily crossed in summer, but in spring or after heavy rains you most likely will need to turn around and return via the way you just came (this is also a good idea if you prefer not to ride with the cars on the busy Kancamagus).

After crossing the river you will have a short stretch of single-track before reaching pavement at 8.8 miles. Turn left onto the Kancamagus Highway, which has a narrow shoulder and occasionally heavy traffic. On your way to Bear Notch Road, you will pass several hiking trails and two campgrounds, as well as the Passaconaway Historic Site—the homestead of pioneer Russell Colbath built in the early 1800s. At 11.5 miles turn left onto Bear Notch Road for the final 1.0-mile climb back to your car.

Alternate trip: To add 3.3 miles of single-track adventure to this otherwise tame ride, turn right onto an unmarked jeep trail on the right immediately after crossing a small brook 2.8 miles from Bear Notch Road. (This will

Taking the proper safety precautions, including wearing a helmet, is essential for an enjoyable ride.

be the second unmarked trail after you pass the Brunel Trail on the right.) This trail will take you around the north side of Birch Hill, climbing sometimes steeply over a rocky trail that is moderately technical most of the time. About 1.2 miles after leaving Rob Brook Road you cross the Sawyer Pond Trail (no bikes) and continue to climb until you reach an old clearcut at 1.5 miles. The forest is beginning to grow back, but some good views can still be seen up to Green's Cliff. After the clearcut, continue straight at a trail junction where the trail reenters the forest and begins its descent back to Rob Brook Road. The trail descends somewhat steeply over rocks, roots, and wooden snowmobile bridges for about 1.0 mile. The remainder of the loop is fairly level with a good riding surface until you reach Rob Brook Road. From here you can turn left to return to the car, or turn right to continue onto the Swift River and the Kancamagus Highway.

TRIP 39
BEEBE RIVER ROAD

Aerobic Level: Moderate
Technical Difficulty: Easy
Distance: 17.2 miles up and back
Elevation Gain: 1,100 feet
Estimated Time: 5 hours, 30 minutes
Maps: AMC White Mountain Trail Map #4: L5, L6, K6, USGS
Plymouth and Squam Mountains Quadrangles

This long ride will give you plenty of opportunities for riverside photo and snack stops.

Directions
Take Exit 27 (Blair Bridge) off I-93. Head east on Blair Road, crossing US 3, and turn left on NH 175 after 0.8 mile. In another 0.6 mile, park on the left in the old Campton Town Hall parking lot.

Trip Description
The Beebe River Road winds along the Beebe River on the southern edge of the White Mountains, just north of Squam Lake. Cars are not allowed on this gravel road, although you may see an occasional logging truck since most of the land along this route is privately owned and currently being managed for timber production. Despite the signs of logging activity, this is still a beautiful trip that passes through a covered bridge and next to a horse farm on its way to the rushing waters of the Beebe River. Beginning at the old town hall in Campton, this trip includes about 2.0 miles of riding on pavement, although automobile traffic will not be a problem. The Beebe River Road makes a barely noticeable climb on its way to Sandwich Notch Road in the White Mountain National Forest. The return ride back down the Beebe River Road is about as easy as it gets. (It is also possible to ride a difficult 20.0-mile loop by combining the Beebe River and Sandwich Notch Roads with NH 49 and NH 175. See trip 37)

From the old town hall turn left onto NH 175 and then turn right at the second right, which is Hog Back Road. It is a steep climb up the first 0.5 mile

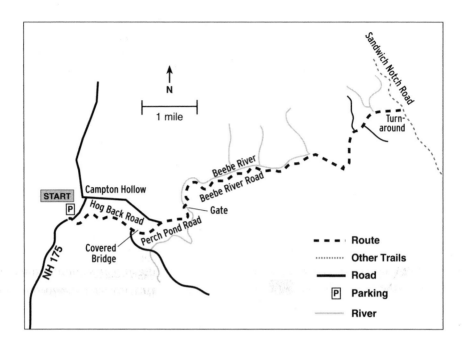

of this dirt road past houses and through forest. At 1.0 mile turn right onto Perch Pond Road and enjoy the easy riding on pavement. At 1.6 miles the road turns to dirt after you turn left and cross the Beebe River on a covered bridge—a gateway to the pastoral scenery of a New England horse farm. In the distance you can see the Squam Mountains, a low ridge of peaks that rise above the northern shores of Squam Lake. At 2.0 miles turn left onto pavement and make a very steep climb past houses and stone walls. The climb eases at 2.3 miles; turn right. The road soon becomes dirt again as it passes Avery Road and a small family cemetery before descending to the Beebe River Road at 2.8 miles.

Turn left onto the Beebe River Road, which is soon blocked by a metal gate. Walk your bike past the gate and leave civilization behind. Since the Beebe River Road is maintained for logging trucks, it is a wide road with a good gravel surface and moderate grades. Shortly after passing the gate, the road meets up with the river and stays close to it for the rest of the ride. At 3.2 miles a great swimming hole is below a small cascade, complete with spots in the shade provided by white pine. At 5.1 miles you pass a logging road and an old building foundation on the left. This foundation is most likely left over from the first half of the twentieth century when the Beebe

You'll want to take periodic breaks during your bike rides to enjoy your surroundings.

River area was originally logged. In 1916 a logging railroad was built along the Beebe River. The first round of logging in this area provided logs for a high diversity of uses: lumber, pianos, textile bobbins, paper, and fuel. By 1942 the railroad was decommissioned as the forest was played out. Due to the recuperative powers of New Hampshire's forests, a second round of logging is now possible.

Near the 6.0-mile mark you enter a cool, dark hemlock grove and sounds of the river find their way up to you from below the road. At 6.4 miles you pass a small waterfall that is worth visiting. At 7.0 miles stay to the left as another logging road goes to the right and crosses the river. By now you should have noticed that a variety of wildlife travels along the river corridor. Signs of moose and coyote are common on the road and hawks often soar high above. Ruffed grouse forage among the hardwoods, feeding on acorns, beechnuts, and other seeds they find on the forest floor. Crow-sized pileated woodpeckers are common, as they seem to thrive on the second-growth forests of central New Hampshire.

At 7.7 miles you pass a sign that signifies you are entering the national forest. Beebe River Road ends 8.6 miles from the old Campton town hall. Here, Sandwich Notch Road leads south to Sandwich and north to Waterville Valley. Before turning around for the return trip, walk across the bridge to the right on Sandwich Notch Road and check out the waterfall.

Tips for Making Great Photos

As you explore the places described in this book, you will undoubtedly be inspired to snap a few photos. Here are a few tips to help you bring back pictures that match the beauty of the White Mountains.

- *Shoot in the good light.* While we all usually time our hikes so that we reach that great view just in time for a lunch break, the bright light of high noon on a sunny day is actually a terrible time to take landscape photos, as the light has a washed-out blue tone to it and is high in contrast (with overly bright whites and too many black shadows). The best light of the day is during the first hour after sunrise and the hour before sunset when contrast is low and the light has a warm glow. This makes it tough to shoot nice scenic shots from the summits unless you spend the night nearby in an AMC hut or at a high backcountry campsite like Liberty Springs on Mount Liberty or the Perch on Mount Adams. The good news is that those beautiful rich green forests you hike through photograph great all day long on days with overcast light. Add a polarizing filter to the front of your lens to really saturate those forest scenes.
- *Get close.* Getting close with your camera lets you emphasize your subject, which in turn helps viewers of your photograph feel like they are really there in the scene, giving the image more impact. Make sure your main subject is big enough in the frame to look like your main subject. We especially like using wide-angle lenses for close-ups. These lenses let you focus on subjects less than a foot away from the camera, making them appear large in your viewfinder, while also capturing some of the background scenery in order to create a real sense of place.

This photographer set up her tripod on a fallen pine to take a shot of the rushing waters of Cascade Brook.

- *Anchor wide shots.* Whether you get very close or not, using wide-angle lenses helps involve your viewer with your subject, creating a real sense of place by taking advantage of these lenses' large depth of field. (Depth of field is the amount of your photograph that appears to be in focus. For example, if you focus your camera on a tulip, not only will the tulip be in focus, but part of the scene in front of the tulip and behind the tulip will also be in focus. This is the depth of field of the image. You get more depth of field with wide-angle lenses and less with telephoto lenses. You also get more depth of field with smaller apertures like F16 than with larger apertures like F4.) Wide-angle shots work best if they have a strong foreground feature as well as an interesting background. By including a foreground feature that "anchors" the scene, and by using a small aperture to maximize depth of field, your viewers will be able to feel like they were standing there with you when you shot the photo.

- *Simplify.* Keep you compositions simple. The outdoors is full of distracting elements that you need to crop out of your compositions, preferably before you download any images to your computer. Pick the most important two or three elements in the scene and make sure everything else is minimized or eliminated completely from view. If there is something in the scene that doesn't help tell your story, keep it out of your picture. Viewers shouldn't have to hunt around a photo to figure out what it is about. Also, pay attention to the background and edges of your photo and be sure they are clean and don't take away focus from your main subject.

- *Shoot sharp.* Nothing detracts from the beauty of a photo more than blurry subject matter (unless of course you are shooting fast action and want it to look blurry). We almost always shoot with a tripod in order to minimize camera shake. We also use a cable release and the mirror lock-up feature on the camera to further reduce camera shake when shooting with a tripod. If you insist on not using a tripod (and it is a challenge to carry a tripod into the backcountry, especially on a bike), try to use a shutter speed of at least 1/60 second or faster. Also, shoot with the lowest ISO setting on your camera to reduce the amount of noise in your image. Noise is comparable to grain in film, and having less noise in an image allows you to make bigger enlargements.

TRIP 40
SHELBURNE TO EVANS NOTCH

Aerobic Level: Strenuous
Technical Difficulty: Easy
Distance: 37.2 miles round-trip
Elevation Gain: 2,200 feet
Estimated Time: 3 to 4 hours
Maps: AMC White Mountain Trail Map #5: F12, F13, USGS Gilead,
    Speckled Mountain, Wild River, and Shelburne Quadrangles

**This long ride on back roads takes you past mountain views
and along the scenic Wild River.**

Directions
From NH 16 and US 2 in Gorham (the southern intersection), drive east
on US 2 for 3.6 miles and park at the Appalachian Trail parking area on the
right.

Trip Description
This relatively long ride follows back roads for most of its length. It meanders through a typical northern New Hampshire landscape of fields and
woodlands before venturing into the deep woods of Evans Notch as it parallels the beautiful Wild River. The ride is on pavement for a little more than
half the ride, and hard-packed gravel for the remainder. While the mileage is
long, the elevation gain of 2,200 feet is well spread out and not too taxing,
though there is a sustained but gradual climb during the Wild River section.
If you are pressed for time and want to cut your mileage down, you can spot a
second car at several spots along Route 113 or on Wild River Road and make
this a one-way trip.

From the parking area on US 2, ride west on US 2 for 0.2 mile and turn
right onto North Road. The road soon crosses the Androscoggin River, just
below the Shelburne Hydropower Dam. After crossing the river, the road
curves to the right and parallels the river. In fact, you'll never be more than
a mile from the river for the next 9 miles or so. The ride on North Road rolls

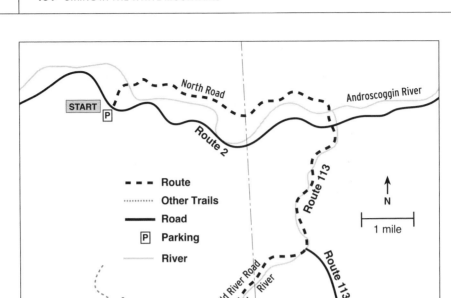

gently up and down for most of its length, passing the occasional house or farm. At 4.0 miles, go straight at an intersection with Meadow Road. The road soon passes some open meadows with nice views of Mount Moriah, and continues along as a quiet, curvy, road through a rural landscape.

In another 4.0 miles, you'll get some nice views of the river and then reach Bridge Road at 9.0 miles. Turn right here and follow the road over the Androscoggin to US 2. Turn right on US 2 for the short ride to ME 113 at 9.6 miles, where you should turn left. As you ride along 113 you immediately enter intimate woodlands, while curving along the fast-flowing Wild River. The Wild River valley is hemmed in by cliffs and steep mountainsides on both sides, which further enhances the rugged nature of the scenery. At 12.6 miles, turn right on the dirt and gravel Wild River Road.

At this point you are in the former logging town of Hastings, Maine, which in the late nineteenth century was home to a sawmill, general store,

The paved portion of this trip offers the opportunity for a speedy ride.

and several hundred people, many of whom harvested timber in the Wild River valley. By 1903, the forest was played out, and the town was completely deserted by 1918. Today, the forest has reclaimed the landscape and all you will find of Hastings is the occasional stone cellar hole.

Continuing with the ride, the road follows the river through northern hardwoods on a good dirt road with a gradual uphill grade. The river is wide and fast, swelled by the waters of numerous brooks that tumble down the slopes of the Carter-Moriah and Baldface Ranges. On the way to the end of the road at 18.6 miles, you will pass a couple of beaver ponds and forest service roads, but for the most part, the landscape doesn't change much. The road ends at the Wild River Campground, where you can take a break and make use of the facilities, which are complete with running water.

It was previously possible to continue from here on a mountain bike by riding on the Wild River Trail, but in 2007, the Forest Service created the Wild River Wilderness Area, where bikes are off-limits. Feel free to hike the trail though if you want to explore the Wild River further. You can use the same route you came in on to make the return trip. You can also opt to take US 2 instead of North Road back to your car, but North Road is much quieter, and avoids the narrow shoulders, high speeds, and heavy traffic of US 2.

3

Paddling in the White Mountains

WHILE THE WHITE MOUNTAINS are not as rich in paddling opportunities as the Lakes Region to the south, a few ponds surrounded by beautiful scenery make for peaceful paddling. All of the lake and pond trips in this chapter are suitable for both solo paddlers and families. These trips also provide excellent wildlife-watching opportunities—loons, ducks, beaver, and occasionally osprey, deer, moose, and river otters can be spotted in the waters within the White Mountain National Forest. The river trips listed require some experience on moving water and are best done with a group of paddlers that includes a boat or two of paddlers experienced in river rescue techniques.

Safety and Etiquette for Quietwater Paddling

To ensure a safe and comfortable quietwater paddling experience, consider the following safety tips:

- Know how to use your canoe or kayak. Small lakes and ponds are the perfect place for inexperienced paddlers to learn, but if you are new to the sport, you should have someone show you some basic paddling strokes and impress upon you how to enter and exit your boat. New paddlers should consider staying close to shore until they are more comfortable with their paddling skills. Luckily, some of the most interesting aspects of the trips in this chapter are found along the shoreline.

- Turn around *before* the members of your party start feeling tired. Paddling a few miles after your arms already are spent can make for cranky travelers. All of the lake and pond trips in this book start and end at the same location, so you can easily turn around at any time.

- Make sure everyone in your group is wearing a life jacket or personal flotation device (PFD) that fits properly and securely. It is easy to tip a canoe accidentally, especially if the notorious White Mountain winds kick up 2-foot waves, since you can be as far as 0.5 mile from shore.
- Be cautious around motorboats on Conway Lake and Lake Tarleton, where large boats may create big wakes. Turn the bow of your boat into the waves if you are afraid of getting swamped by the wake of one of these larger boats; do not assume that bigger boats can see you. Kayaks especially can be hard to spot in bright sunlight or fog, so it might be up to you to get out of the way.
- Pay close attention to the winds. Winds as gentle as 10 MPH can create some fairly large waves on some of the ponds. With the mountains making their own weather, be prepared for a calm day to turn suddenly choppy. Bring a windbreaker, as it can get cold in a canoe in the lightest of winds. Long Pond and Upper Kimball Pond are small and narrow enough to paddle on windy days without too much difficulty.
- Stay off the water if thunderstorms are nearby. Lightning is a serious danger to boaters. If you hear a thunderstorm approaching, get off of the water immediately and seek shelter. For a current weather forecast, call the AMC weather phone at 603-466-2721 (option 4).

Bring the following supplies along with you to make the trip more comfortable:

✓ One or two quarts of water per person depending on the weather and length of the trip
✓ Even for a short, one-hour paddle, it is a good idea to bring some high-energy snacks like nuts, dried fruit, or snack bars. Bring a lunch for longer trips.
✓ Map and compass—and the ability to use them
✓ Extra clothing: Rain gear, wool sweater or fleece jacket, wool or fleece hat in a waterproof bag
✓ Headlamp or flashlight, with spare batteries and lightbulb
✓ Sunscreen and hat
✓ First-aid kit: Adhesive bandages, gauze, nonprescription painkiller
✓ A trash bag
✓ Toilet paper

✓ Pocketknife

✓ Binoculars for wildlife viewing

In addition to the no-impact techniques described in this book's introduction, please keep the following things in mind while paddling:

- Give wildlife a wide berth. Lakes and ponds are much different than forests in that wildlife has less of an opportunity to hide from humans. The summer months see numerous people in the water, and the ducks, heron, and loons waste a good deal of energy just swimming or flying away from curious boaters. If you spot wildlife, remain still and quiet and let the animals decide whether or not to approach you. Use binoculars if you want a closer view. In spring, steer clear of loons nesting along the shore.

- Respect private property. Much of the land surrounding the ponds in this chapter is private property. Most of the put-ins are on or adjacent to private property, so please act with respect in order to ensure future access for paddlers. Take a map that shows the national forest boundaries. Do not land your boat on private property, and speak quietly when paddling near homes and cottages.

- Respect the purity of the water. Some of the ponds in the White Mountains are used for drinking water by the surrounding communities. If you need to relieve yourself, do so on land, at least 200 yards from the shoreline.

- Sound carries a long way on the water, so try to keep your conversations quiet in order not to disturb other paddlers or nearby hikers.

- Boats are responsible for the movement of nonindigenous species, like the zebra mussel, between water bodies and river systems. To prevent the spread of nonindigenous plants and animals, make it a habit to drain all of the water out of your canoe or kayak, visually inspect your boat for unwelcome hitchhikers, and rinse your boat off with a hose once you return home.

The river trips in this book encounter mainly quickwater and Class I rapids, which are navigable by most boaters under normal conditions. However, moving water requires a greater level of boating experience and we recommend anyone planning to do the river trips in this book to receive training in whitewater paddling techniques, including self-rescue.

TRIP 41
UPPER KIMBALL POND

Difficulty: Quietwater
Distance: 3.4 miles round-trip
Estimated Time: 2 hours
Maps: AMC White Mountain Trail Map #5: H12, USGS North
Conway East Quadrangle

This easy paddle provides good mountain views and excellent bird-watching opportunities.

Directions
From the intersection of NH 16 and River Road in North Conway, head north on NH 16 for 1.8 miles and turn right onto Hurricane Mountain Road. Follow Hurricane Mountain Road until it ends in 6.0 miles. Turn left onto Green Hill Road, following the sign for Chatham. The put-in will be on the right in another 2.0 miles. Alternatively, from US 302 and ME 113 in Fryeburg, Maine, take ME 113 north. In 1.2 miles turn right, staying on ME 113. In another 0.9 mile turn left onto Green Hill Road. The put-in will be on the right in 5.5 miles.

Trip Description
Fed by the mountain streams high up the slopes of Mount Kearsarge and Hurricane Mountain, Upper Kimball Pond is a small pond on the Maine-New Hampshire border south of Evans Notch. With a few unobtrusive camps, the pond is a relatively quiet place to spend a few hours dipping your paddles into the water while taking in the characteristically beautiful White Mountain scenery. A little more than 150 acres in size, the pond is small enough for a short family outing, but it has enough diversity to keep most people interested for at least a couple of hours. Motorboats and large waves are rarely a problem here. Most of the land surrounding this pond is private property, so please act in a respectful manner.

Put in next to the dam and paddle up a narrow passage before entering the main part of the pond. Find your way to the southern end of the pond by following either shoreline. The western shoreline is less developed, while the eastern shoreline has better views of Mount Kearsarge and other peaks.

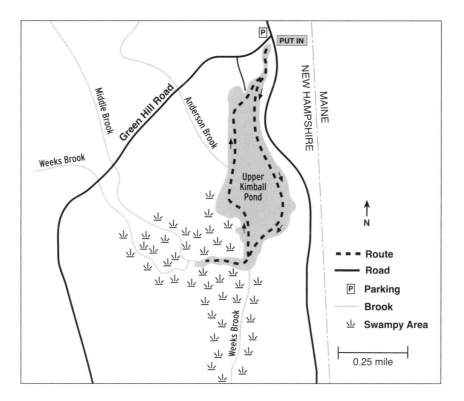

At the southern end of the pond you will enter a shallow, marshy area that bends to the right, leaving any signs of civilization behind. Here you can paddle among tall reeds, grasses, and cattails, and around the purple blooms of pickerelweed and the round, yellow flowers of water lilies. On a warm summer day you are bound to see a variety of swallows and flycatchers, all feeding on the plentiful insects (that might be feeding on you). During the twilight hours you might spot a beaver swimming or a mink patrolling the shore.

Larch trees and sheep laurel grow in the poor soils surrounding the marsh. In fall, these plants react in the opposite manner to what you might expect. Sheep laurel, a 1- to 3-foot-tall shrub with pink flowers in the summer, keeps its leaves and stays green throughout the winter, while larch trees, conifers that resemble other evergreens, drop their inch-long needles after they turn yellow in the fall. In New England, both species are common in poorly drained, boggy areas.

Once you are confronted with primarily boggy areas and you can no longer find navigable water, just head back to the main part of the pond and follow either shore back to the parking area.

TRIP 42
MOUNTAIN POND

Difficulty: Quietwater
Distance: 1.7 miles round-trip plus a 0.3-mile portage
Estimated Time: 1 hour
Maps: AMC White Mountain Trail Map #5: G12, USGS Chatham
 Quadrangle

Take this paddle on a remote pond for excellent views of the surrounding mountains.

Directions

From the intersection of NH 16 and River Road in North Conway, drive north on NH 16 for 3.7 miles and turn right onto Town Hall Road. In 0.1 mile go straight at a stop sign, follow the road until the 2.5-mile mark, and take the left fork. Go straight at an intersection 5.9 miles from NH 16, and take a right into a parking area in another 0.7 mile.

Trip Description

The fact that you have to carry your boat for about 0.3 mile before putting it in the water makes Mountain Pond the quietest of the quietwater trips in this book. It is worth the effort, as you will find solitude and excellent views on this small pond that sits 1,500 feet above sea level. The solitude is especially welcome if you had to fight the traffic through the nearby strip of outlet malls in North Conway. If you are looking for some pond-side back-country camping, you can spend the night in a lean-to on the northern side of the pond. Primitive camping is allowed in the forest surrounding the pond. Be sure to practice no-impact camping techniques to ensure a pristine experience for the next visitor. For more information on camping in this area, contact the Saco Ranger District at 33 Kancamagus Highway, Conway, NH 03818; 603-447-5448.

From the parking area you will need to carry your boat to Mountain Pond via the Mountain Pond Trail. The trail is wide with good footing and reaches a fork just before the pond. Turn left and in another 25 yards follow a side trail to the right. This will take you to the put-in at the western edge of the pond. Near the put-in is a marshy area that is good habitat for ducks

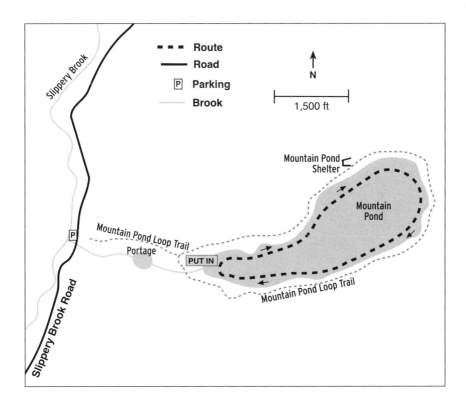

and frogs, especially bullfrogs and green frogs. The rest of the pond is surrounded by rocky shoreline, with sheep laurel, alder, and blueberries reaching out over the water. Bird-watchers might spot northern bird species in the surrounding boreal forest when they are not gazing at the views of North and South Doublehead and South Baldface.

It is easy to spot a boreal forest—just look for the evergreens. Around Mountain Pond, you will see primarily red spruce, balsam fir, and white pines, with some paper birch as well. The boreal forest is the northernmost forest ecosystem in the world as it circles the globe across North America, Europe, and Asia. Though characterized by evergreens, the specific species that make up the boreal forest are different in different parts of the world. In the White Mountains, the boreal forest is predominantly red spruce and balsam fir, with paper birch often growing in disturbed areas. Other evergreens sometimes present are white and red pines, white and black spruce, and eastern hemlock. Not much grows in the dark understory of a boreal forest, but in spring you might come across wildflowers like star flowers and wood sorrel.

Ferns growing in the understory of a spruce fir forest.

Spruce and fir trees are remarkably adapted to survive the long winters of the high latitudes. Their conical, Christmas tree shape sheds the heavy snows of winter so that their branches are not damaged. The short growing season makes it inefficient to grow new leaves every year, so the trees' needles stay on year-round and go dormant during the winter. The needles are protected by a thick wax on the outside and a sugary fluid on the inside that acts much like antifreeze and prevents frost damage. The way needles are arranged on the tree has been shown to prevent wind chill and evaporation, and actually helps keep the trees warmer in winter. The needles can quickly begin photosynthesizing in spring when temperatures rise.

If you want to get an inside look at the boreal forest around Mountain Pond, your best bet is to use the hiking trail that circles the pond. It takes about an hour and a half to complete this hike.

TRIP 43
CHOCORUA LAKE

Difficulty: Quietwater
Distance: 3.3 miles round-trip
Estimated Time: 2 hours
Maps: AMC White Mountain Trail Map #3: K10, USGS Lake
Quadrangle

See loons, pines, and spectacular views of Mount Chocorua.

Directions

From the intersection of NH 16 and NH 113 in Tamworth, drive north on
NH 16. There are two parking options. The first is to turn left in 1.6 miles
onto Chocorua Lake Road and park in the lot on the left. This lot has a small
picnic area on the lake as well as a portable toilet. The other option is to
continue for an additional 0.6 mile and turn left onto a narrow road on conservation land that borders the eastern shore of the lake; park off to the
side before reaching the signs that indicate parking for Tamworth residents
only.

Trip Description

Chocorua Lake is familiar to travelers on NH 16 who approach the White
Mountains from the south. The view of craggy Mount Chocorua from the
lake is one of the most famous in New England. Despite the presence of
NH 16 on the east and several well-concealed cottages on its western shore,
Chocorua Lake manages to have a wild feel. While the mountain commands
attention, paddlers on Chocorua Lake are soon drawn to the smaller details of nature—the colorful blooms of water lilies and sheep laurel, the calls
of loons, and the swooping of swallows. At 220 acres the lake is relatively
small, but winds can pick up and create some big waves, making it necessary to monitor the weather. In good weather, however, this is a great place
for family paddling. Much of the western shore of Chocorua Lake is private
property, so if you need to take a break and get out of your boat, do so on the
conservation land on the eastern and southern shores.

Being somewhat pear shaped with no deep coves, Chocorua Lake is easy
to navigate. By just following the shoreline in either direction you can see the

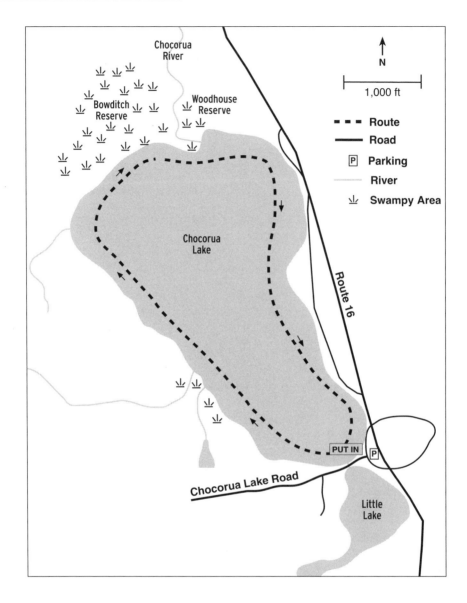

whole lake in a couple of hours. While NH 16 borders the lake on the east, tall stands of red and white pine help to keep the road from your mind. Nature lovers will want to head to the western and northern shores of the lake where marshy coves are filled with lilies and pickerelweed. Loons nest here and insect-loving birds like tree swallows, flycatchers, and cedar waxwings can usually be seen feeding above the lake on warm summer days. The north

This sole kayaker glides through the water as fog rises from Lake Chocorua.

end of the lake is bordered by swampy land owned by The Nature Conservancy. Here you will find an old beaver dam, sheep laurel and other heaths, as well as small birds like swamp sparrows and yellowthroats flitting about the undergrowth.

At the southern outlet of the lake you can paddle under the bridge to Little Lake, a much smaller body of water that is a good place to watch for painted turtles and green frogs. Both Chocorua Lake and Mount Chocorua are named after an Abenaki Indian chief from the eighteenth century, who was immortalized in numerous writings and paintings in the nineteenth century. The first published account of Chocorua was written by Henry Wadsworth Longfellow in 1825. His poem, *Jeckoyva*, described the tragic tale of a Penacook hunter (the Penacooks were a band of Abenakis who lived in central New Hampshire) falling to his death from the summit of Mount Chocorua. A few years later, painter Thomas Cole climbed the peak and wrote a tale in which white settlers killed Chocorua on the mountain's summit.

The Common Loon: Symbol of Wilderness

Perhaps no other animal in New England symbolizes wilderness like the common loon, a bird known for its beauty and its calls, which include laughs, yodels, and wails. The loon is a primitive, highly successful bird that has lived on earth for more than 50 million years. Once common on lakes and ponds across the northern United States, loon populations have declined dramatically in the last century—New Hampshire's population is only 50 percent of what it was 100 years ago. This decline is due to degradation of loon habitat through development and pollution. Loons are only slightly tolerant of human activities, and they are especially susceptible to lead poisoning (from fishing tackle) and mercury poisoning (from airborne pollutants). The common loon is currently listed as a threatened species in New Hampshire, where the population is thought to be about 450 adult birds. You are likely to see loons on any of the quietwater trips listed in this chapter.

Common loons are easy to identify. A common loon has a black head and bill, bright red eyes, a white and black striped collar, a white chest and belly, and a black and white checkered back. They are large, stout birds, about 32 inches long and weighing as much as 13 pounds. Unlike most birds, which have hollow bones for easy flight, loons have solid bones, giving them the mass needed to dive easily for fish. In addition, their feet are set far back on their bodies to help them dive, and internal air sacks allow them to control their diving speed and depth. Loons have been found diving to depths of 200 feet, as they search for fish, amphibians, crayfish, and even leeches. Adult loons prefer fish, especially perch, suckers, catfish, and sunfish.

The same characteristics that make diving so easy for loons also make it hard for them to take off and fly. Without a breeze to fly into, a loon may need to run several hundred yards on the surface of a lake before it can become airborne. Loons spend winters in waters along both the Atlantic and Pacific coasts, and fly to inland lakes and ponds as soon as the ice melts in early spring. Loons need a lot of space, and lakes smaller than about 100 acres can usually accommodate only one nesting pair. Loons are not very adept at moving on land and build their nests right on the shoreline, usually on islands or other places surrounded by water like partially submerged logs or muskrat lodges. These spots are prone

Loons can be easily identified by their black head, white chest, and checkered back.

to flooding and loons often lose their nests during periods of heavy rain. Loons usually lay two eggs in early June and the chicks hatch about one month later. Disturbing loons while they are incubating can cause them to leave the nest, which puts the eggs at risk for chilling (the embryo can die within 30 minutes if left unattended) or being taken by predators such as fox, raccoons, skunk, and crows.

In June and July be especially careful not to disturb loons while enjoying your quietwater paddles. Loon chicks can swim almost immediately, but they often ride on their parents' backs in order to rest and avoid predators like eagles, gulls, large fish, and snapping turtles. The parents feed the chicks until they start to dive for fish and other food at about 8 weeks of age. By the time they are 12 weeks old they can usually fly, and they will often migrate a few weeks after their parents leave for the ocean in late October or early November. Wintering loons may be seen anywhere along the New England coast; young loons will remain at sea for three or four years before returning inland to breed.

Loons are cherished for their calls as much as their beauty. Common loons have four distinct calls: tremolo, wail, yodel, and hoot. The *tremolo*, which loons use when disturbed or annoyed, is a danger call that sounds similar to a human laugh. When intruders ignore a tremolo call, loons will stand up, violently kick the water, and flap their wings. The *wail* is the haunting cry often heard at night, which loons use to establish contact with a family member. This call is often the first contact humans have with loons, and it is forever etched in the memory of anyone who has attended summer camp on a lake in the North Country. Male loons use the *yodel* as a territorial song, warning intruding males that they have ventured into hostile territory. Each male has its own unique yodel, which is usually a long call that lasts up to six seconds and increases in volume. The last of the loon calls is the *hoot*, a short call used to locate other family members and check on their safety.

Four other species of loons live in North America, but the common loon is the only one that breeds south of Canada; however, it is possible to spot a red-throated loon off the New England coast, particularly in northern Maine. Red-throated loons have gray heads and a red throat patch and are slightly smaller than common loons. Efforts to protect loons appear to be working, as their population seems to have stabilized in much of their range. New Hampshire recently banned anglers from using lead sinkers, and the preliminary results show that fewer loons are dying due to lead poisoning. Education efforts aimed at preventing the disturbance of loons while nesting also seem to be working. Often you will see buoys marking loon nesting areas in lakes with boat traffic— make sure to avoid these areas when you encounter them. Every little bit helps, and with wise pollution-control measures and education efforts, we should be hearing loon calls for generations to come.

TRIP 44
CONWAY LAKE

Difficulty: Quietwater
Distance: 7.5 miles round-trip
Estimated Time: 4 hours
Maps: AMC White Mountain Trail Map #5: J12, USGS Conway
Quadrangle

See mountain views and miles of varied wildlife-filled shoreline.

Directions
From the intersection of NH 16 and NH 153 in Conway, head south on NH 153. In 4.4 miles turn left onto Potter Road. The put-in will be on the left in 1.4 miles just beyond a small one-lane bridge.

Trip Description
Conway Lake is a big lake by White Mountain standards, and provides miles of pine-covered shoreline filled with nooks and crannies that are fun to explore. This trip takes you to the southern half of the lake, which is well suited to quietwater paddling because of its two narrow and secluded finger-like coves. Except for a 0.25-mile stretch of waterfront camps and a large commercial campground on the western shore, the lake is relatively undeveloped and provides excellent opportunities for bird-watching and solitude. You might be lucky enough to spot a moose, beaver, or mink in the quieter coves. Since it is larger than other lakes in the region, Conway Lake does receive its share of motorboats that leave large wakes—on summer weekends plan an early morning paddle to avoid the noise. Its size also means fairly large waves can kick up on windy days, so check the weather forecast before you start your day and be prepared to turn around if the weather turns bad.

The fun starts as you launch into the larger, eastern finger at the southern end of the lake. The shallow, marshy area teems with insect-eating birds like swallows and kingbirds. As you get into the deeper water you will pass islands covered in red pine; at least one of these islands has a pair of nesting loons. If

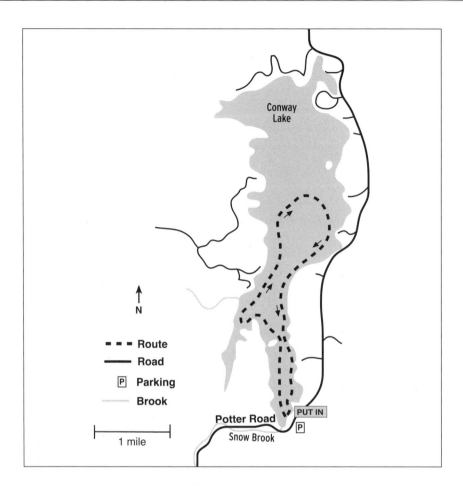

you stick to the left shore you will find yourself turning into the completely undeveloped western finger after about 1.2 miles. As you continue the forest begins to close in and you feel like you are on a remote stretch of river. It is a great place to watch for flycatchers, warblers, cedar waxwings, white-tailed deer, and moose. Near the southern end of the finger is a fairly large beaver lodge built on the bank of the lake. Early morning paddlers are likely to be startled by the loud slap of a beaver tail hitting the surface of the water.

Once you reach the end of the western finger, turn around and head up the left shoreline into the main part of the lake. This is the less-than-quiet stretch of developed shoreline, but quick paddling will put you back in quiet-water territory in no time. You can explore this shoreline and its numerous

The trunk diameter of red pines generally does not exceed 1 meter.

coves for as long as you wish. One good turnaround spot is a large island about an acre in size that is covered by tall red pine with an understory of blueberries. Unless you plan to paddle most of the day, circle this island, head straight across the lake to the eastern shore, and follow the shore back to the put-in (keeping the shoreline on your left). Along the way you will be rewarded with scenic mountain views from the shade of tall white pine.

TRIP 45
LONG POND

Difficulty: Quietwater
Distance: 2.5 miles round-trip
Estimated Time: 1 hour, 30 minutes
Maps: AMC White Mountain Trail Map #4: I2, USGS East Haverhill
Quadrangle

This is an easy paddle on one of New Hampshire's most scenic ponds.

Directions

From I-93 in Lincoln take Exit 32 and head west on NH 112. In 11.5 miles follow the road to the left as it is joined by NH 116. In 0.9 mile turn left onto NH 116. In another 1.7 miles turn left onto Long Pond Road (marked on some maps as North and South Road). In 2.4 miles turn right, following a sign for Long Pond. The pond is at the end of this road in another 0.6 mile.

Trip Description

There are at least eight Long Ponds in New Hampshire, but none of them compare to the one in Benton in the western part of the White Mountain National Forest. Long Pond personifies quietwater paddling—it is remote, filled with wildlife, completely undeveloped, and surrounded by mountains. Despite its relatively small size (124 acres), Long Pond has plenty of shore-line to cover, since it is almost 1.0 mile long and has several spruce-covered islands. You easily can spend an entire morning or afternoon here explor-ing the coves, watching wildlife, and taking in the views of Mount Moosi-lauke. Backcountry camping is allowed in the surrounding forest, but not on the islands in the pond. (For more information about backcountry camping around Long Pond, contact the Ammonoosuc/Pemigewasset Ranger District at RFD #3, Box 15, Route 175, Plymouth, NH 03264; 603-536-1310.)

There is really no need for us to explain a route in Long Pond, as it is small enough to just put your boat in and start paddling. The only thing to watch out for is the dam to the right of the put-in—do not paddle over it! The

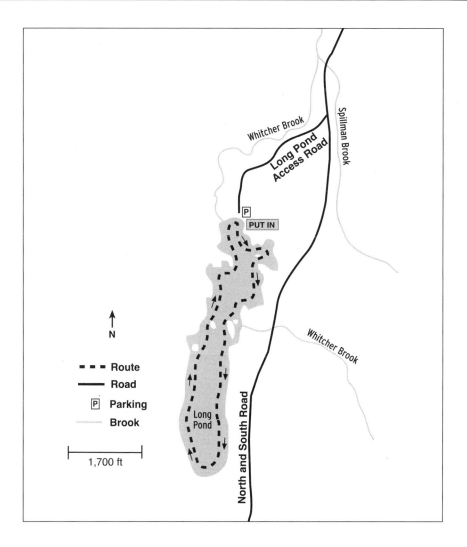

shorelines of the pond and its islands are a great place to watch for all kinds of wildlife—great blue heron, osprey, mergansers, otters, mink, and beaver. We once watched a trio of moose feeding in the afternoon sun on the eastern shoreline. Surrounding the pond are a few marshy coves, but mostly you will find banks supporting tall spruce with an understory of sheep laurel, hobble-bush, and alder. The slopes rising up beyond the shoreline are covered with hardwoods, putting on a brilliant display of color at the end of September and beginning of October.

The view from this dock on Long Pond is extensive and relaxing.

Though shallow (its average depth is only 4 feet), Long Pond sits above 2,000 feet, keeping the water cool enough to sustain a population of eastern brook trout, the only trout native to New Hampshire streams. Fishing is popular here from a platform next to the dam at the north end of the lake, but you can also paddle out a fly rod in your kayak and cast for brookies while soaking in the bigger views from out in the middle of the pond.

If you are in the mood to tackle more than one trip in a day, Long Pond is relatively close to other trips in this book, including a paddle on Lake Tarleton (trip 46) and a hike up Mount Moosilauke (trip 19).

Amphibious Exploration

The White Mountains are home to a variety of toads, frogs, and salamanders, which can be found on virtually any trip into the mountains during spring and summer. Toads and frogs are the most commonly seen, particularly American toads, which seem to use hiking trails as their main habitat during the late-summer months. Some amphibians breed in vernal pools, small ponds and pools that fill with water for only a few months in spring and early summer. These temporary bodies of water are relatively safe places for amphibians to breed, as they are devoid of fish that prey on the eggs and larvae of amphibians. Small frogs like spring peepers and wood frogs use vernal pools, as do spotted, Jefferson's, and blue-spotted salamanders. Larger frogs such as bullfrogs and green frogs do not use vernal pools, as their tadpoles can take more than a year to mature into adult frogs.

New Hampshire is home to eight species of frogs, two species of toads, ten species of salamanders, and one species of newts. While it is relatively easy to find toads and frogs, salamanders can seem nonexistent at times. Rest assured, they are plentiful—in fact if you gathered up all of the salamanders in the White Mountains, they would outweigh all of the moose. In the White Mountains the amphibians you are most likely to encounter are listed below:

- *Spring peepers* are more likely to be heard than seen. Considered a chorus frog, but also exhibiting characteristics of tree frogs, spring peepers fill the night air in spring with their loud chorus of frog song. They prefer small, often temporary bodies of water near trees. These tiny frogs are less than an inch long and are usually brown or gray with a dark "X" on their backs.
- *Bullfrogs* are the largest frogs in the United States, measuring from 3 1/2 to 6 inches in length. They are either green, or brown and gray with a green background. They can be found in lakes, ponds, bogs, and streams, and have a voracious appetite, eating almost anything that they can swallow including small snakes.
- *Green frogs* are smaller than bullfrogs, measuring 2 1/4 to 3 1/2 inches in length, and tend to be greenish-brown in color. In rare cases they may be blue. Green frogs tend to like shallower water than bullfrogs, spending their time in brooks, small streams, and along the edges of lakes and ponds.

Wood frogs range from 2 to 3 inches in length. Female wood frogs are slightly larger than their male counterparts.

- *Pickerel frogs* are 1 3/4 to 3 inches in length and have square spots arranged in two parallel rows down their backs. They often have bright yellow or orange coloring on their hind legs. Pickerels prefer the clear, cold waters of sphagnum bogs, rocky ravines, and meadow streams.
- *Wood frogs* are slightly smaller than pickerels but have an unmistakable robber's mask, a dark patch around the eye. Wood frogs are generally brown, blending in well with leaf litter on the forest floor. They spend a lot of their time in moist woods, away from water.

- *American toads* are the only toads that live in the White Mountains, but they are very conspicuous on hiking and biking trails, especially in late summer when you might see dozens of young toads less than half an inch in length. They are 2 to 4 inches in length and generally tan or brown in color with a highly variable pattern of spots, ranging in color from gray, olive, and brown to brick red. One or two warts also appear on their larger spots.

- *Red-spotted newts* and *red efts* are actually different forms of the same species. Red efts are the juvenile land form of the red-spotted newt, which can be seen hanging suspended in shallow ponds throughout the White Mountains. After a heavy rain red efts can be quite conspicuous, venturing out in broad daylight in large numbers. Red efts are bright orange-red in color with black-bordered red spots and range in size from 1 3/8 to 3 3/8 inches. Efts remain on land for one to three years before returning to the water and transforming into adult red-spotted newts.

- *Redback salamanders* are common in leaf litter and under decaying logs in moist areas of the forest. They are 2 to 4 inches in length and dark gray in color with a wide red stripe down their back. Some members of this species do not have the red stripe and are called leadbacks. Like most salamanders, redbacks thrive on insects.

Frogs have been found recently throughout the United States (including New Hampshire) with severe physical deformities, most commonly having extra sets of legs. Scientists have discovered that one cause of these deformities is a parasitic flatworm. While it has yet to be proven, scientists hypothesize that pollution may be an additional cause. Breathing through their moist skin, all amphibians may be especially susceptible to acid rain, airborne pollutants such as mercury, and chemicals that disturb the endocrine system like dioxin and PCBs.

TRIP 46
LAKE TARLETON

Difficulty: Quietwater
Distance: 3.5 miles round-trip
Estimated Time: 2 hours
Maps: AMC White Mountain Trail Map #4: J1, USGS Warren
Quadrangle

See views of Mount Moosilauke and paddle along some of New Hampshire's most recently protected undeveloped shoreline.

Directions

From the intersection of NH 25 and NH 25C in Warren, take NH 25C west for 5.0 miles and turn right onto a dirt road with a small sign that says "Road to Public Waters." The put-in is in a few hundred yards at the end of the road.

Trip Description

Lake Tarleton is located on the far western edge of the White Mountain National Forest, only a few miles from the Vermont border. While the western shore is home to a few houses and a large summer camp, the lake's eastern shore is undeveloped and fun to explore. In 1994, the undeveloped character of Lake Tarleton was threatened by plans to build a resort on the lake, which would have compromised both water quality and the viability of the surrounding forest as wildlife habitat. By the summer of 2000 more than 5,500 acres of the forest surrounding the lake (and three smaller nearby lakes) had been protected by a coalition of environmental groups, the federal government, and the state of New Hampshire. Due to these efforts, Lake Tarleton is home to loons and osprey, bears, and moose. Loons nest on the lake; take care not to disturb them, especially when they are nesting or with their young.

Motorboats and waterskiing are allowed on the lake, but traffic is usually light on all but the busiest summer weekends. On busy days plan an early morning paddle to ensure a peaceful time on the lake. While you can choose

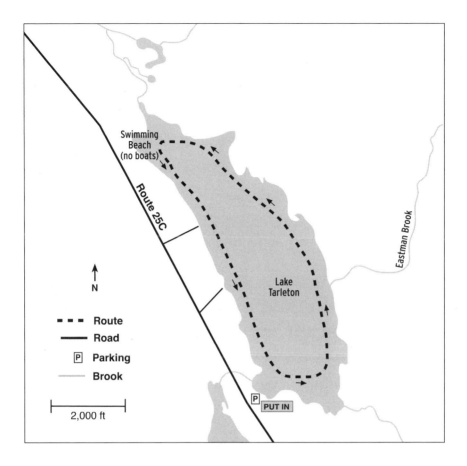

any route, the most immediate rewards are found by following the shore to the right of the put-in. From here you soon will reach the eastern edge of the lake and encounter a few coves filled with pickerelweed and yellow water lilies. Most of the lake is surrounded by a northern hardwood forest, punctuated by the occasional tall white pine or spruce. You will hear bird song from the forest joined by the chatter of kingfishers and the calls of loons on the lake.

The northern hardwood forest around Lake Tarleton is like that found in many places in the White Mountains, especially below 2,000 feet in elevation. A northern hardwood forest is dominated by three species—American beech, sugar maple, and yellow birch—and it is the transition forest between the boreal forests to the north and the oak-hickory forests to the south.

Covering more than 300 acres, Lake Tarleton is one of the largest lakes in the White Mountains and is mostly undeveloped.

Depending on elevation, soil types, and local climate, there may be trees from these other forest habitats present in a northern hardwood forest, such as red spruce, paper birch, red oak, and white pine. The understory of this forest is populated by striped maple, a favorite food of moose, and hobblebush, with its broad round leaves and showy white flowers. White-tailed deer, red squirrels, porcupines, and snowshoe hares are common in a northern hardwood forest, as are the yellow-bellied sapsucker, red-eyed vireo, black-throated blue warblers, brown creeper, and the hermit thrush. Black bears also frequent this productive forest in search of beechnuts, acorns, and other tasty vegetarian treats. It is the red, yellow, and orange of the northern hardwood forest that is responsible for northern New England's spectacular fall foliage displays.

In addition to coves filled with heaths, frogs, and wild roses, Lake Tarleton provides good views toward Mount Moosilauke and the surrounding peaks. At the north end of the lake is a public beach, recently purchased by the state. Landing or launching a boat from the beach is prohibited, but if you feel like a swim after your paddle, drive 1.2 miles north to the beach parking area.

TRIP 47
PEARL LAKE

Difficulty: Quietwater
Distance: 1.5 miles round-trip
Estimated Time: 1 hour
Maps: AMC White Mountain Trail Map #4: G2, USGS Sugar Hill
    Quadrangle

This quietwater paddle is in the rural western foothills of the Whites.

Directions

From downtown Lisbon, head east on US 302 for 0.3 mile and turn right on Savageville Road. As you climb the hill up from US 302, turn right at the fork in 0.3 mile. In another 0.1 mile, turn left on Pearl Lake Road. In another 2.1 miles, turn right on Scotland Road and park in about 100 yards at the put-in on the left.

Trip Description

Pearl Lake is small and out of the way, nestled in the foothills to the west of the Cannon-Kinsman Range. If you are in the Franconia or Littleton area, it makes a great early morning or evening paddle with beautiful rural New Hampshire quiet and the possibility for some productive bird-watching. Though you will see some houses and fields on your paddle, the lake is undeveloped and managed for conservation by the Lisbon Conservation Commission.

Since this a small lake, you can paddle any route you want and never be far from your car. We usually paddle it in a clockwise direction and spend the bulk of our time in the wetlands on the eastern and southern shorelines. Right away there are views of the surrounding 2,000-foot hills, with glimpses of the taller peaks of the western Whites in the distance. Near the put-in is the outlet of the lake, where it flows into Pearl Lake Brook, a small tributary of the Ammonoosuc River. During the summer of 2008, the 14-foot high, 21-foot long Pearl Lake Brook Dam was removed in order to improve water quality in the brook and improve the ecological health of the brook for resident and migrating aquatic species.

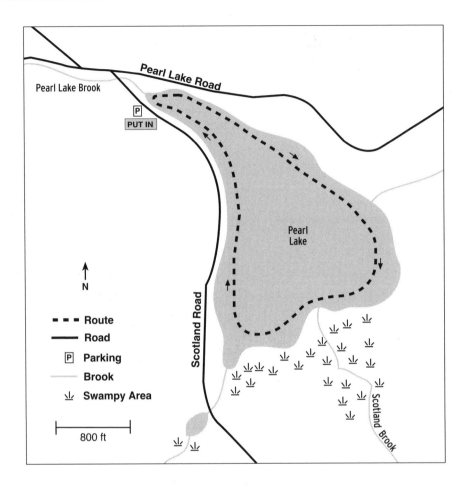

Pearl Lake Brook and the Ammonoosuc River are tributaries of the Connecticut River, the longest river in New England. The Connecticut forms the entire border between New Hampshire and Vermont, draining about one-third of the land mass of both states. Of the 7 million-plus acres in the watershed, more than 4 million acres remain undeveloped and unprotected, creating a big opportunity for future conservation efforts. Ten federally endangered or threatened species live in the watershed, including bald eagles and peregrine falcons and aquatic species like the dwarf wedge mussel, which rely on the free-flowing nature of the mainstem and tributaries like the Ammonoosuc River and Pearl Lake Brook. Dam removals like the one on Pearl Lake Brook are important steps in the efforts to conserve this species.

Pearl Lake is a good canoeing option for families.

While paddling Pearl Lake, you will most likely encounter the loons that live on the lake in summer, feeding on fish, including the rainbow trout that are stocked by the state of New Hampshire. You can also find good bird-watching among the cattails on the eastern and southern ends of the lake, where the shallows merge into a forest of tall white pines and northern hardwoods. Look for great blue herons and smaller birds like marsh wrens, sparrows, swallows, and woods warblers combing the edge of the forest for insects.

As you follow the shoreline back toward the put-in, the lake's character changes as the western shore is rocky and wooded below the steep slopes of Pond Hill. The shoreline is also closely followed by Scotland Road, but its scarce traffic will hardly be a distraction to your quietwater paddle.

TRIP 48
PEMIGEWASSET RIVER—WOODSTOCK TO THORNTON

Difficulty: Flatwater, quickwater, Class I
Distance: 12.3 miles
Estimated Time: 5 hours
Maps: AMC White Mountain Trail Map #4: J4, K4, K5, USGS
Woodstock and Plymouth Quadrangles

A long, enjoyable paddle takes you through the beautiful White Mountain countryside.

Directions to Put-in

From I-93 take Exit 30 in Woodstock and drive north on US 3. In 1.1 miles turn right onto an unmarked side road. In another 0.3 mile turn right onto NH 175 and make an immediate right onto Death Valley Road. The put-in is at the end of the road.

Directions to Take-out

From the put-in drive back to NH 175 and turn left (north). Take your first left, drive the 0.3 mile back to US 3 and turn left. Follow US 3 for 9.6 miles and turn left onto NH 49. The take-out is on the right in 0.2 mile just before NH 49 crosses the river.

Trip Description

Paddling this section of the Pemigewasset River requires that paddlers be comfortable maneuvering a boat on fast-moving water, as there are some sections in the first half of the trip with quick water and some Class I rapids. Most of the rest of the trip has negligible current, which requires a fair amount of paddling just to keep moving forward. The reward for all of this paddling is a long day spent enjoying beautiful White Mountain scenery. This trip can be tedious during summer's low water levels, as you will have to get out and drag your boat over rocks in shallow sections. Plan your trip in spring or within a day or two of a heavy summer rain. To check the water level look for the gauge near the put-in; it is about 100 yards upstream on an old bridge abutment. A level between 3 and 6 feet should make for decent paddling. A reading above 6 feet might make for stronger water conditions

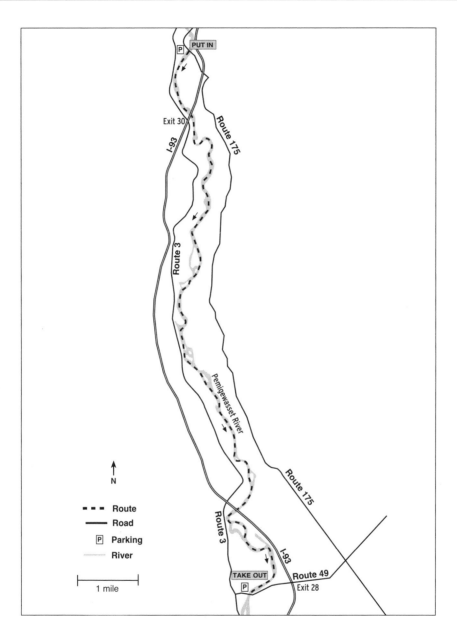

than are comfortable for many paddlers. If you are unsure of paddling conditions, check with local outfitters in Lincoln.

The trip starts out with easy Class I rapids and a few rocks that require some maneuvering. These are the hardest rapids of the trip, and after passing a golf course at about the 2.0-mile mark, you mostly encounter quick

Although you will encounter rapids, you will find that the Pemigewasset River is mostly gentle along this trip.

water with a few short Class I sections usually confined to bends in the river and under bridges. Some of these river bends are tight with fast-moving water, creating the possibility of strainers on the outside bank. Start with your stern pointed at the inside bank of these turns and use a few back-paddle strokes to keep it there as the river pulls you toward the outer bank. For the most part this trip is an easy paddle; you can enjoy good views upstream of the western White Mountains while you float past a forest of northern hardwoods and tall white pine. You also will find plenty of beaches where you can rest in the sun.

After passing under a bridge at about the 5.0-mile mark you can expect the river to get flatter as you go, alternating between quickwater and flatwater sections. Navigation choices are easy, as you can choose to paddle safely on either side of any island you encounter. At about the 9.0-mile mark you will pass under an iron railroad bridge and then the two lanes of I-93. After I-93 the river splits—either direction is fine, but the right channel takes you past some interesting rock ledges as it winds through a series of narrow turns. After passing under another bridge at 12.3 miles the take-out is immediately on your right.

TRIP 49
SACO RIVER—NORTH CONWAY TO CONWAY

Difficulty: Flatwater, quickwater, Class I
Distance: 8.5 miles
Estimated Time: 4 hours
Maps: AMC White Mountain Trail Map #5: I11, USGS Conway,
North Conway East, and North Conway West Quadrangles

This easy paddle close to town offers great scenery.

Directions to Put-in

From the intersection of NH 16 and River Road in North Conway (near the Eastern Slope Inn), head west on River Road. Park at the First Bridge Conservation Area, which will be on your right in 0.4 mile just before the river. It is actually easier to put in on the other side of the river on the left, but once you unload your boat there, you should park at the conservation area parking lot.

Directions to Take-out

From the put-in head west on River Road for 0.6 mile and turn left onto West Side Road. In another 6.1 miles turn left onto the first road after the Swift River covered bridge (also on your left). In about 50 yards turn left again at a stop sign. The take-out will be in another 0.1 mile on the right just after crossing the Saco River on a covered bridge. The take-out is part of the Davis Park Conservation Area.

Trip Description

The Saco River has something for everyone, from technical whitewater die-hards to flatwater enthusiasts paddling with boats full of tents and coolers. This trip is somewhere in between—an easy day trip that consists mostly of quickwater and flatwater paddling through the scenic countryside of North Conway and Conway. There is also one short stretch of Class I whitewater at the very end of the trip that requires the ability to maneuver a fast-moving boat around a few rocks (follow the safety guidelines at the beginning of this chapter). This trip is best run at medium water levels in May and early June,

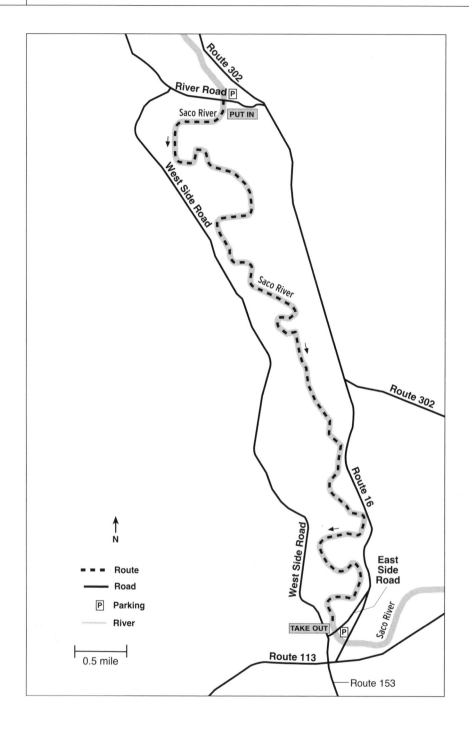

Although rocks line the edges of the Saco River, it is a welcoming place for a paddle.

or after a heavy summer rain. Later in the year the river can be very shallow, requiring paddlers to get out and drag their boats over sand and gravel bars. Unfortunately, there is no gauge for reading water levels at this time.

The paddle along this stretch of the Saco is a slow-moving, peaceful trip where you may be rewarded with wildlife sightings such as great blue heron, mergansers, kingfishers, and other birds. Besides invertebrates and other fish, these birds may be fishing for native eastern brook trout. If you want to try your luck at hooking a brookie, take note that this part of the river is a fly-fishing-only area (and that you need a state fishing license). Brook trout thrive in the cold (below 68 degrees) waters of mountain streams and rivers, which are usually very clean (which the Saco is) and high in oxygen content.

Eastern brook trout also are called squaretail or speckled trout, as their tails are almost square and their sides are usually sprinkled with red spots ringed in blue. They can grow to weigh up to 4 pounds, though most brook trout in White Mountain streams are small and rarely exceed 6 inches in length. Besides being the only native trout in the White Mountains, eastern brook trout are the only naturally reproducing trout in the Whites, as rainbows and browns need to be stocked.

This trip follows the river as it meanders for 8.0 miles through northern hardwood forests and past farms, providing beautiful views of the surrounding hills and mountains. About 2.0 miles from the put-in you will pass the AMC Moose Campground (advanced reservations required; see Appendix D). At about the halfway point you will pass under a railroad bridge. You know you have reached the end of the trip when the water gets bumpy and the Swift River enters on the right. The take-out will be on the left, immediately after you pass under the covered bridge.

If you are looking for an overnight camping adventure on the Saco other than that offered by the AMC campground, check out the opportunities offered by Saco Bound in Conway. It provides boat shuttle services as well as private campgrounds along the river in nearby Maine.

Art and the White Mountains

In August of 1826, the Willey family, homesteaders in Crawford Notch, was killed by a landslide, caused by a dry summer followed by torrential rains. The Willeys had left their house to either escape the landslide or the rising waters of a flooding Saco River. Ironically, as they perished in the slide, their house (and the family dog) was left untouched. When this tragic story made its way to Boston, New York, and beyond, it inspired writers and painters of the young American nation to explore the region in their art and in person. For the following half-century, the region became perhaps the most important community of landscape artists in the country, and inspired works by some of America's most influential painters of the nineteenth century, including Thomas Cole, Albert Bierstadt, and Winslow Homer.

The dominant style of the era was the romantic and lushly lighted landscapes of the Hudson River School of painters, initiated by Cole. Their paintings often explored spiritual themes, but with nature itself as the subject. As Americans felt pride in their new nation and expanded westward, paintings of the White Mountains mirrored the optimism and patriotism of the time. Paintings of the White Mountains dominated the American art scene of the time, and played a role in defining America's self-identity. These paintings were often of such iconic White Mountain features as Crawford Notch, Mount Chocorua, Mount Washington, and Franconia Notch. Chocorua became the most painted mountain in the region (and probably the entire country), due to its classical Alp-like conical summit and the legend of the Native American chief after whom the mountain is named. Cole painted many canvases of the mountain over several decades, even depicting the mountain complete with a waterfall and palm trees in "Garden of Eden."

Benjamin Champney, a New Hampshire native, began visiting the White Mountains in 1838 and founded what would become known as the White Mountain School of painting with John Casilear and John Kensett in the 1850s. He drew other artists to the North Conway area and soon summers found the region dotted with painters *en plein air* in what was the first true artists' colony in America. (Another colony later formed in Waterville Valley.) This was the period that Winslow Homer painted in the region as well. Depicting the mountains as a romantic, bucolic, and unspoiled landscape, the painters of this time period undoubtedly played a large role in the growth of the White Mountains as a tourist haven, as engravings and prints of their paintings were mass-produced and distributed throughout America's big cities.

Also encouraging visitation to the White Mountains were photographs by Samuel Bemis, and Albert Bierstadt's brothers Charles and Edward. In fact, the Whites are considered the first place in America where landscape photography was practiced, though the importance of the White Mountains to the art of photography never reached the level it attained for painters. In any event, tourism peaked in the Whites in the late nineteenth century just as the artists' colonies peaked, and the mountains have been a draw for tourists and wilderness seekers ever since. However, the importance of the White Mountains as an art scene dwindled in the twentieth century, as travel to the dramatic western American landscapes became commonplace.

TRIP 50
NORTHERN FOREST ODYSSEY—
ANDROSCOGGIN RIVER AND UMBAGOG LAKE

Difficulty: Quietwater
Distance: 9.0 miles out and back
Estimated Time: 5 hours
Maps: USGS Umbagog Lake North Quadrangle

A true wilderness paddle takes you through New Hampshire's wild Northern Forest.

Directions

From the intersection of NH 16 and NH 26 in Errol, head east on NH 26 for 0.2 mile, where you should turn left on North Mountain Pond Road. The put-in is at the end of the road in 1 mile.

Trip Description

While technically not in the White Mountains, this is by far the wildest and longest quietwater paddle available for those visiting the Whites, and for paddlers who relish wildlife watching, it is well worth the hour-long drive from the Gorham, N.H., area. This trip follows 3 miles of the Androscoggin River and then explores the shallow, wildlife-rich marshy area where the Androscoggin meets Umbagog Lake and the Magalloway River. Along the way, it is common to see moose, loon, and osprey, and during most of the summer, you are also likely to see bald eagles that nest in the area. This is a long paddle that can be even longer if the winds are above 12 or 15 miles per hour, so wear a healthy dose of sunscreen and bring plenty of water and snacks to keep your energy level high. If you paddle beyond the marshy area described in this trip, venturing into the open water of Umbagog Lake, you will encounter large waves in windy conditions and should attempt the paddle only if you have proper sea kayaking training and self-rescue skills.

From the put-in, follow the river upstream, to the right (go left and you'll soon float over the Errol Dam!). Thanks to the dam, the current here is negligible, so even though you are paddling upstream, it is an easy, quietwater effort. NH 16 follows the north bank of the river for the first three-quarters of

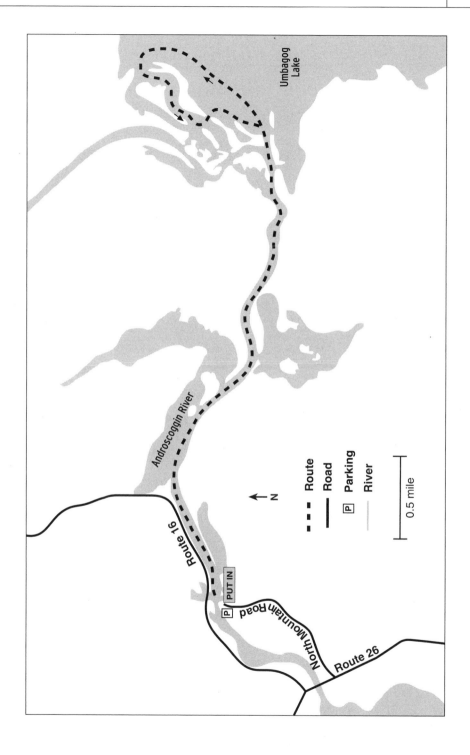

You will find fragrant water lillies where Umbagog Lake enters into the Androscoggin River.

a mile, but you will soon paddle into quiet, undeveloped extensive wetlands. After about 1.2 miles there will be a pair of islands—stay to their right to remain in the main river channel. In another half mile, there will be an entrance to an extensive cove, known as Sweat Meadows, on the right. Stay in the main channel and follow the river through the low-lying landscape of alders and the occasional paper birch, spruce, and pine trees.

About 3 miles from the put-in, the Androscoggin River ends. To the left is the Magalloway River and straight ahead is Umbagog Lake. Paddle past the mouth of the Magalloway and then follow the shorelines of the islands to the left. This shallow, island-studded part of the lake is known as Leonard Pond and is worth an hour or two of exploration. On the higher islands, you will see remote camping sites managed by Umbagog State Park (for camping information, check with park headquarters on NH 26 at the southern end of the lake or visit the New Hampshire State Parks website at www.nhparks. state.nh.us/).

In the Leonard Pond area, you will be treated to expansive lake and mountain views as well as loons plying the waters. Near the center of this area you will see a roped-off section of the lake that surrounds an island with a tall white pine that is home to a bald eagle nest. Most years the nest is home to a family of eagles and you should have no problem viewing the birds during the summer months. Osprey also nest in the area, and it is common to see eagles and osprey harassing each other over territory and fish. The water is dotted with blooming water lilies and on a calm summer day, it is an idyllic place to spend the afternoon watching the wildlife.

Umbagog has long been considered one of the jewels of the Northern Forest, which consists of 26 million acres of relatively undeveloped forest that stretches from upstate New York across Vermont, New Hampshire, and Maine. In 1992, the Lake Umbagog National Wildlife Refuge was established and since then more than 20,500 acres of critical habitat around the lake has been conserved. For more information about the refuge, visit its website, www.fws.gov/northeast/lakeumbagog/index.htm.

To complete your trip, paddle back through Leonard Pond and follow the Androscoggin River to the right and back to the put-in.

Appendix A: Wildlife Viewing

Wildlife is abundant in the White Mountains of New Hampshire, as are the opportunities for viewing. Here are some of the many places you can visit in the White Mountains to observe the outdoor residents of the region.

Lake Umbagog National Wildlife Refuge

Directions: The headquarters is located on NH 16, 5.5 miles north of Errol.

What you'll see: Common loons are plentiful and moose are often seen snacking on aquatic vegetation. Ospreys, moose, eastern kingbirds, belted kingfishers, and great blue herons are also commonly seen.

Thirteen-Mile Woods Scenic Area

Directions: The 13-mile stretch of road extends along NH 16 south from Errol.

What you'll see: In the early morning or late evening, you will most likely see moose. In the summer, you will find Cape May, blackpoll, and yellow-throated warblers. You should also watch for evening grosbeaks, boreal chickadees, and northern three-toed woodpeckers.

Pondicherry Wildlife Refuge

Directions: From downtown Whitefield, follow NH 116 east for about 2 miles to Hazen Road. Turn right onto Hazen Road, and follow it about a mile to the sign for the Mount Washington Regional Airport. Turn left onto Airport Road, and follow the road for about 1.5 miles. Turn left into a small parking area with a kiosk and trailhead.

What you'll see: Pondicherry Wildlife Refuge is a great place to go for bird-watching. Here you'll find a wide variety of birds: green-winged teal, ring-necked ducks, American bitterns, northern harriers, rusty blackbirds, pie-billed grebes, American black ducks, wood ducks, and great blue herons, among others.

Route 26 Wildlife Viewing Area

Directions: From the junctions of NH 16 and NH 26 in Errol, drive west on NH 26 for 9.8 miles. The parking lot is on the left.

What you'll see: Moose and deer are plentiful in the spring and early summer. You may also find mourning, chestnut-sided, and common yellowthroat nesting in the shrubs. Purple finches and kinglets live in the spruce and fir trees.

Appendix B: Recommended Reading

Guide Books

Bolnick, Bruce, Doreen, and Daniel. *Waterfalls of the White Mountains: 30 Hikes to 100 Waterfalls*. Backcountry Publications, 1999.

Buchsbaum, Robert. *AMC's Best Day Hikes in the White Mountains*. Appalachian Mountain Club Books, 2006.

Daniell, Gene, and Steve Smith. *White Mountain Guide, 28th Edition*. Appalachian Mountain Club Books, 2007.

Fiske, John. *AMC River Guide: New Hampshire/Vermont, 4th Edition*. Appalachian Mountain Club Books, 2007.

Heid, Matt. *AMC's Best Backpacking in New England*. Appalachian Mountain Club Books, 2008.

Hudson, Judy, Doug Mayer, and Steve Smith. *Randolph Paths 8th Edition*. Randolph Mountain Club, 2005.

Wilson, Alex. *AMC Quiet Water New Hampshire and Vermont: Canoe and Kayak Guide, 2nd Edition*. Appalachian Mountain Club Books, 2001.

History/Stories

Brown, Dona. *A Tourist's New England: Travel Fiction 1820–1920*. University Press of New England, 1999.

Brown, Rebecca A. *Women on High: Pioneers of Mountaineering*. Appalachian Mountain Club Books, 2002.

Crawford, Lucy. *History of the White Mountains*. Durand Press, 1999.

Howe, Nicholas. *Not Without Peril: 150 Years of Misadventure on the Presidential Range of New Hampshire*. Appalachian Mountain Club Books, 2001.

McGrath, Robert. *Gods in Granite: The Art of the White Mountains*. Syracuse University Press, 2001.

Monkman, Jerry and Marcy. *White Mountain Wilderness*. University Press of New England, 2005.

Mudge, John T. B. *The White Mountains: Names, Places, and Legends*. Durand Press, 1995.

Sargent, William. *A Year in the Notch: Exploring the Natural History of the White Mountains*. University Press of New England, 2001.

Nature

Kiel, Warren. *The Butterflies of the White Mountains of New Hampshire*. Falcon Press, 2003.

Slack, Nancy G. and Allison W. Bell. *AMC Field Guide to the New England Alpine Summits, 2nd edition*. Appalachian Mountain Club, 2006.

Van Diver, Bradford. *Roadside Geology of Vermont and New Hampshire*. Mountain Press, 1987.

Waterman, Laura and Guy. *Backwoods Ethics: Environmental Issues for Hikers and Campers*. Countryman Press, 1993.

Appendix C:
Environmental Organizations

Appalachian Mountain Club
617-523-0655
www.outdoors.org

Appalachian Trail Conservancy
304-535-6331
www.appalachiantrail.org

Friends of Tuckerman Ravine
603-367-4417
www.friendsoftuckerman.org

Leave No Trace
800-332-4100
www.lnt.org

The Nature Conservancy
603-224-5853
www.tnc.org

Northern Forest Alliance
802-223-5256
www.northernforestalliance.org

Northern Forest Center
603-229-0679
www.northernforest.org

Sierra Club
415-977-5500
www.sierraclub.org

Society for Protection of New
Hampshire Forests (SPNHF)
603-224-9945
www.spnhf.org

The Trust for Public Land
617-367-6200
www.tpl.org

The Wilderness Society
207-626-5553
www.wilderness.org

Appendix D: Lodging

Literally hundreds of choices for lodging exist in and around the White Mountains. They range from basic campgrounds to very expensive, luxurious hotels and inns. Here are some resources to help you find the place that's right for your needs:

Appalachian Mountain Club
603-466-2727
www.outdoors.org/lodging

State of New Hampshire Division of Tourism
800-FUN IN NH
www.visitnh.gov

Bethlehem Chamber of Commerce
603-869-3409
www.bethlehemwhitemtns.com

Conway Village Chamber of Commerce
603-447-2639
www.conwaychamber.com

Country Inns in the White Mountains
603-447-2818
www.countryinnsinthewhitemountains.com

Franconia Notch Chamber
of Commerce
603-823-5661
www.franconianotch.org

Jackson Chamber of Commerce
800-866-3334
www.jacksonnh.com

Lincoln/Woodstock Chamber of Commerce
603-745-6621
www.linwoodcc.org

Littleton Chamber of Commerce
603-444-6561
www.littletonareachamber.com

Mount Washington Valley Chamber of Commerce
877-948-6867
www.mtwashingtonvalley.org

New England Inns & Resorts
603-964-6689
www.newenglandinnsandresorts.com

Northern White Mountain Chamber of Commerce
800-992-7480
www.northernwhitemtnchamber.org

White Mountain Attractions
800-FIND MTS
www.visitwhitemountains.com

Index

About the Authors

KNOWN FOR THEIR CONSERVATION WORK IN NEW ENGLAND'S WILD PLACES, Jerry and Marcy Monkman have spent the last fifteen years artfully documenting the mountains, forests, and coastlines that define the region. In 2002, they were awarded a communications award by the Northern Forest Alliance in recognition for their "vision and excellence in chronicling the story of the Northern Forest through photography." Authors of six books, including three AMC Discover guides, their work has appeared in publications worldwide and their client list includes *National Geographic Adventure*, Audubon, *Men's Journal*, *The Washington Post*, *Outdoor Photographer*, L.L. Bean, Princess Cruises, and The Nature Conservancy. Jerry and Marcy live in Portsmouth, N.H., with their daughter Acadia and their son Quinn.

The Appalachian Mountain Club

Founded in 1876, the AMC is the nation's oldest outdoor recreation and conservation organization. The AMC promotes the protection, enjoyment, and wise use of the mountains, rivers, and trails of the Northeast outdoors.

People

We are nearly 90,000 members in 12 chapters, 16,000 volunteers, and more than 450 full time and seasonal staff. Our chapters reach from Maine to Washington, D.C.

Outdoor Adventure and Fun

We offer more than 8,000 trips each year, from local chapter activities to major excursions worldwide, for every ability level and outdoor interest— from hiking and climbing to paddling, snowshoeing, and skiing.

Great Places to Stay

We host more than 150,000 guest nights each year at our AMC lodges, huts, camps, shelters, and campgrounds. Each AMC Destination is a model for environmental education and stewardship.

Opportunities for Learning

We teach people the skills to be safe outdoors and to care for the natural world around us through programs for children, teens, and adults, as well as outdoor leadership training.

Caring for Trails

We maintain more than 1,700 miles of trails throughout the Northeast, including nearly 350 miles of the Appalachian Trail in five states.

Protecting Wild Places

We advocate for land and riverway conservation, monitor air quality, and work to protect alpine and forest ecosystems throughout the Northern Forest and Highlands regions.

Engaging the Public

We seek to educate and inform our own members and an additional 2 million people annually through AMC Books, our website, our White Mountain visitor centers, and AMC Destinations.

Join Us!

Members support our mission while enjoying great AMC programs, our award-winning *AMC Outdoors* magazine, and special discounts. Visit www.outdoors.org or call 617-523-0636 for more information.

THE APPALACHIAN MOUNTAIN CLUB
Recreation • Education • Conservation
www.outdoors.org

The AMC New Hampshire Chapter

The AMC New Hampshire Chapter offers a wide variety of hiking, backpacking, climbing, paddling, and skiing trips each year, as well as social, family, and young member programs and instructional workshops. The chapter also maintains trails throughout the state. The AMC maintains the Appalachian Trail in the White Mountains from Woodstock, N.H., to Grafton Notch in Maine, as well as huts, campsites, and shelters along the AT.

To view a list AMC activities in New Hampshire and other parts of the Northeast, visit trips.outdoors.org.

AMC Book Updates

AMC Books strives to keep our guidebooks as up-to-date as possible to help you plan safe and enjoyable adventures. If after publishing a book we learn that trails are relocated or route or contact information has changed, we will post the updated information online. Before you hit the trail, check for updates at www.outdoors.org/publications/books/updates.

While hiking or paddling, if you notice discrepancies with the trail description or map, or if you find any other errors in the book, please let us know by submitting them to amcbookupdates@outdoors.org or in writing to Books Editor, c/o AMC, 5 Joy Street, Boston, MA 02108. We will verify all submissions and post key updates each month.

AMC Books is dedicated to being a recognized leader in outdoor publishing. Thank you for your participation.

AMC BOOKS & MAPS

EXPLORE THE POSSIBILITIES

More Books from the Outdoor Experts

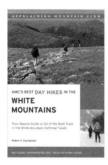
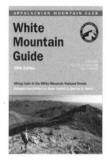
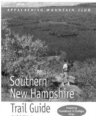